BIRTHRIGHT

THE COMING POSTHUMAN APOCALYPSE
AND THE USURPATION OF ADAM'S DOMINION
ON PLANET EARTH

TIMOTHY ALBERINO

ALBERINO
PUBLISHING

Alberino Publishing
Bozeman, MT 59718

Edited by Lara Kennedy
Cover design by Timothy Alberino and Rafael Andres
Interior design by Timothy Alberino

Scripture references are from the following sources:

The Holy Bible, King James Version.

New King James Version®, copyright © 1982 by Thomas Nelson. Used by permission. All rights reserved.

The Holy Bible, English Standard Version, copyright © 2001 by Good News Publishers. Used by permission. All rights reserved.

New American Standard Bible, copyright © 1960, 1962, 1963, 1968, 1971, 1972, 1973, 1975, 1977, 1995 by The Lockman Foundation. Used by permission.

The Holy Bible, New International Version®, NIV®, copyright © 1973, 1978, 1984, 2011 by Biblica®, Inc. Used by permission. All rights reserved worldwide.

Revised Standard Version of the Bible, copyright © 1946, 1952, and 1971 by the Division of Christian Education of the National Council of the Churches of Christ in the United States of America. Used by permission. All rights reserved.

The Revised Standard Version of the Bible: Second Catholic Edition, copyright © 1965, 1966 by the Division of Christian Education of the National Council of the Churches of Christ in the United States of America. Used by permission. All rights reserved.

New Revised Standard Version Bible: Catholic Edition, copyright © 1989, 1993 by the Division of Christian Education of the National Council of the Churches of Christ in the United States of America. Used by permission. All rights reserved.

The Christian Standard Bible, copyright © 2017 by Holman Bible Publishers. Used by permission. Christian Standard Bible® and CSB® are registered trademarks of Holman Bible Publishers. All rights reserved.

Common English Bible, copyright © 2011 by Common English Bible. All rights reserved. Used by permission.

Jubilee Bible 2000, copyright © 2013, 2020 by Ransom Press. All rights reserved.

Geneva Bible, 1599 Edition. Published by Tolle Lege Press. All rights reserved.

The Septuagint version of the Old Testament (Brenton).

The Book of Enoch (R. H. Charles).

ISBN: 9798556521193

To my wife, Jasmine, and my sons,
Arazan, Ardorblaze, Avendrake, Attilio, and Axel.

Contents

Acknowledgments

Let me begin by saying that this book would never have been accomplished without the love and devotion of my darling wife, Jasmine, whose continual encouragement fortified my resolve to stay the course and finish the task.

I would also like to thank Gary Heavin for the many Cuban cigars that helped to stimulate my cerebral cortex during ponderous hours of endless typing. Gary has stayed with me (literally) through the deserts, mountains, and jungles of this journey. Without his support and mentorship, I would be half the man I am today.

And finally, I am indebted to David Flynn, whose brilliant insights illumined the path of the present work. Though, sadly, Flynn passed away before I had the chance to know him, I feel as if I have been handed the baton to continue in his career. Perhaps it is not coincidental that he and I share the distinction of being identical twins and that we are both aficionados of the great Isaac Newton, whose portrait looks down on me even as I write these words.

In the same way that Newton's work revolutionized our understanding of the universe, it is my sincere desire that the contents of this book will serve to reorient our place within it.

A Note from the Author

The book you hold in your hands was conceived on the banks of a black-water tributary to the River Mazan, itself a tributary to the mighty Napo, in the Amazon jungle. There I paced, a young man nineteen years old, engulfed in a sea of foliage, contemplating the glory of Eden, the fall of Adam, and the gospel of Christ.

These were the most formative days of my life. I had dropped out of Midpark High School in Middleburg Heights, Ohio, during the first week of my senior year and set out for the Peruvian Amazon. I was driven into the jungle by an insatiable appetite for adventure and an ardent desire to encounter God. Both of these longings would be thoroughly satisfied in the extraordinary events that followed, but that is another tale for another book.

The writing of this book has been fraught with difficulty. During the two years it took me to complete the manuscript, I was called away on a six-month expedition to Peru (one of the most arduous I had ever undertaken), I suffered through a three-month-long illness, and I lost my father to a protracted battle with cancer.

Aside from these adversities, I was faced with the daunting mental task of coalescing many complex subjects, each one worthy of its own book, into a cohesive narrative in which all of the various pieces fit together like a jigsaw puzzle. In truth, I had originally intended to organize the subject matter into two or three volumes. However, upon further consideration, I determined that it was essential for the reader to comprehend the confluence of themes in a single volume so as to preserve the continuity of the story they tell.

C. S. Lewis famously converted to Christianity after realizing that the gospel of Christ was not merely a set of doctrines and moral precepts but the heroic story of mankind, a myth that just so happens to be true. It was none other than his Oxford colleagues and fellow Inklings Hugo Dyson and J. R. R. Tolkien who persuaded him to consider things from this perspective. As a boy pining for adventure, enamored of *The Chronicles of Narnia* and *The Lord of the Rings*, I, too, began to see the gospel as a heroic story—an epic saga filled with dramatic battles, valiant deeds, treacherous villains, and victories snatched from the jaws of defeat.

In today's society, the Bible is generally regarded as an archaic book of Jewish fables with little relevance to modern man. Christian celebrities have attempted to remedy this perception by renovating the text of scripture for contemporary application, resulting in an endless slew of superficial self-help flummery. What so many fail to realize is that the Bible is not a collection of quaint bedtime stories nor a guidebook for attaining "Your Best Life Now," but a coded communication to mankind from the Creator of the universe preserved *through* and *for* all ages.

The late Chuck Missler would often describe the sixty-six books of the Bible, penned by more than forty different people over a period of several thousand years, as a highly integrated message system from an extraterrestrial source outside of time. Like a hologram, a facet of the message is encoded on every page that, when illumined by the light of the Spirit, projects a multidimensional portrait of its divine Author and communicates his plan to redeem, reconcile, and restore the sons and daughters of Adam to the glory of their original estate in the family of God.

I pray that you will discover in the following pages a newfound fascination for the gospel of Christ, the greatest story ever told, and a renewed affection for Jesus of Nazareth, the greatest hero humanity has ever known.

Timothy Alberino

Chapter 1

THE ELDER RACE

The story of mankind begins in the beginning, but not in the very beginning. The beginning of our story marks the appearance of a new sentient species in the universe, one specifically designed to inhabit the earth. It does not mark the beginning of all other species inhabiting other worlds, nor the beginning of the earth itself.

Before we venture a gaze toward the dateless horizon of ages long past, we should take a moment to defog our spectacles of the conceptual brume clouding the view beyond the tip of our nose. If you are like me, you have been subjected throughout your life to a continual reinforcement of vacuous religious concepts regarding the nature of the cosmos and the beings that inhabit it—concepts which neither clarify nor satisfy the questions that percolate in the inquisitive mind.

The sheer vastness of the universe compels us to contemplate the significance—or insignificance—of our place within it. Suspended in the vacuum of space, we feel small and alone, but the biblical narrative assures us that we are not.

Man is not alone in the cosmos, nor is his existence a random occurrence. Like a decorative float rounding the bend in a parade, his appearance was carefully coordinated in the procession of time. Although his participation is of great importance, the parade was not organized in his honor, and his float was not first in the procession.

If we are to understand our place in the universe, then we must surrender our need to be the center of it. Man was not conceived with the universe, and the universe was not created for man. We were born *into* the cosmos, not with it—thrust into the fray of a complex political, societal, and martial conflict involving incomprehensibly intelligent agencies of exceedingly ancient origin.

Christians, by and large, tend to adopt an anthropocentric (human-centric) perspective of the universe that places man, like the axle of a wheel, at the center of all things. In this view, man is both the principal protagonist of creation and its primary purpose. All other sentient creatures in created order are ancillary characters in the story of mankind.

This presumptuous appraisal of the human race has engendered a condescending attitude in the minds of many Christians concerning their extraterrestrial elder siblings, the *sons of God*, even demoting them to our servants, or worse, dismissing them altogether.

For reasons unwarranted, the term *extraterrestrial* is anathema in the seminary classroom. However, a simple definition of the word should suffice to exorcise its imagined demons. An extraterrestrial is a being whose provenance is not Planet Earth. Notice that I did not say *residence*. *Provenance* is where you come from. *Residence* is where you reside. It is entirely possible for beings of extraterrestrial provenance to be residing on Earth (as we shall see), a concept which necessitates the defining of another associated term—*alien*.

Due to its inherent ambiguity, the word *alien* requires context. In the cosmological sense, an alien is a foreign being from an extraterrestrial world. However, generally speaking, any nonhuman being of advanced intelligence may be considered alien to the human species, regardless of its provenance. For example, if we should discover a race of nonhuman beings inhabiting the interior of our planet, or a parallel dimension, we would be accurate in describing them as aliens, even though we are essentially coinhabiting the same space.

With our terms thus defined, we may venture the question: *Do extraterrestrials and/or aliens exist within the biblical paradigm?*

The answer is, unequivocally, *yes*.

This should come as no surprise to students of the scriptures. The biblical narrative unapologetically introduces us to a race of beings that are clearly alien (in every sense of the word), indisputably extraterrestrial, and incalculably ancient. Indeed, these attributes are intentionally exemplified in one of the epithets most often used to describe them, the *morning stars*. The extraterrestrial provenance of the morning stars is plainly communicated to Job by the Maker himself:

> "Where were you when I laid the foundations of the earth? Tell me, if you have understanding. Who determined its measurements? Surely you know! Or who stretched the line upon it? To what were its foundations fastened? Or who laid its cornerstone, when the morning stars sang together, and all the sons of God shouted for joy?"[1]

We may deduce two logical conclusions from these verses: first, that they are not referring to literal stars but the sentient sons of God, and second, that these sons of God are older than the earth itself, since they were present to witness its primordial formation.

The motif of the morning star in biblical parlance is meant to convey preexistence and preeminence. In John's Revelation, Jesus declares, "I am the root and the offspring of David, the bright and morning star."[2] While writing to the brethren in Colossae, Paul affirms the preeminence of Christ: "He is the head of the body, the church, who is the beginning, the firstborn from the dead, that in all things he may have the preeminence."[3]

As the firstborn (not only from the dead, but over all creation), Jesus is the original morning star and the preeminent Son of God. These epithets are more than descriptions of his attributes; they are proper titles assigned to the person of Christ alone. When employed in an informal and broader context, the connotation of the terms remains the same, but the persons they denote are of a different estate. The *morning stars* and *sons of God* are children of the dawn, the second-born sons in the family

---

[1] Job 38:4–7 (New King James Version).
[2] Revelation 22:16 (NKJV).
[3] Colossians 1:18 (NKJV).

of God. They represent an elder race of beings that are both preexistent and preeminent in relationship to all others, save the Son of God himself, the first and foremost over all creation.

Very little is disclosed about the morning stars, but by virtue of their designations, we may surmise that they are, to some degree, akin to the firstborn Son and ancient beyond reckoning. As we have seen, the exceptional agedness of the *elder race*[4] (as we shall refer to them hereafter) is assumed in the biblical narrative, since they were a party to the formation of Planet Earth, an event that likely took place many millions of years ago.

The age of the earth, and the universe around it, is hotly disputed in both theological and secular circles. On the short end of the spectrum, Young Earth Creationists argue an approximate age of six thousand years for both, while proponents on the long end of the spectrum contend that the earth has existed for at least 4.5 billion years, and the universe for about 14 billion years. An assumption is made by Young Earth Creationists that the earth and the universe came into existence with the conception of mankind, even simultaneously, as if the universe were made for the earth and the earth for man. Born from the anthropocentric perspective, this ideology tends to make of man, in the minds of its adherents, the fulcrum upon which creation itself pivots. It has inflicted the Christian with a kind of tunnel vision, rendering phenomena occurring in the peripheral of his anthropocentrism impossible to conceptualize, much less comprehend. But the scriptures by no means constrain us to such a view.

Rather than supporting an anthropocentric perspective of the universe, the biblical paradigm expressly conveys a Christocentric (Christ-centric) perspective. By making ourselves the center of all things, we supplant the Son of God, who is not only the primal source of the universe but its primary purpose. Paul articulates the correct view with supreme elegance:

---

[4] "Elder" to signify that they are older than mankind, and "race" to delineate them from the other sentient beings in the universe. (How else should we describe them if not a race?) The reader who is versed in the works of J. R. R. Tolkien will recognize a similarity in the term *elder race* with Tolkien's "Eldar" race, otherwise known as the Elves. According to the lore of *The Silmarillion*, the immortal Eldar ("People of the Stars") were the first and eldest of the children of Ilúvatar (an adaptation of the Hebrew God Yahweh) and are considered to be fairer and wiser than men, their younger siblings. Tolkien's depiction of the tall, fair-skinned, blond-haired Elves is an obvious allusion to the morning stars in the biblical narrative.

He is the image of the invisible God, the firstborn over all creation. For by him all things were created that are in heaven and that are on earth, visible and invisible, whether thrones or dominions or principalities or powers. All things were created through him and for him. And he is before all things, and in him all things consist.[5]

Notice that all things were created not only *through* him but *for* him. The Son of God is the first cause, the initial singularity,[6] and the intrinsic purpose of the universe. He is the Alpha and the Omega, the first and the last, the beginning and the end.[7] The universe was not made for the earth, and the earth was not made for man. It was all made for Jesus, the firstborn and beloved Son of the Father—the apple of his eye.

Notice also that Paul references thrones, dominions, principalities, and powers when referring to things created in heaven and on the earth. These terms are indicative of a vast kingdom with many realms. There is a plurality of thrones, a plurality of dominions, and a plurality of principalities.[8]

In light of the Christocentric perspective clearly conveyed in the scriptures, we may comfortably disassociate the creation of the universe with the creation of mankind, as man was not its purpose. Moreover, the fact that the morning stars were present to witness the primordial formation of Planet Earth presumes a pre-Adamic paradigm. The pre-Adamic controversy is entirely inconsequential when man is properly positioned within the order of creation. It is perfectly logical to infer that nonhuman intelligent beings were inhabiting other worlds in the cosmos before Adam was created on Earth. Indeed, the inference is made by the writer of Hebrews:

---

[5] Colossians 1:15–17 (NKJV).

[6] The Big Bang theory postulates that the universe emerged from an initial singularity of infinite density and gravity and that before this event, space and time were nonexistent.

[7] See Revelation 22:13.

[8] There exists a persistent mythology among Evangelicals concerning the word *principality*, which is widely regarded by these to be the title of a high-ranking demonic being. However, a principality does not denote an entity but rather a realm governed by a prince.

God, who at various times and in various ways spoke in time past to the fathers by the prophets, has in these last days spoken to us by his Son, whom he has appointed heir of all things, through whom also he made the worlds [or ages].[9]

And again,

By faith we understand that the worlds were prepared by the word of God [Son of God], so that what is seen was not made out of things which are visible.[10]

In concert with Paul's letter to the Colossians identifying Christ as the creator of thrones, dominions, principalities, and powers, the writer of Hebrews (perhaps Paul himself) reaffirms a plurality of realms, which were both *made through* and *relegated by* the Son of God, the Prince and heir of the kingdom. Like the morning stars themselves, these primordial worlds preexisted the age of man, whose appearance corresponded with the relegation of a new realm (renovated from an old one).

John, in a vision concerning the end of the age (which we will analyze later), beholds Jesus returning to the earth astride a white horse, with the armies of heaven in train; his head is adorned with many crowns, and his thigh is emblazoned with the title *King of kings and Lord of lords*.[11]

When titles of regency are directly juxtaposed in the text, in this case *kings* and *lords*, they often reflect two distinct realities—the *terrestrial* and the *extraterrestrial*, the *human* and the *nonhuman*. The terrestrial realm is the domain of the human race, governed by human kings, but other realms more ancient than the earth are governed by the lords (or *princes*) of the elder race. Extraterrestrial thrones, dominions, and principalities were appointed by the Son of God, the *Prince of princes*,[12] long before the creation of mankind.

The pre-Adamic landscape is one of empire. The system of government

---

[9] Hebrews 1:1–2 (NKJV).
[10] Hebrews 11:3 (New American Standard Bible).
[11] See Revelation 19.
[12] *Prince of princes* is a title ascribed to the Son of God in Daniel 8.

presented in the biblical narrative is an absolute monarchy. There is a kingdom of heaven (kingdom of God) and a high King who sits on a throne and before whom all tremble and pay obeisance.[13] Other, lesser thrones, configured in the hierarchy of the empire, are occupied by the King's delegates, princes and regents who do his bidding. The kingdom has a court, a council, and an army. It has councilors, courtiers, couriers, and warriors. There is a royal family and a ruling class. Rebellions are incited by disaffected factions and put down with decisive force. Insurgencies are formed and vie for their own piece of the imperial landscape. In their most fundamental aspects, the visible thrones and dominions of terrestrial governance are reflections of their invisible extraterrestrial counterparts, including (and perhaps especially) in the aspect of war.

The language of scripture is laced with martial overtones. The right hand of God, his preeminent Son, is often portrayed as a man of war[14] and mighty in battle.[15] Isaiah declares, "The Lord will go forth like a warrior, he will arouse his zeal like a man of war. He will utter a shout, yes, he will raise a war cry. He will prevail against his enemies."[16] On the eve of the Jericho assault, he appeared to Joshua with a sword drawn in his hand as commander of the armies of heaven.[17] He is later depicted fighting against the enemies of Israel, even hurling hailstones down upon the Amorites, killing more of them himself than did Joshua and his forces.[18]

Over and over again, we are inculcated with the idea that there is a conflict raging in the cosmos. Jesus declared, "The kingdom of heaven suffers violence, and the violent take it by force."[19] In the Book of Revelation, John describes a battle of heroic proportions breaking out in heaven

---

[13] The Son of God is the King of heaven. His supreme authority over all other potentates in the cosmos is emphasized in the various titles of dominion ascribed to him (e.g., King of kings, Lord of lords, Prince of princes, etc.).

[14] See Exodus 15.

[15] E.g., Psalm 24:8.

[16] Isaiah 42:13 (NASB).

[17] See Joshua 5.

[18] See Joshua 10.

[19] Matthew 11:12 (NKJV). This esoteric declaration has been the subject of much controversy over the centuries. What violence does the kingdom of heaven suffer? With an imperial view in mind, it is easy to envision the violence and persistence of a rebel insurgency making continual incursions into the kingdom and perhaps even gaining territorial dominance through successful campaigns.

between opposing angelic factions: on the one side, Michael and his angels, and on the other, the dragon, who draws a third of the heavenly host into his rebellion.[20] The relentless violence and malevolence of the insurgency is manifest in the dreadful prison devised for their incarceration.[21] The very term *heavenly host* (or *host of heaven*) is connotative of an organized military force trained and equipped for war. One of the titles most frequently ascribed to God in the Old Testament is "Lord of Armies."[22]

Armies are only necessary when a plurality of opposing factions exists and the borders of a sovereign domain are threatened by enemy incursion, and domains amount to more than the armies that protect them. What is the kingdom of heaven if not a civilization? And what is a civilization if not the organization of a complex society peopled by intelligent beings?

The scriptures refer to the citizens of this celestial civilization as *angels*. Reference to angels in the biblical narrative is ambiguous by design. In consequence of this intentional ambiguity, many fanciful notions have been concocted regarding the nature and function of the elder race. The Church of Rome, for example, has fabricated an entire angelic mythology, modeled in the Greco-Roman style, complete with the figures of heroic angels sculpted in marble and painted on sanctuary walls. The anatomical depictions of these heavenly beings are the product of pure fantasy. The great cathedrals of Europe are covered in the sensual physiques of angelic females adorned in feathery wings and the pedophilic portraits of chubby cherubim, usually depicted in the nude. Like the demigods of the Greco-Roman pantheon, the angels and saints of the Roman Catholic Church are revered as minor deities.

Human history bears witness to the fact that men are oft inclined to worship what they cannot comprehend. Hence, the veneration of heavenly bodies—the sun, moon, and stars—and of the elemental forces of nature—water, wind, and fire—is an ever-present characteristic of primitive cultures. Considering this proclivity to prostrate before the unexplained, it is not profitable for men of antiquated knowledge to be acquainted with beings of superior intelligence, especially when they

[20] See Revelation 12.
[21] See Matthew 25.
[22] *Yahweh Tsebaoth*, meaning "Lord of Hosts" or "Lord of Armies," occurs more than 240 times in the Hebrew Scriptures.

are operating advanced technology. Man is at a disadvantage in such an encounter, susceptible to deception and manipulation. The scriptures record several occasions that highlight the danger implicit in these interactions. Even John, who broke bread with the resurrected Christ, fell down at the feet of an angel to worship him. The angel's recoil is revealing:

> "You must not do that! I am a fellow servant with you and your brothers who hold to the testimony of Jesus. Worship God."[23]

His alarm is not unwarranted. The temptation to be worshipped by mankind had led—and leads still—to the ruination of his comrades, many of whom were chained in the infernal penitentiary for precisely this transgression. Interaction between our worlds can be just as hazardous for angels as for men. The prohibition of contact is strictly enforced, as much for their benefit as for ours. When the human condition is finally rectified at the resurrection and mankind is restored to his original estate, fellowship between our races will be renewed. Until then, we must be content with what little enlightenment has been granted us regarding our elder siblings.

Scant as the information is, logical inferences may be deduced from what is disclosed in the scriptures.

Much confusion has been propagated by self-proclaimed *supernaturalists*, who appeal to special revelation and religious superstition in the formulation of their own proprietary blends of angelology. These individuals have managed to make of angels a servile race of winged attendants whose sole purpose is to comfort and protect them or to do their bidding. Like the Catholic Church, they have assigned rank and duty to a florid panoply of angelic beings inhabiting the fantasy land of their imaginations. Fortunately, most of their delusions can be dispelled with a cursory examination of the word *angel*.

Rendered as *mal'ak* in the Hebrew and *angelos* in the Greek, *angel* simply means "messenger; an envoy; one who is sent." Hence, *angel* is a description of occupation rather than classification or kind. The word does not supply any insight into the provenance or nature of the person

---

[23] Revelation 19:10 (English Standard Version).

it denotes. Neither is it applied exclusively to heavenly beings. When functioning in the capacity of messengers and envoys, human beings are also referred to as angels in the biblical text.[24]

On the rare occasion that messengers of extraterrestrial provenance are dispatched to communicate with the inhabitants of Earth, they always have the appearance of men. So much do they resemble us—or rather, *we* resemble them—that the writer of Hebrews, while reminding the Church not to neglect the entertainment of strangers, includes the curious addendum, "for by so doing some have unwittingly entertained angels."[25]

Quite contrary to Renaissance imagery, there are no occurrences of female angels recorded in the scriptures.[26] In fact, a feminine form of the Greek word *angelos* does not even exist. In addition, except in the context of prophetic iconography, or in the case of seraphim and cherubim (which are symbolic creatures subject to interpretation), angels are never depicted with wings. We do, however, often find them in possession of technology, such as vehicles of conveyance and weapons of war.[27] It is also apparent that angels eat and drink, as they do so with both Abraham and Lot in the eighteenth and nineteenth chapters of Genesis. The children of Israel ate the bread of heaven (what they called *manna*) during their wanderings in the wilderness of Sinai. The Hebrews considered manna to be the sustenance of angels, as the Psalmist writes:

> Yet he commanded the skies above and opened the doors of heaven, and he rained down on them manna to eat and gave them the grain of heaven. Man ate of the bread of the angels; he sent them food in abundance.[28]

Feasting is a prominent feature of the kingdom of heaven. While

---

[24] In Numbers 20, for example, Moses dispatches messengers to the king of Edom. The word for messengers in this instance is *mal'ak*, the very same used for heavenly "angelic" messengers.

[25] Hebrews 13:2 (NKJV).

[26] In Zechariah 5:9, two female entities with wings are depicted in the context of prophetic iconography and, as such, should not be interpreted as literal beings. It should be noted that, although there is no textual support for their existence, the scriptures do not necessarily preclude the possibility of female angels.

[27] E.g., 2 Kings 2; 1 Chronicles 21.

[28] Psalm 78:23–25 (ESV).

marveling at the faith of the centurion, Jesus remarked, "I say to you that many will come from the east and the west, and will take their places at the feast with Abraham, Isaac and Jacob in the kingdom of heaven."[29] John was instructed by the angel to write, "Blessed are those who are invited to the marriage supper of the Lamb."[30] On the eve of his crucifixion, the Lord drank wine from the chalice before passing it to his disciples with the pronouncement, "I will not drink again of the fruit of the vine until that day when I drink it new in the kingdom of God."[31]

Even the risen Christ ate and drank. While the two men who had encountered him on the road to Emmaus were recounting their tale to the apostles, suddenly Jesus appeared in their midst:

> But they were startled and frightened and thought they saw a spirit. And he said to them, "Why are you troubled, and why do doubts arise in your hearts? See my hands and my feet, that it is I myself. Touch me, and see. For a spirit does not have flesh and bones as you see that I have." And when he had said this, he showed them his hands and his feet. And while they still disbelieved for joy and were marveling, he said to them, "Have you anything here to eat?" They gave him a piece of broiled fish, and he took it and ate before them.[32]

This passage is highly intriguing. After inviting his disciples to touch the flesh of his hands and feet (still bearing the marks of the crucifixion), Jesus asks for something to eat in order to further prove his corporeality. The risen Christ is the firstborn from the dead and the forerunner of what man is to become at the resurrection. The glorified body is a *physical* human body. Clearly, the consumption of food and drink is not merely the exercise of fallen flesh, nor is it exclusive to the terrestrial realm.

The biblical narrative informs us that some angels deliver messages, some engage in warfare, some execute the judgment of God, and some

---

[29] Matthew 8:11 (New International Version).
[30] Revelation 19:9 (ESV).
[31] Mark 14:25 (ESV).
[32] Luke 24:36–43 (ESV).

minister to the children of men, but we are never explicitly told *who* or *what* exactly they are. The question seems to be left for us to extrapolate—so let's extrapolate: the angels of heaven have a spoken and written language; they keep records; they sing and compose music; they eat and drink; they possess, wield, and (assumedly) build technology; and they are the subjects of a kingdom, complete with a complex system of government and a standing army. These are the hallmarks of society and culture. It is therefore rational to conclude that the nonhuman angelic beings depicted in the scriptures are the citizens of an advanced extraterrestrial civilization that predates our own.

Mankind did not invent civilization; he inherited it. The benchmarks of a civilized society—sophisticated bureaucracy, social hierarchy, a criminal justice system, refined spoken and written language, technological advancement, military organization, and so forth—were already existent in the universe before Adam emerged from the earthen clay. In truth, we are the beneficiaries of the elder race, the recipients of their societal institutions, and the coinheritors of their kingdom. We are also the coinheritors of their condemnation should we follow in their rebellion.

Whereas the ambiguity of the word *angel* does little to illumine the silhouette of our extraterrestrial predecessor, the term *son(s) of God* (*b'nai Elohim*) is much more elucidative, uniting the elder race and the human race in extraordinary ways. *Sons of God* is always and *only* used in the Old Testament to denote the nonprocreated children of God (that is to say, beings who were not conceived in a womb, such as angels and Adam). It is a familial designation of one's paternity and estate. The term carries over into the New Testament, where it maintains its Old Testament meaning but is now applicable to the sons of men who, through Christ, can become the sons of God:

> But as many as received him [Jesus], to them gave he power to become the sons of God, even to them that believe on his name: Which were born, not of blood, nor of the will of the flesh, nor of the will of man, but of God.[33]

---

[33] John 1:12–13 (King James Version).

The above verse has been mangled and twisted to undergird all kinds of strange theology, but the meaning is explicit if we allow the term *sons of God* to retain its original context. Those who are born not of blood nor of the will of the flesh nor of the will of man *are* the sons of God. Human beings do not yet qualify to this estate, as we are all the product of procreation by means of sexual intercourse (the will of the flesh). John is not saying that those who believe in Christ are *already* the sons of God, but rather, they are given power to *become* the sons of God. This power is the hope of the gospel—the *resurrection*.

Notice how Jesus replies when the Sadducees, who denied the resurrection, tried to entangle him in a parable related to a widow who had been the wife of seven husbands before her death. "Whose wife," they inquired, "does she become at the resurrection?":

> Jesus answered and said to them, "The sons of this age marry and are given in marriage. But those who are counted worthy to attain that age, and the resurrection from the dead, neither marry nor are given in marriage; nor can they die anymore, for they are equal to the angels and are sons of God, *being sons of the resurrection.*"[34]

By misinterpreting the meaning of the term *sons of God* in the Old Testament—as nearly all seminaries do in order to sidestep the inconvenient realities of Genesis 6—we have misconstrued the gospel, awarding to Christians now that which can only be attained through the transformative power of the resurrection. Being "born again" is not merely the regeneration of the heart and mind but of the body as well. Only the power of the resurrection can truly effectuate a new birth. Believers in Christ Jesus are on a trajectory to become the sons of God, equal to the angels in respect to their immortal condition and membership in the divine family, which is essentially the restoration of mankind to the patrimony and purpose of his original estate—to Adam, the son of God. (We shall enlarge on this point in a later chapter.)

---

[34] Luke 20:34–36 (NKJV), emphasis added.

The sons of God in heaven and on the earth are destined to be united in Christ in what is essentially a family reunion, since mankind was conceived as a son in the beginning. This remarkable reality is insinuated by the Lord himself in the Parable of the Prodigal Son:

> "There was a man who had two sons. The younger one said to his father, 'Father, give me my share of the estate.' So he divided his property between them.
>
> "Not long after that, the younger son got together all he had, set off for a distant country and there squandered his wealth in wild living. After he had spent everything, there was a severe famine in that whole country, and he began to be in need. So he went and hired himself out to a citizen of that country [a swineherd], who sent him to his fields to feed pigs. He longed to fill his stomach with the pods that the pigs were eating, but no one gave him anything.
>
> "When he came to his senses, he said, 'How many of my father's hired servants have food to spare, and here I am starving to death! I will set out and go back to my father and say to him: Father, I have sinned against heaven and against you. I am no longer worthy to be called your son; make me like one of your hired servants.' So he got up and went to his father.
>
> "But while he was still a long way off, his father saw him and was filled with compassion for him; he ran to his son, threw his arms around him and kissed him.
>
> "The son said to him, 'Father, I have sinned against heaven and against you. I am no longer worthy to be called your son.'
>
> "But the father said to his servants, 'Quick! Bring the best robe and put it on him. Put a ring on his finger and sandals on his feet. Bring the fattened calf and kill it. Let's have a feast and celebrate. For this son of mine was dead and is alive again; he was lost and is found.' So they began to celebrate.
>
> "Meanwhile, the older son was in the field. When he came near the house, he heard music and dancing. So he called one of the servants and asked him what was going on.

'Your brother has come,' he replied, 'and your father has killed the fattened calf because he has him back safe and sound.'

"The older brother became angry and refused to go in. So his father went out and pleaded with him. But he answered his father, 'Look! All these years I've been slaving for you and never disobeyed your orders. Yet you never gave me even a young goat so I could celebrate with my friends. But when this son of yours who has squandered your property with prostitutes comes home, you kill the fattened calf for him!'

"'My son,' the father said, 'you are always with me, and everything I have is yours. But we had to celebrate and be glad, because this brother of yours was dead and is alive again; he was lost and is found.'"[35]

There are five characters in this parable: the father, the older son, the younger son, the servants, and the swineherd. The protagonist of the story is the younger son, an archetype of Adam, who squanders the coinheritance of his father's estate which he shares with his elder brother. The squalor that befalls the younger son is symbolic of the wages of sin and the consequence of estrangement from the family. Due to his impoverishment, the prodigal son becomes subject to a swineherd, the archetype of Satan. Recognizing the depravity of his condition, he repents of his folly and decides to return to his father's house in the hope that he might be received back, if only as a lowly servant.

(Note that not all those who are in the Father's house are sons. The servants, though employed in the house, are not members of the family. This circumstance implies that there are other sentient creatures inhabiting the cosmos who, though citizens of the kingdom, are not the sons of God. Because they are not sons, they would not be created in the image and likeness of the Elohim. The variety of species among these beings may be as diverse as the animal life on Earth.)

When the father sees his son approaching, he runs out to meet him. The son, assuming his father would be fuming with displeasure, is

---

[35] Luke 15:11–32 (NIV). On the surface, this parable relates to the reunion of Judah and Israel, but the deeper meaning pertains to the reunion of mankind in the family of God.

surprised to find him brimming with joy and kissing his face. The father escorts his son home and adorns him in new clothes (representative of the righteousness of Christ and the resurrection), placing a ring on his finger (the seal of his house). A fattened calf is slaughtered, and a great celebration ensues, with feasting, music, and dancing.

The older son, who has always been with the father (in heaven), is bewildered. Why should they celebrate the return of his younger sibling, who foolishly squandered his portion of the inheritance? The father's answer conveys the message of the gospel: "because this brother of yours was dead and is alive again; he was lost and is found."

If anyone should doubt that the Parable of the Prodigal Son concerns the reuniting of the family of God (i.e., the elder race and the human race), consider that in the two preceding parables (namely, the Parable of the Lost Sheep and the Parable of the Lost Coin), Jesus remarks that there will be joy in heaven among the angels over every sinner who repents.[36] The sons of God rejoice at the repentance of their sundered siblings, because they know that soon we will be reinstated in the family of God, and the fellowship of Eden will be renewed.

In his letter to the Ephesians, Paul provides us with a fitting summation of the themes presented in this chapter:

> To me, who am less than the least of all the saints, this grace was given, that I should preach among the Gentiles the unsearchable riches of Christ, and to make all see what is the fellowship of the mystery, which from the beginning of the ages has been hidden in God who created all things through Jesus Christ; to the intent that now the manifold wisdom of God might be made known by the church to the principalities [realms] and powers in the heavenly places, according to the eternal purpose which he accomplished in Christ Jesus our Lord . . . For this reason I bow my knees to the Father of our Lord Jesus Christ, from whom the whole family in heaven and earth is named.[37]

---

[36] See Luke 15:7, 10.
[37] Ephesians 3:8–11, 14–15 (NKJV).

In view of these remarkable revelations, it is appropriate that we regard the morning stars as our elder siblings and fellow servants of the King, since we are destined to be sons of God together with them in the kingdom. Their civilization is the predecessor and prototype of ours, inasmuch as our world is but the shadow of theirs.

Chapter 2

SHADOWS OF REALITY

We have established so far, through the exercise of deductive reasoning, that the human race, indigenous to Planet Earth, is the younger sibling of an elder race whose provenance and habitation are elsewhere in the cosmos. Before we examine the origin of this scenario, let us indulge in a brief digression concerning the nature of the universe itself, which we will find useful for the comprehension of forthcoming topics.

We must now embark on a road of speculation.

The lecture halls of universities across the civilized world are still echoing in the aftermath of the Atomic Age and ringing with the names of its luminaries (Bohr, Rutherford, Schrodinger, Heisenberg, Planck, Einstein, Oppenheimer, Pauli, Feynman, etc.), whose pioneering work permanently altered our conception of reality. Thanks to the genius of these men (and others besides), we now know that the world in which we live is quite different from what we perceive it to be. Atoms, for instance, are primarily composed of empty space, which means that matter is not really solid after all—a fact that boggles the mind. The surprises at the subatomic level are even more baffling. The bizarre behavior of quantum mechanics forces us to conclude that what we behold to be real may only be the shadow of reality—a three-dimensional projection of a ten-dimensional universe lurking in the peripheral of our perception.

Even the definition of time has undergone a profound transformation over the last century. In a consoling letter to the family of his deceased friend, Albert Einstein famously penned the observation, "People like us, who believe in physics, know that the distinction between past, present, and future is only a stubbornly persistent illusion."[1] Einstein's theory of relativity—and indeed, the compendium of twentieth-century physics—has taught us that when contemplating the nature of the universe, perception is the problem.

Before Albert Einstein, there was Paul of Tarsus, who discerned the crux and cure of our perceptual predicament:

> For our knowledge is imperfect and our prophecy is imperfect;
> but when the perfect comes, the imperfect will pass away.
> When I was a child, I spoke like a child, I thought like a child, I
> reasoned like a child; when I became a man, I gave up childish
> ways. For now we see in a mirror dimly, but then face to face.
> Now I know in part; then I shall understand fully, even as I
> have been fully understood.[2]

When considered in the context of his letter to the Corinthians, it is apparent that Paul is alluding here to the resurrection. Man's ability to perceive the universe around him is hamstrung by the present deficiency of his degenerate condition. Entropy's slow grind has gradually worn away at the built-in capabilities of human biology, both mind and body. As a result, we suffer from a kind of perceptual cataract—we see as in a mirror, dimly.[3]

Before the invention of reflective glass in the nineteenth century, mirrors were made of polished metal, providing the viewer with only the faintest impression of his features. In the same way, our perceptual impairment permits us to discern little more than the pallid contours of reality. However, when the imperfections of our biology are rectified at the resurrection and the perfect comes, we will perceive the full spectrum

---

[1] Quoted in Freeman Dyson, *Disturbing the Universe* (London: Pan Books, 1979), 193. Einstein was writing to the family of Michele Besso, the Swiss engineer, who was one of his most intimate friends.

[2] 1 Corinthians 13:9–12 (Revised Standard Version).

[3] The KJV renders it as, "we see through a glass, darkly," which is precisely the impairment caused by cataracts.

of the dimensional totality in which we abide, as did the progenitors of our race. For now, we must suffer to see the world in shadows.

Men who see the world in shadows was one of Plato's most ingenious thought experiments. In his "Allegory of the Cave," a group of prisoners are condemned to endure a most peculiar punishment: they have been chained up in a cave since infancy, facing a solitary wall and unable to turn their heads. Their comprehension of the world outside the cave, whose opening is directly behind them, is derived exclusively from the fleeting shadows cast upon the wall. Plato explains their extraordinary predicament through a dialogue between Socrates and Glaucon:

> "And now," I [Socrates] said, "let me show in a figure how far our nature is enlightened or unenlightened: Behold! human beings living in an underground cave, which has a mouth open towards the light and reaching all along the cave; here they have been from their childhood, and have their legs and necks chained so that they cannot move, and can only see before them, being prevented by the chains from turning round their heads. Above and behind them a fire is blazing at a distance, and between the fire and the prisoners there is a raised way; and you will see, if you look, a low wall built along the way, like the screen which marionette players have in front of them, over which they show the puppets."
>
> [Glaucon replied,] "I see."
>
> "And do you see," I said, "men passing along the wall carrying all sorts of vessels, and statues and figures of animals made of wood and stone and various materials, which appear over the wall? Some of them are talking, others silent."
>
> "You have shown me a strange image, and they are strange prisoners."
>
> "Like ourselves," I replied. "And they see only their own shadows, or the shadows of one another, which the fire throws on the opposite wall of the cave?"
>
> "True," he said. "How could they see anything but the shadows if they were never allowed to move their heads?"

"And of the objects which are being carried in like manner they would only see the shadows?"

"Yes," he said.

"And if they were able to converse with one another, would they not suppose that they were naming what was actually before them?"

"Very true."

"And suppose further that the prison had an echo which came from the other side, would they not be sure to fancy when one of the passers-by spoke that the voice which they heard came from the passing shadow?"

"No question," he replied.

"To them," I said, "the truth would be literally nothing but the shadows of the images."

"That is certain."

"And now look again, and see what will naturally follow if the prisoners are released and disabused of their error. At first, when any of them is liberated and compelled suddenly to stand up and turn his neck round and walk and look towards the light, he will suffer sharp pains; the glare will distress him, and he will be unable to see the realities of which in his former state he had seen the shadows; and then conceive someone saying to him, that what he saw before was an illusion, but that now, when he is approaching nearer to being and his eye is turned towards more real existence, he has a clearer vision, what will be his reply? And you may further imagine that his instructor is pointing to the objects as they pass and requiring him to name them, will he not be perplexed? Will he not fancy that the shadows which he formerly saw are truer than the objects which are now shown to him?"

"Far truer."

"And if he is compelled to look straight at the light, will he not have a pain in his eyes which will make him turn away to take in the objects of vision which he can see, and which he will conceive to be in reality clearer than the things which are now being shown to him?"

"True," he said.

"And suppose once more, that he is reluctantly dragged up a steep and rugged ascent, and held fast until he's forced into the presence of the sun himself, is he not likely to be pained and irritated? When he approaches the light his eyes will be dazzled, and he will not be able to see anything at all of what are now called realities."

"Not all in a moment," he said.

"He will require to grow accustomed to the sight of the upper world. And first he will see the shadows best, next the reflections of men and other objects in the water, and then the objects themselves; then he will gaze upon the light of the moon and the stars and the spangled heaven; and he will see the sky and the stars by night better than the sun or the light of the sun by day?"

"Certainly."

"Last of all he will be able to see the sun, and not mere reflections of him in the water, but he will see him in his own proper place, and not in another; and he will contemplate him as he is."

"Certainly."[4]

Plato's clever allegory is a fitting illustration of our predicament. We, as the prisoners chained up in the cave, are presently constrained by the perceptual impairment of our condition and, like them, are forced to see the world in shadows. When we are finally released from our bonds and liberated from the damp dark of the cave, we will be dazzled and dismayed by the dimensional splendor of all those things we had formerly experienced in silhouette.

Paul and Plato were articulating the same problem, but their solutions were quite different. For Plato, intellectual enlightenment would ultimately

---

[4] Plato, *The Republic: The Complete and Unabridged Jowett Translation* (New York: Vintage, 1991), Book VII.

liberate man from the cave. For Paul, only the resurrection could remedy man's degenerate condition. Paul, as we shall see, was correct. No amount of enlightenment can break the chains of sin and death that bind us to the grave.

Plato could not have known that his "Allegory of the Cave," written in the fourth century BC, would be scientifically substantiated in the twenty-first century, at least as it relates to the nature of the universe. The prevailing theory among physicists today is that the universe comprises many dimensions, only three of which (plus time) are directly perceivable to us.[5] It turns out, then, that a shadow is a fitting representation of this reality. A shadow casts a two-dimensional silhouette of a three-dimensional object. In essence, it is a darkened and flattened facsimile of a luminous, multifaceted world—a world that cannot be directly perceived by those condemned to see in shadows.

In physics, an extraspatial environment consisting of more than three dimensions is called a hyperdimensional space, or hyperspace. The hyperspace theory of the universe is supported by one of the most profound epiphanies of modern physics—*the laws of nature become simpler and more elegant when expressed in higher dimensions*. This statement also happens to ring true when applied to matters of theology. Much of the "supernatural" activity recurrent in the biblical narrative is demystified when read against the backdrop of a hyperdimensional universe. Consider, for example, the episode recorded in the sixth chapter of 2 Kings. The Syrian army had encircled the city of Dothan with horses and chariots in the dark of night, intent on capturing the prophet Elisha. Seeing that they were hopelessly ensnared, Elisha's servant bemoaned, "Alas, my master! What shall we do?"

> So he [Elisha] answered, "Do not fear, for those who are with us are more than those who are with them." And Elisha prayed, and said, "Lord, I pray, open his eyes that he may see." Then the Lord opened the eyes of the young man, and he saw.

[5] See Alan Boyle, "Physicists Probe the Fifth Dimension," *NBC News*, June 6, 2006, Mysteries of the Universe, http://www.nbcnews.com/id/13070896/ns/technology_and_science-science/t/physicists-probe-fifth-dimension/#.Wlu-nExFz-g.

And behold, the mountain was full of horses and chariots of fire all around Elisha.[6]

Notice that Elisha prayed for his servant's eyes to be opened, not that the invisible army of horses and chariots be made visible. This is because the angelic army was not *invisible*, but rather *imperceivable*. Elisha's servant, and presumably the inhabitants of Dothan, were simply unable to perceive the full spectrum of the dimensional world encompassing them.[7]

The ability of certain beings to appear and disappear at will, traverse through solid objects, and inhabit a host body (as in demon possession) is perfectly explicable when an extraspatial environment is assumed.

"Imagine being able to walk through walls," muses Michio Kaku, a professor of theoretical physics at The City College of New York.

> You wouldn't have to bother with opening doors; you could pass right through them. You wouldn't have to go around buildings; you could enter them through their walls and pillars and out through the back wall. You wouldn't have to detour around mountains; you could step right into them. . . . Imagine being able to disappear or reappear at will. Instead of driving to school or work, you would just vanish and rematerialize in your classroom or office. . . . Imagine having x-ray eyes. You would be able to see accidents happening from a distance. After vanishing and rematerializing at the site of any accident, you could see exactly where the victims were, even if they were buried under debris. . . . No secrets could be kept from us. No treasures could be hidden from us. No obstructions

---

[6] 2 Kings 6:15–17 (NKJV).

[7] It is also important to note that the machinery of the angelic army was most certainly not composed of horses and chariots. The biblical writers had to rely on familiar references when attempting to describe visions of extraterrestrial technology. Chariots were the most sophisticated vehicles of conveyance known to them and, as such, provided the most conceivable correlation. Men of that age could not even conceptualize horseless chariots—let alone air- and spacecraft—and would have had great difficulty describing the mechanisms that powered them. It is also illogical to assume that the elder race, apparently capable of incredible technological feats, would be utilizing horses and chariots for conveyance, a form of transportation that even man abandoned long ago in favor of more efficient means.

could stop us. We would truly be miracle workers, performing feats beyond the comprehension of mortals. . . . What being could possess such God-like power? The answer: a being from a higher-dimensional world.[8]

It is important to delineate the difference between an extraspatial environment and an entirely dichotomous dimensional world. While the former is encountered every day, the latter exists only in science fiction. When we observe goldfish swimming in a pond, for example, we are not looking into another world but another facet of the world we already inhabit.

The hyperspace theory is a useful lens through which to contemplate the unperceived facets of the universe, but some have used it as a prism through which to divide the universe into a strata of dimensional planes. It is assumed, for instance, that angels and demons are spiritual beings inhabiting higher dimensions, while human beings with physical bodies inhabit the lower ones.[9] This may at first appear biblically sound, until we recall that the resurrected Christ was capable of performing the incredible feats described by Dr. Kaku while still having a body of flesh and bones—a human body. Indeed, according to John, we who believe in Christ are destined to become like him and will, consequently, be capable of the same feats:

> Beloved, we are God's children now, and what we will be has not yet appeared; but we know that when he appears we shall be like him, because we shall see him as he is.[10]

We shall see him as he is when our perceptual cataract is removed at the resurrection. The purpose of the resurrection is not to promote us to

---

[8] Michio Kaku, *Hyperspace: A Scientific Odyssey Through Parallel Universes, Time Warps, and the 10th Dimension* (New York: Oxford University Press, 1994), 45–46.
[9] The stratification of the universe into spiritual and physical planes is by no means a new concept. Nearly every religious institution that has arisen in the course of time has incorporated some version of the view into the corpus of their teaching. The mysteries of the occult and the doctrines of the New Age are especially concerned with one's ascension to higher planes of existence.
[10] 1 John 3:2 (ESV).

a higher dimensional plane but to restore us to the blueprint of Adam, the original human being. It is the author's contention that Adam was able not only to perceive the dimensional totality of the natural world but to traffic in it, much like his elder siblings, until his eyes were darkened because of sin.

Those who are condemned to see the world in shadows will be forced to formulate a description of reality based on insufficient information and, therefore, contrivance. Human history verifies the axiom, "In the absence of knowledge, superstition prevails." Impaired perception impedes comprehension and breeds fabrication. We find the gaps in our knowledge irritating and uncomfortable, like a road riddled with potholes, and so we fill them in with fabrications to make the ride smoother. The rutted highway of human knowledge is mended with all sorts of contrivances concerning the nature of the universe, a query that for many centuries was beyond investigation. The tools of modern science have enabled us to repave the road, in a manner of speaking, and to upend, one by one, the falsities of our former ignorance. But the road is long, and the work is slow.

We must concede that our current conception of the universe is still infantile. Like a child staring bewilderedly at a blackboard chalked from end to end with the esoteric figures of a complex mathematical formula, we are able to recognize some of the numbers and symbols but cannot hope to comprehend the equation, much less solve it. But rather than accept the irreducible complexity before us, many Christians have endeavored to reduce what they cannot comprehend into facile religious concepts that they can. This "Sunday school reductionism" tends to transform profound truths into coloring book illustrations and connect-the-dot puzzles. Instead of illuminating the problem with the lamp of logic and admitting our ignorance, we tend to obscure the problem beneath a canopy of nebulous abstractions, commending ourselves with the false satisfaction of having "solved" it.

Sunday school reductionism is perhaps best exemplified in a concept we have come to call the *supernatural*. In true reductionist form, we have managed to devise a catch-all term with which to define the anomalous phenomena we do not understand so that we may pretend as if we do. Consequently, we have transgressed the boundaries of logic by creating a contradiction in nature that does not exist—the *super*-natural. This amorphous term has supplied us the brush with which to paint in broad strokes over every occurrence that cannot be explained by traditional scientific methods. It has emboldened its wielder with an ill-conceived conception of the cosmos derived from presumption rather than knowledge.

To the degree that our knowledge of the natural world increases, so the breadth and scope of the supernatural must necessarily decrease, until it is no more. It is a simple equation: when the mechanism behind a given supernatural occurrence is understood, it ceases to be *super* and is only then *natural*. It is expedient, therefore, that we discard supernatural explanations in favor of scientific ones, insofar as they can be formulated. At the very least, the admission of ignorance is better than the pretense of knowledge.

Defining what we cannot perceive as supernatural has engendered many foolish and injurious superstitions throughout history that have greatly inhibited knowledge and proliferated ignorance. Before the invention and utility of the microscope, it was commonly believed that diseases were caused by foul air or demonic spirits.[11] It was not until we could peer into the microscopic world that we finally identified the true culprit—germs. The problem was one of perception. Our inability to perceive the microbial world led to the fabrication of superstitious conclusions. Equally so, superstitions regarding the supernatural inevitably result from our inability to perceive the dimensional totality encompassing us. These hidden facets of reality, though invisible to our sensory faculties, are nevertheless perfectly natural within the context of a hyperdimensional universe.

It may surprise the reader to learn that the word *supernatural* is not in the Bible, nor can it be found in any extrabiblical text. In fact, it is an invention of medieval theology, derived in the sixth century from the Latin word *supernaturalis*, meaning "beyond nature." The adjective

---

[11] In some cases, demonic spirits do cause physical maladies. Modern medical science, of course, has totally ruled out such a condition, but it is true, nevertheless. The author has witnessed authentic demonic possession firsthand, as have many others around the world. When an unclean spirit inhabits a human host, it can, and usually does, afflict the host physically and mentally. However, these cases are exceedingly rare, as they are contingent on the presence of a disembodied spirit, of which there is limited supply.

form of *supernatural* implies an infraction of the laws of nature and an interruption of natural processes—in a word, chaos. It engenders the conceptualization of two distinct worlds—the *natural* and the *supernatural*—which constitutes an irreconcilable contradiction for adherents of scripture.

The scriptures describe the Son of God as the craftsman of the universe and the architect of the laws that govern it. According to the writers of the New Testament, Jesus *is* the Singularity—the first cause and catalyst of the Big Bang.[12] Everything in the universe, visible and invisible, from the largest star to the smallest quark, was created through him and for him, and in him all things consist. The biblical paradigm does not portray two distinct creations, one for the natural world and one for the supernatural, but a singular universe in which all things abide and are bound together by synergistic forces. Some of the universe is discernible through human perception (the visible), but the preponderance of created order is imperceivable (the invisible). This perceptual *black matter* is not beyond nature but simply beyond the perceptive limitations of our degenerate condition.

Paul is not the only apostle to describe Jesus as the Singularity; John affirms the doctrine in the Book of Revelation:

> "And to the angel of the church in Laodicea write: 'The words of the Amen, the faithful and true witness, the beginning of God's creation.'"[13]

And in the opening remarks of his gospel, he writes,

> In the beginning was the Word, and the Word was with God, and the Word was God. He was in the beginning with God. All things were made through him, and without him nothing was made that was made.[14]

---

[12] In the author's opinion, Christians ought to embrace Big Bang cosmology, as it is quite congruent with the doctrine of scripture. Whether through an explosion or a spoken word, all matter and energy emerged from a singular source, a singularity—the Son of God.

[13] Revelation 3:14 (ESV).

[14] John 1:1–3 (NKJV).

Word in the passage above is derived from the Greek *logos*, meaning "a word, uttered by a living voice."[15] A spoken word results from the modulated vibration of a voice.

John's conception of the Word through whom the world was spoken into existence is surprisingly concordant with the leading candidate for the elusive "theory of everything" that Einstein was pursuing before his death. The theory of everything (unified field theory) is the Holy Grail of theoretical physics—the consummate description of the universe that elegantly binds the forces of nature (strong nuclear, weak nuclear, electromagnetism, gravity) into a unifying symmetry. "If we discover a complete theory," wrote Stephen Hawking in *A Brief History of Time*, "it would be the ultimate triumph of human reason—for then we should know the mind of God."[16] When refined, Hawking's postulation is closer to the mark: the discovery of a unified field theory will reveal not the *mind* of God but the *Word* of God.

Among the many propositions for a theory of everything, only one has withstood the fastidious scrutiny of physicists and mathematicians over the decades—string theory. In short, string theory posits that the universe, at its most fundamental level, is composed of vibrating filaments, or strings. The way in which these strings vibrate determines the nature and action of the elementary constituents of the material world. In other words, the essence of matter can be likened to music. Dr. Kaku, the cofounder of string field theory, explains,

> The subatomic particles we see in nature—the quarks, the electrons—are nothing but musical notes on a tiny vibrating string. What is physics? Physics is nothing but the laws of harmony that you can write on vibrating strings. What is chemistry? Chemistry is nothing but the melodies you can play on interacting vibrating strings. What is the universe? The universe is a symphony of vibrating strings. And then, what is the mind of God that Albert Einstein eloquently wrote

---

[15] See "Strong's G3056 - *logos*." Blue Letter Bible, accessed on April 12, 2020, https://www.blueletterbible.org/lang/lexicon/lexicon.cfm?Strongs=G3056&t=KJV.

[16] Stephen Hawking, *A Brief History of Time* (New York: Bantam Books, 1998).

about for the last thirty years of his life? . . . It is cosmic music resonating through eleven-dimensional hyperspace.[17]

An essential question arises when considering the fascinating implications of string theory: What caused the strings to vibrate in the first place? *Energy* is the simplest answer. But can we define the source of that energy? Do the strings vibrate with the unmodulated violence and chaos of the Big Bang? Or is their vibration the result of a more discreet and harmonizing force?

Explosions, by definition, are disorganized and inharmonious. They are the agents of chaos rather than order. Because the laws of physics express the elegance and harmony of an implicit order, chaos cannot be their source. Beautiful symphonies are not created by throwing instruments against the wall. The instruments, like the elemental strings of the universe, must first be carefully tuned by a skillful hand and then played according to the implicit order of a musical composition if they are to harmonize into a symphony.

What makes string theory so elegant is that it describes each particle in the Standard Model as a uniquely tuned vibration of the string. In the same way that different vibrations in a guitar string correspond to different notes, the different vibrations of the elemental strings correspond to different elemental particles (e.g., electrons, photons, gluons, etc.).

String theory gives new meaning to the theological argument of *fine-tuning*, which posits that the extreme precision observed in the mechanisms that make the universe possible must be the result of intelligent design (i.e., a *conscious tuner*). If string theory is correct, then the precision of these mechanisms is precisely the result of tuning in the musical sense.

The difference of being in tune and out of tune is the difference between a shriek and a song. When we shriek with fright or excitement, we produce an unmodulated and unmelodious noise through our voice, like that of an explosion. When we sing, we are consciously modulating the vibration of our vocal cords in order to produce (or attempt to produce) the notes requisite for a given melody. A chorus of singers produce

---

[17] "Michio Kaku: The Universe Is a Symphony of Vibrating Strings," produced by Big Think, May 31, 2011, https://www.youtube.com/watch?v=fW6JFKgbAF4.

harmony through the coordinated modulation of many vibrating vocal cords. In the same way, the coordinated modulation of vibrating elemental strings results in a harmonious universe.

Harmony. Symmetry. Order. Elegance. These words, often used by physicists, mathematicians, and cosmologists to describe the universe, are the hallmarks of beautiful music. When the antipodes of these words are intoned—discord, imbalance, chaos, ugliness—they do not describe the natural world nor the laws that govern it. It is plausible, then, that the elemental mechanisms of the universe were precisely tuned through the conscious modulation of a voice, the vibration of which still reverberates through the subatomic matrix of matter and energy binding the laws of nature into a unifying symmetry. In other words, the universe is resonating with the Word of God, just as the psalmist wrote:

> The heavens declare the glory of God; the skies proclaim the work of his hands. Day after day they pour forth speech; night after night they reveal knowledge. They have no speech, they use no words; no sound is heard from them. Yet their voice goes out into all the earth, their words to the ends of the world.[18]

Solomon, peering into the deep before time, allegorizes the Word of God as *Wisdom*, the master craftsman, through whom the Father created the heavens and the earth:

> "The Lord possessed me at the beginning of his way, before his works of old. I have been established from everlasting, from the beginning, before there was ever an earth. When there were no depths I was brought forth, when there were no fountains abounding with water. Before the mountains were settled, before the hills, I was brought forth; while as yet he had not made the earth or the fields [or *outer places*], or the

---

[18] Psalm 19:1–4 (NIV). As an intriguing aside, creation through a voice is described by C. S. Lewis in *The Magician's Nephew*; Aslan—an archetype of the Son of God—sings and roars Narnia into existence.

primeval dust of the world. When he prepared the heavens, I was there, when he drew a circle on the face of the deep, when he established the clouds above, when he strengthened the fountains of the deep, when he assigned to the sea its limit, so that the waters would not transgress his command, when he marked out the foundations of the earth, then I was beside him as a master craftsman; and I was daily his delight, rejoicing always before him, rejoicing in his inhabited world, and my delight was with the sons of men."[19]

When the Word became flesh and dwelt among us, he was a carpenter crafting works of wood with his hands, revealing to us the essence of his nature. The miracles he performed demonstrated that he had the power to mend and manipulate the architecture of matter, which he himself had designed. He was telling us who he was, telegraphing to the crowds that followed him, *the Maker is walking in your midst.*

When Peter, James, and John ascended to the summit of Mount Hermon with Christ,[20] he transfigured before them—his face shone like the sun, and his clothes radiated with white light. Moses and Elijah appeared to converse with him. As the disciples gaped in wonder, suddenly a cloud overshadowed them and a voice thundered the pronouncement, "This is my beloved Son. Hear *him!*" When the cloud passed, only Jesus remained.[21] The message was clear: Moses and Elijah represent the law and the prophets—the word of God in print—but Jesus is the living Word *through* whom and *for* whom all things exist.

> For from him and through him and to him are all things. To him be glory forever.[22]

The biblical narrative propounds a theory of everything in which the laws of nature are bound together within the unifying symmetry of a

---

[19] Proverbs 8:22–31 (NKJV).
[20] Mount Hermon (also known as Sirion and Senir) is the highest peak in the Anti-Lebanon Mountains, which straddle the border between Syria and Lebanon.
[21] See Matthew 17; Mark 9; Luke 9.
[22] Romans 11:36 (ESV).

singular universe created through and upheld by the Word of God. Like two sides of the same coin, every component of created order, visible and invisible, whether thrones or dominions or principalities or powers, are synergistic parts of the same universe and equally subject to the laws that govern it. Ergo, there is no power beyond nature except for the Father and his Only Begotten Son, the Singularity, through whom the continuum of space and time was created. Christ is all, and in all.[23]

As a postscript to the concepts presented in this chapter, let us take a moment to consider the residence of the soul.

The problem of where exactly our soul (or consciousness) resides may be resolved with the addition of a fourth spatial dimension. That our anatomy is composed of more than the three dimensions directly perceivable to us seems to be insinuated in a disturbing phenomenon depicted in the biblical narrative—demonic possession.

Demonic possession is a baffling condition. Apparently, some facet of human biology can be inhabited by parasitical spirits who hijack the body of their host. This unsettling circumstance is not unlike a carjacking. Imagine you are idling at a red light, when suddenly, several masked men approach your vehicle and force their way inside. One of them enters through the driver-side door, shoving you into the adjacent passenger seat. You now have unwanted company traveling with you, and they have the wheel. Depending on the strength of the intruders, you may be able to wrangle back into the driver's seat and regain control of the vehicle, but the company remains.

It is easy to visualize these masked intruders sitting inside of a car, but where do they reside when the vehicle is your body? Do some inhabit the large intestine and others the small? Perhaps some demons prefer the spleen or kidneys? These scenarios would be equivalent to our hypothetical carjackers occupying the gas tank or carburetor of your engine rather than the seats in the passenger compartment, which is obviously absurd.

Like a car, the vehicle of your biology must have a seat for the soul— a passenger compartment of sorts—from which the brain and, by

---

[23] See Colossians 3.

extension, other bodily functions are controlled and into which demonic spirits can intrude and comfortably reside.

It is entirely plausible that a fourth spatial dimension is concealed within—or without—human biology: an imperceivable appendage designed to house the soul. This fourth-dimensional compartment would not necessarily be constrained within the three-dimensional proportions of your body but might represent a commodious space large enough to accommodate multiple souls. Christ's encounter with the Gadarene demoniac possessed by a legion of unclean spirits clearly demonstrates that the biology of a single human being is capable of housing many demons, who are themselves the disembodied souls of angel-human hybrids. It also demonstrates that animals are equipped with the same extraspatial compartment, as the demons were quite content to inhabit swine. (We will revisit this scene in a later chapter.)

Consciousness is an indication that there is more to biology than meets the eye. It may ultimately prove that human beings, and indeed all conscious creatures, are inherently hyperdimensional.

Chapter 3

REBELLION, WAR, AND RUIN

I f the immeasurable vastness of the universe compels us to contemplate the significance of our place within it, then its unfathomable agedness obliges us to consider things in our absence. Since we know that the existence of mankind does not extend infinitely into the past but had a beginning in the course of time, we may presume that eons of untold history had unfolded on unknown worlds long before Adam graced the stage.

"All the world's a stage, and all the men and women merely players."[1] We shall enlarge Shakespeare's metaphor to encompass all the universe and include all its players, human and otherwise. Within this cosmic theater, mankind is the latest performer on the stage. His part in the play is the continuation of a tale long in the telling and, like any good story, follows the plotline of the previous act, with all the intrigue and consequence of its characters. The curtain closed on many a performance before it opened for the human race.

In order to fully appreciate the significance of our first act, we must examine the cataclysmic events that preceded it.

The earth and distant extraterrestrial worlds are reeling in the wake of rebellion, war, and ruin. A powerful insubordinate prince, personified as the *dragon*, the *serpent*, the *devil*, and the *satan*, has mounted an unsuccessful insurrection against the kingdom of heaven in a battle of

---

[1] William Shakespeare, *As You Like It*, Act II, Scene VII.

unimaginable destruction. Upon his defeat, the dragon (our preferred handle for him hereafter[2]) and his confederates were exiled to the earth's interior as punishment for their crimes.

Intimations of the dragon's sedition are disguised within the prophetic utterances of scripture. In the twenty-eighth chapter of Ezekiel, for instance, he wears the mask of Tyre's contemptuous king:

> "Son of man, raise a lamentation over the king of Tyre, and say to him, thus says the Lord God: 'You were the signet of perfection, full of wisdom and perfect in beauty. You were in Eden, the garden of God; every precious stone was your covering, sardius, topaz, and diamond, beryl, onyx, and jasper, sapphire, emerald, and carbuncle; and crafted in gold were your settings and your engravings. On the day that you were created they were prepared. You were an anointed guardian cherub. I placed you; you were on the holy mountain of God; in the midst of the stones of fire you walked. You were blameless in your ways from the day you were created, till unrighteousness was found in you. In the abundance of your trade you were filled with violence in your midst, and you sinned; so I cast you as a profane thing from the mountain of God, and I destroyed you, O guardian cherub, from the midst of the stones of fire. Your heart was proud because of your beauty; you corrupted your wisdom for the sake of your splendor. I cast you to the ground; I exposed you before kings, to feast their eyes on you.
>
> By the multitude of your iniquities, in the unrighteousness of your trade you profaned your sanctuaries; so I brought fire out from your midst; it consumed you, and I turned you to ashes on the earth in the sight of all who saw you. All who

---

[2] The author prefers the *dragon* moniker because it is more definitive than the terms *devil* (meaning "accuser") and *satan* (meaning "adversary"), which are not proper names but descriptive appellations assigned to anyone acting in these roles, and especially to the chief of all accusers and adversaries—the Devil with a capital D and Satan with a capital S. This infamous character is treated rather like Voldemort from the Harry Potter series, who is evasively referred to as "You-Know-Who" and "He Who Must Not Be Named"; in other words, he is so contemptible and dangerous that the mention of his actual name is forbidden.

know you among the peoples are appalled at you; you have come to a dreadful end and shall be no more forever."[3]

It is evident that this lamentation does not regard the human king of Phoenician pedigree but rather the inhuman power behind his throne—a being of ancient provenance who was in Eden, the garden of God. Ezekiel's king of Tyre is none other than the defiler of Eve, "that serpent of old, who is the Devil and Satan."[4]

The former prominence of the fallen dragon prince is plainly disclosed in the title "guardian cherub." In contrast with the term *angel*, the *cherub* denomination is never applied to human beings in the biblical text. Contrary to popular conception, *cherub* is a designation of rank rather than a classification of species. The chimeric depictions of cherubim (and seraphim) found throughout the scriptures are not meant to be taken as literal diagrams of their anatomy but iconographic portraits of their attributes. For example, Ezekiel's description of cherubim having four faces (human, lion, ox, eagle) and four wings and full of eyes all around conveys the attribute of vigilance.[5] Like the Praetorian Guard of the Roman Empire, the cherubim princes are wardens of the King whose throne they guard (or *cover*, hence the wings) and watchers over the affairs of the kingdom (hence the eyes).[6]

That the dragon walked in the midst of the "stones of fire" is of interest. Although there is little evidence to support the postulation, the stones of fire may be emblematic of the planets in our solar system. The nine precious stones that served as his "covering" (or perhaps, his *dominion*) may correspond to the eight planets in our solar system, plus one that was obliterated. The residue of this missing planet is evidenced in the asteroid

---

[3] Ezekiel 28:12–19 (ESV).

[4] Revelation 20:2 (NKJV).

[5] There is certainly a more profound interpretation of the faces, wings, and eyes of the cherubim that relates to the four cardinal points of the mazzaroth (zodiac) and the brightest of its stars: Fomalhaut, in Aquarius (man); Regulus, in Leo (lion); Anteres, in Opheocus (eagle); and Alderberan in Taurus (bull). More often than not, prophetic iconography is associated with the signs of the mazzaroth, its various constellations, and its astronomical implications, which is a complex subject well beyond the bounds of the present work.

[6] In the author's opinion, cherubim and seraphim are simply different titles for the same order of beings, who hold the highest office in the kingdom of heaven.

belt, located between the orbits of Mars and Jupiter, and could provide the context for the declaration, "I destroyed you, O guardian cherub, from the midst of the stones of fire."

The language of Ezekiel's lamentation suggests that the dragon was the most illustrious of the morning stars and chief among the cherubim. In a fairy-tale twist of fate, the love of his own beauty became a fatal attraction. As has been the case with many a human potentate, the mighty cherub prince was corrupted by the glory and power of his privileged estate.

The height of the dragon's pride and the depth of his downfall are advertised in Isaiah 14:

> "How you are fallen from heaven, O Lucifer [*bright star*], son of the morning [*morning star*]! How you are cut down to the ground, you who weakened the nations! For you have said in your heart: 'I will ascend into heaven, I will exalt my throne above the stars of God; I will also sit on the mount of the congregation on the farthest sides of the north; I will ascend above the heights of the clouds, I will be like the Most High.' Yet you shall be brought down to Sheol, to the lowest depths of the Pit.
>
> "Those who see you will gaze at you, and consider you, saying: 'Is this the man who made the earth tremble, who shook kingdoms, who made the world as a wilderness and destroyed its cities, who did not open the house of his prisoners?'"[7]

Here we find the origin of the stubborn misnomer *Lucifer* ("light-bearer"), a contrivance of the Latin Vulgate derived from the Hebrew *heylel*, meaning "shining one" or "bright star" and erroneously rendered by Jerome as a proper name. A critical point escapes those who have adopted the Lucifer epithet from the Vulgate: the purpose of the text is not to christen the dragon with a new name but to identify him as a morning star. To say that he is a "light-bearer" is missing the mark. He is an apostate son of God fallen from among the elder race.

---

[7] Isaiah 14:12–17 (NKJV).

The Masoretic translation (from which the above passage is extracted) describes Lucifer as having "weakened the nations," for which he was consequently "cut down to the ground." It is worth noting the slight variation in the Septuagint's[8] rendering of the same verse:

> How has Lucifer [the bright star] that rose in the morning, fallen from heaven! He that sent orders to all the nations is crushed to the earth.[9]

This reading paints the portrait of an imperious renegade prince commanding the forces of a galactic rebellion before being deposed from his throne and exiled to Planet Earth.

It is easy to pass over the dragon's betrayal with a careless wave of the hand, as if he possesses some intrinsic penchant for devilry to which we are immune. But the sedition of our elder sibling should not be so lightly considered, as his vices tend to run in the family.

Betrayal, by definition, can only be committed by one who has been taken into confidence. Satan was not always the infamous villain he is today. Once upon a time, he was a worshipful warden of the kingdom delighting in the favor of the King and basking in the adulation of his compatriots. He was the exemplar of a son before he became the symbol of a sinner—the very personification of betrayal among the morning stars.

Among men, betrayal is known by another name. Judas Iscariot was numbered with the twelve disciples of Christ, the most intimate of all his associates on Earth. Judas fellowshipped daily with Jesus for several years, witnessing every sign of his divinity, before betraying him to the Sanhedrin for thirty pieces of silver.

On the eve of his crucifixion, Jesus identified his betrayer by dipping a piece of bread in wine and handing it to Judas, evoking the lamentation of David: "Even my close friend in whom I trusted, who ate my bread, has

---

[8] The Septuagint (LXX) is the Greek translation of the Hebrew Old Testament, compiled by seventy (or seventy-two) Jewish scribes in Alexandria, Egypt, roughly three hundred years before Christ. By the first century AD, the Septuagint was widely circulated throughout the Greek-speaking world of the Roman Empire and was most certainly the text favored by the apostle Paul and the early church.

[9] Isaiah 14:12 (LXX, Brenton).

lifted his heel against me."[10] Although the betrayal of Judas Iscariot was certainly a fulfillment of this prophecy, he was not the close friend to whom Jesus referred.

Judas was always a fraud. He pilfered from the money bag and feigned concern for the poor. Jesus knew this and made it plain: "Did I not choose you, the twelve, and one of you is a devil?"[11] Judas was deliberately chosen to be the vessel of destruction through whom a far more ancient and sinister associate of the Son of God could reenact his betrayal, as manifested in the scene that follows:

> When Jesus had said these things, he was troubled in spirit, and testified and said, "Most assuredly, I say to you, one of you will betray me." Then the disciples looked at one another, perplexed about whom he spoke.
>
> Now there was leaning on Jesus' bosom one of his disciples, whom Jesus loved. Simon Peter therefore motioned to him to ask who it was of whom he spoke.
>
> Then, leaning back on Jesus' breast, he said to him, "Lord, who is it?"
>
> Jesus answered, "It is he to whom I shall give a piece of bread when I have dipped it." And having dipped the bread, he gave it to Judas Iscariot, the son of Simon. Now after the piece of bread, Satan entered him. Then Jesus said to him, "What you do, do quickly."[12]

Judas moved quickly indeed.

That very night, he led the Roman cohort and officers of the Temple guard into the garden of Gethsemane to arrest Jesus of Nazareth. When he pressed his lips to the Messiah's cheek, identifying him to his captors, it was no mere mortal kiss of betrayal. That familiar voice that once sang in the chorus of heaven could now be heard in the treacherous words, "Greetings, Rabbi."

---

[10] Psalm 41:9 (ESV).
[11] John 6:70 (NKJV).
[12] John 13:21–27 (NKJV).

The tragic betrayal of the cherub prince is a pivotal theme in the story arc of the Bible, the consequence of which bears on every chapter from Genesis to Revelation. In truth, the tale of mankind cannot be properly told unless set against a cosmic backdrop of cataclysm and desolation.

The Book of Genesis begins with a planet engulfed in water and darkness—a dreadful scene that resonates with divine retribution. Many eminent theologians throughout the centuries were convinced that the inaugural verses of the biblical narrative describe the earth in a state of utter desolation postjudgment. Not least among them, George H. Pember, writing in the nineteenth century, was perhaps the most eloquent proponent of the view.[13]

In his classic work, *Earth's Earliest Ages*, Pember contends that the prevailing conception among Christians regarding the primordial creation of Planet Earth does not conform to Hebrew cosmology but was adopted from the pagan doctrine of chaos. The doctrine of chaos maintains that the earth was an "unformed and confused bulk," suspended like a lump of clay in the void of space until it was molded by the hands of the gods. The motif of *order out of chaos* is central to the origin myths of many ancient cultures, including the Greeks and Romans, and in Pember's appraisal had infiltrated the Christian interpretation of Genesis. He writes,

> This doctrine [the doctrine of chaos], ancient and widespread as it was in the time of our Lord, did not fail to influence the real as well as the spurious Christians. Among the last mentioned, the important sects of the Gnostics believed in the eternity and intrinsic evil of matter; but, unlike the Heathen, they taught that the Supreme Being also existed from eternity. The orthodox Christians escaped the greater error altogether; but, nevertheless, gave clear testimony to the influence of the

---

[13] Born in 1836 and deceased in 1910, George Hawkins Pember was a highly regarded English theologian affiliated with the Plymouth Brethren. His literary works include *The Antichrist, Babylon, and the Coming of the Kingdom*; *The Great Prophecies of the Centuries Concerning Israel and the Gentiles*; and *Mystery Babylon the Great*, among others. *Earth's Earliest Ages* is considered by many to be his magnum opus and has been celebrated through the years as a classical masterpiece.

popular belief in their interpretation of the commencing chapter of Genesis. For they made the first verse signify the creation of a confused mass of elements, out of which the heavens and earth were formed during the six days, understanding the next sentence to be a description of this crude matter before God shaped it. And their opinion has descended to our days. But it does not appear to be substantiated by Scripture, as we shall presently see, and the guile of the serpent may be detected in its results.[14]

Pember believed that the theologians of his day (the nineteenth century), confronted as they were with newly discovered geologic indications of an exceedingly old Earth, had been baited into the fool's errand of proving that the earth was in fact young, an exercise, he argues, that had encumbered the precious time and talent of many able minds:

For how great a contest has it provoked between the Church and the World! How ready a handle do the geological difficulties involved in it present to the assailants of Scripture! With what perplexity do we behold earth gloomy with the shadow of pain and death ages before the sin of Adam! How many young minds have been turned aside by the absolute impossibility of defending what they have been taught to regard as Biblical statements! And lastly, in carrying on the dispute, how much precious time has been wasted by able servants of God, who would otherwise have been more profitably employed![15]

Order out of chaos is a Luciferian creed and a fundamental tenet in the doctrine of the mystery schools (of which we shall have more to say later), whose devotees are dedicated to the proposition that Yahweh is a tyrant—the author of darkness and chaos—and Lucifer is a hero, the bringer of illumination and order.

Genesis conveys the antithesis of the Luciferian creed: *chaos out of order.*

---

[14] George H. Pember, *Earth's Earliest Ages* (Crane, MO: Defense Publishing, 2012), 16–17.
[15] Pember, *Earth's Earliest Ages*, 17.

In the beginning, God created perfect order, but chaos was born of disobedience, which, when fully matured, wrought destruction and desolation. The story of mankind begins with the reformation and restoration of the order that God had originally purposed on Planet Earth.

In the Masoretic text, the first two verses of Genesis read as follows: "In the beginning God created the heaven and the earth. And the earth was without form, and void; and darkness was upon the face of the deep."[16] Pember argues that the translation of the phrase "the earth was without form, and void" is not the most accurate rendering from the Hebrew but "a glaring illustration of the influence of the chaos-legend."[17] He notes that Julius Fürst (a respected nineteenth-century Hebrew scholar) renders the term "without form" (*tohu*) as "ruin" or "desolation" and the word "void" (*bohu*) as "emptiness" or "that which is empty." To buttress the point, Pember explains that the Hebrew words *tohu* and *bohu* are only found together in two other passages of scripture, and in both cases they are explicitly employed to describe the perfect ruination wrought by the wrath of God:

> In a prophecy of Isaiah, after a fearful description of the fall of Idumea [Edom] in the day of vengeance, we find the expression, "He shall stretch out upon it the line of confusion, and the stones—or, as it should be translated, the plummet—of emptiness." Now "confusion" and "emptiness" are, in the Hebrew, the same words as those rendered "without form, and void." And the sense is, that just as the architect makes careful use of line and plummet in order to raise the building in perfection, so will the Lord to make the ruin complete.
>
> There is, then, no possibility of mistaking the meaning of the words in this place, and the second passage is even more conclusive. For, in describing the devastation of Judah and Jerusalem, Jeramiah likens it to the preadamite destruction, and exclaims: "I beheld the earth, and, lo, it was without form, and void; and the heavens, and they had no light. I beheld the

---

[16] Genesis 1:1–2 (KJV).
[17] Pember, *Earth's Earliest Ages*, 21.

mountains, and, lo, they trembled, and all the hills moved lightly. I beheld, and, lo, there was no man, and all the birds of the heavens were fled. I beheld, and, lo, the fruitful place was a wilderness, and all the cities thereof were broken down at the presence of the Lord, and by his fierce anger. For thus hath the Lord said, The whole land shall be desolate; yet will I not make a full end."[18]

Continuing his observations, Pember notes that the Hebrew verb *hayah,* translated as *was* in verse 2 ("And the earth *was* without form, and void," emphasis added), can also be rendered "to become." An example of this rendition is supplied in the history of Lot's wife, of whom we are told, "she *became* [*hayah*] a pillar of salt."[19] He concludes,

> But if any further evidence be needed to prove that our verse does not describe a chaotic mass which God first created and afterwards fashioned into shape, we have a direct and positive assertion to that effect in the forty-fifth chapter of Isaiah: for we are there told that God did not create the earth a *tohu.* This word, therefore, whatever meaning be assigned to it, cannot at least be descriptive of the earliest condition of earth. But our translators have obscured the fact by rendering *tohu* "in vain": they can hardly have compared the passages in which it occurs, or they would surely have seen the propriety of translating it in Isaiah's manifest reference to creation by the same word as in Genesis.[20]

Other competent scholars have argued convincingly that the word *and* at the beginning of verse 2 should more accurately be rendered *but.* Credence to this view is provided in the Septuagint, where the *but* rendition is favored in the Greek.[21]

---

[18] Pember, *Earth's Earliest Ages,* 22.
[19] Genesis 19:26 (KJV), emphasis added.
[20] Pember, *Earth's Earliest Ages,* 23.
[21] See Genesis 1:2 (LXX, Brenton).

These textual nuances may at first appear innocuous when considered in isolation, but when the changes are bound together in the verse, we get a very different view of the opening scene in Genesis:

> In the beginning God created the heaven and the earth. *But* the earth *became desolate, and empty*; and darkness was upon the face of the deep.

Our story now begins with a planet wrecked in the aftermath of cataclysmic judgment.

It is my contention that the threads of a galactic war are woven into the oracles of the Hebrew prophets and elsewhere in the scriptures. If we trace these threads, a thematic tapestry emerges, depicting an ancient insurrection that led to the total desolation of the planets in our solar system long before the creation of Adam.

Prophecy is esoteric by design. Oracles are intentionally encrypted with information, like a zipped folder on a computer, and require extraction. Once extracted, they often contain multiple layers of meaning. The surface layers usually pertain to the nation of Israel, or one of the contemporary nations in its vicinity, but the deeper layers sometimes address alien agencies and extraterrestrial events. Such is the case with Edom.

Just as Israel is another name for Jacob, the son of Isaac, so Edom is another name for Esau, his twin brother. The Israelites were the descendants of Jacob and the Edomites the descendants of Esau. Edom was the archenemy of Israel. A peculiar contempt for the Edomites is manifest in the scriptures, as they are the recipients of more pronouncements of judgment than any other nation.[22]

In the same way that the nation of Israel was representative of the kingdom of heaven on Earth, so Edom was representative of its ancient extraterrestrial adversary. The contention between Israel and Edom is an allegory of the war that raged—and rages still—between the kingdom and the insurgency. Indeed, Jacob is christened with the name Israel after

---

[22] See Isaiah 11:14, 34:5–17, 63:1–6; Jeremiah 9:25–26, 25:17–26, 49:7–22; Lamentations 4:21–22; Ezekiel 25:12–14, 35:15; Joel 3:19; Amos 1:11–12, 9:11–12; Obadiah 1:1–21; Malachi 1:4.

physically contending with Yahweh at the fords of the river Jabbok.[23]

The name *Israel* means "Yahweh contends." The name *Edom* means "red." An iconographic portrait of the adversary with whom Yahweh contends is presented to the apostle John in the form of a *red dragon*. When the names and concepts they represent are combined, Israel and Edom convey the cosmic conflict in which mankind is inescapably embroiled: *Yahweh contends with the red dragon.*

The dragon's primordial insurrection led to the destruction of many worlds and the defection of many sons. Among the mutinous morning stars drawn into the rebellion, six apostate princes—likely numbered among the cherubim—joined the dragon with their respective principalities to form a sevenfold confederacy. This unholy union is depicted in John's vision of the red dragon in Revelation 12:

> And another sign appeared in heaven: behold, a great red dragon, with seven heads and ten horns, and on his heads seven diadems.[24]

The dragon's red complexion is indicative of Edom. The seven heads crowned with seven diadems represent seven princes, and the ten horns correspond to the realms (conceivably planets) under their dominion.[25]

When visualizing the seven-headed red dragon of Revelation, we should imagine the head in the center as Satan, the preeminent dragon prince and chief of the confederacy; the other six heads, three on each side, are subordinate to his command.

Fantastical as it may seem in modern times, the figure of the seven-headed dragon was not unfamiliar to the ancient world. In fact, it makes several appearances in the Tanakh (the Hebrew Bible), embodied in the fabled creature *Leviathan.*

Prominently featured in the mythology of the ancient Near East, Leviathan (*Lotan* to the Ugarites and *Mussag* to the Sumerians) was a seven-headed dragon of the sea. The foremost significance of the Leviathan

---

[23] See Genesis 32.

[24] Revelation 12:3 (ESV).

[25] The ten horns may also be symbolic of great authority and power.

motif relates to the Ouroboros (the snake eating its tail) in the sea of the Milky Way, which signals the cataclysmic transition of eons (a complex subject beyond the scope of the present work). Aside from its astronomical implications, Leviathan represents the confederation of apostate dragon princes who dared to contend with the King of heaven in a bygone age:

> How long, O God, is the foe to scoff? Is the enemy to revile your name forever? Why do you hold back your hand, why do you keep your right hand in your bosom?
> Yet God my King is from old, working salvation in the midst of the earth. You divided the sea by your might; you broke the heads of the dragons on the waters. You crushed the heads of Leviathan.[26]

In the cosmology of the ancient world, outer space is universally portrayed as a cosmic sea—the waters above the earth.[27] Dividing the sea and breaking the heads of the dragons on the waters are figures of speech meant to conjure the vision of a galactic war in which the seven apostate princes, and the forces they led into battle, were utterly crushed by the armies of heaven. The Book of Job features a lengthy soliloquy in which Leviathan is dubbed "king over all the sons of pride" and depicted as an indomitable behemoth unable to be subdued, save by the hand of God.[28] Notice, in the passage above, the psalmist's petition that God unleash his right hand against the enemy (Leviathan), who *continues* to revile his name. The right hand of God is clearly an allusion to his Only Begotten Son, who John informs us "is in the bosom of the Father."[29] The Son of God is the King of old who subdued the dragons in the midst of the cosmic sea and threw them down from their lofty thrones.

The insurgency was defeated but not destroyed. Their forces were routed but not eradicated. The dragons would continue to revile the King and resist him on Earth, but they were now princes without a

---

[26] Psalm 74:10–14 (Revised Standard Version, Second Catholic Edition).
[27] As in Genesis 1:6, where God divides the terrestrial waters under the firmament from the cosmic waters above it.
[28] See Job 41 (ESV).
[29] John 1:18 (NKJV).

kingdom—the dethroned and disinherited sons of God doomed to abide the indignation of the Lord forever, with no hope of reconciliation.

Satan had temporarily evaded annihilation, but he would not escape judgment. After seducing the mother of our race in Eden, the dragon's fate was foretold from the very lips of the Maker, in one of the most remarkable prophecies of scripture:

> "I will put enmity between you and the woman, and between your offspring [seed] and hers; he will crush your head, and you will strike his heel."
>
> To the woman he said, "I will make your pains in childbearing very severe; with painful labor you will give birth to children."[30]

I call this the *Dragon Slayer Prophecy*. Like the plotline of a thrilling fantasy novel (that just so happens to be true), it foretells of the dragon's final defeat at the hands of a human being—a son of Adam destined to be born through the virgin womb of a daughter of Eve. (The virgin birth is insinuated in the phenomenon of the woman having seed. Women, of course, do not have seed. This suggests that the seed of the Dragon Slayer would come through the genetic line of the woman—the line of David through Mary—without the need of insemination. The Y chromosome would be supplied by God.)

The Dragon Slayer Prophecy is further elucidated in an oracle of Isaiah, wherein the nation of Israel is portrayed as a pregnant woman travailing to bring forth the Christ:

> And as a woman in travail draws nigh to be delivered, and cries out in her pain; so have we been to thy beloved [the Father's beloved Son]. We have conceived, O Lord, because of thy fear, and have been in pain, and have brought forth the breath of thy salvation [the Christ], which we have wrought upon the earth . . . Go, my people, enter into thy closets, shut thy door, hide thyself for a little season, until the anger of the

---

[30] Genesis 3:15–16 (NIV).

Lord has passed away. For, behold, the Lord is bringing wrath from his holy place upon the dwellers of the earth: the earth also shall disclose her blood, and shall not cover her slain. . . .

In that day God shall bring his holy and great and strong sword upon the dragon, even the serpent that flees, upon the dragon, the crooked serpent: he shall destroy the dragon.[31]

After hearing the pronouncement of his demise at the hands of a human being, the dragon was determined to foil the prophecy at all costs. In a vision corresponding to Isaiah's pregnant woman, John beholds the unfolding of Satan's strategy from Eden to Armageddon.

The vision of the Woman and the Dragon in Revelation 12 consists of three archetypes:

1. A pregnant woman travailing in labor, about to give birth.[32]

2. A dragon poised to devour her offspring as soon as he emerges from the womb.[33]

3. A male child destined to rule the nations with a rod of iron (who, upon his birth, is caught up to the throne of God).[34]

As affirmed in the oracle of Isaiah (and elsewhere), the woman is clearly Israel, but she is also Eve. The male child is clearly the Christ, but he is also Adam. We have already deciphered the identity of the red dragon.

Without getting too far afield into the intricacies of this prophecy and its many correlative passages throughout the scriptures,[35] we can extrapolate the sequence of events communicated in the vision:

---

[31] Isaiah 26:17–18, 20–21; 27:1 (LXX, Brenton).

[32] "A woman clothed with the sun, with the moon under her feet, and on her head a crown of twelve stars. She was pregnant and was crying out in birth pains and the agony of giving birth" (Revelation 12:1–2, ESV).

[33] "And the dragon stood before the woman who was about to give birth, so that when she bore her child he might devour it" (Revelation 12:4, ESV).

[34] "She gave birth to a male child, one who is to rule all the nations with a rod of iron, but her child was caught up to God and to his throne" (Revelation 12:5, ESV).

[35] In addition to its narrative interpretation, the vision of the Woman and the Dragon in Revelation 12 has an astonishing astrological correlation pertaining to the mazzaroth and its various constellations.

a. First, the narrative assumes the defection and downfall of the dragon who, upon being defeated in heaven, was exiled to the earth with his confederates.[36]

b. Whereupon Adam is created and the seed of the Dragon Slayer, the Christ, is prophesied to emerge from the womb of a daughter of Eve.

c. The dragon attempts to thwart the prophecy by corrupting the genome (seed) of mankind through the events that transpire in Genesis 6 (examined in a forthcoming chapter).

d. He nearly succeeds, but the genetic profile of the human species is preserved in Noah and his sons, who are delivered through the Flood to repopulate the earth.

e. After the Flood, the dragon narrows his focus on the line of Adam in the offspring of Abraham, through whom the Christ must come. He sows the seed of Edom in the womb of Rebekah, the wife of Isaac (examined in a forthcoming chapter), and populates the promised land with Nephilimic tribes. When Canaan falls to the Hebrews, he attempts to destroy the nation of Israel through various schemes.

f. Once again, he is unsuccessful. The nation of Israel endures, and Christ is born of the virgin Mary in the line of King David, Adam's rightful heir in accordance with the scriptures.

g. Having failed to prevent the birth of Christ, the dragon attempts to persuade him to abandon his mission and betray his Father in the desert of Judea. However, unlike Satan, Jesus is a faithful son and fulfills the will of his Father by submitting himself to death on the cross.

---

[36] It is of interest to note that Isaiah's parallel prophecy concerning the pregnant woman also records an allusion to the same event: "Who hast humbled and brought down them that dwell on high, thou shalt cast down strong cities, and bring them to the ground [or Earth]" (Isaiah 26:5, LXX).

h. Christ completes his mission and ascends to the throne of God, where he awaits the end of the age. When the age is fully consummated, he will return to the earth to crush the head of the dragon and assume the throne of David, from which he will rule the nations with a rod of iron.

i. Despite his best efforts, the dragon's clever ploys have been frustrated at every turn. He has but one recourse left—to prepare for war.

The fulfillment of the Dragon Slayer Prophecy is now inevitable. In an eleventh-hour bid to forestall his fate, the dragon is rebuilding his ancient strongholds and amassing his forces for a final insurrection.

References to Edom in the scriptures are intended to communicate three interconnected episodes in time: 1) the celestial conflict in the pre-Adamic past, 2) the terrestrial conflict with the nation of Israel during the biblical period, and 3) the battle of Armageddon at the end of the age. All three episodes are synthesized in Isaiah's description of the fall of Edom, which depicts a sanguinary battle fought in a galactic theater of war:

> For the indignation of the Lord is against all nations, and his fury against all their armies; he has utterly destroyed them, he has given them over to the slaughter. Also their slain shall be thrown out; their stench shall rise from their corpses, and the mountains shall be melted with their blood. All the host of heaven shall be dissolved, and the heavens shall be rolled up like a scroll; all their host shall fall down as the leaf falls from the vine, and as fruit falling from a fig tree.
>
> "For my sword shall be bathed in heaven; indeed it shall come down on Edom, and on the people of my curse . . . And he shall stretch out over it the line of confusion [*tohu*] and the stones [plummet] of emptiness [*bohu*]. . . .
>
> They shall call the princes thereof, princes without a kingdom; and all her great ones shall be nothing.[37]

---

[37] Isaiah 34:2–5, 11 (NKJV), 12 (Jubilee Bible 2000).

While the *prima facie* context of this passage pertains to the historical destruction of the Edomite nation, it is hard to miss the apocalyptic landscape of Armageddon at the end of the age and the connotations of a cosmic battle that precipitated the fall of a heavenly host. As noted by Pember, the very same words that Isaiah uses to convey the wrathful ruination of Edom, *tohu* and *bohu*, are employed by the author of Genesis to describe the pre-Adamic desolation of Planet Earth. In other words, the same event led to the retributive destruction of both—the dragon's primordial rebellion.

Obadiah leaves no room for doubt:

> Thus says the Lord God concerning Edom . . . "Arise, and let us rise up against her for battle."
>
> "The pride of your heart has deceived you, you who dwell in the clefts of the rock, whose habitation is high; you who say in your heart, 'Who will bring me down to the ground?' Though you ascend as high as the eagle, and though you set your nest among the stars, from there I will bring you down."[38]

These verses resound with the pomposity of the mighty cherub prince who said in his heart, "I will ascend into heaven, I will exalt my throne above the stars of God." To which God replied, "You shall be brought down to Sheol, to the lowest depths of the Pit."

The Song of Deborah, memorialized in the Book of Judges, describes the King of heaven marching against the dragon on the galactic battlefield of Edom:

> "Hear, O kings! Give ear, O princes! . . . Lord, when you went out from Seir, when you marched from the field of Edom, the earth trembled and the heavens poured, the clouds also poured water; the mountains gushed [melted] before the Lord . . .
>
> They fought from the heavens; the stars from their courses fought."[39]

---

[38] Obadiah 1:1, 3–4 (NKJV).
[39] Judges 5:3–5, 20 (NKJV).

As previously mentioned, when titles of regency are directly juxtaposed in the biblical text, in this case, *kings* and *princes*, they often signal a distinction of realms and rulers, the terrestrial and the extraterrestrial, kings of the human race and their elder race counterparts. The oracles of Edom are intended to convey the scope and nature of a cosmic conflict that began long ago on extraterrestrial worlds but is destined to culminate on Earth at the battle of Armageddon.

If we compare the prophecy of Isaiah 63, looking back to the battle of Edom, with the vision of John in Revelation 19, looking forward to the battle of Armageddon, a clear correlation emerges. Both of these passages portray the King of heaven making war, his raiment stained in blood as he treads the winepress of God's wrath.

Writes Isaiah,

> Who is this coming from Edom, from Bozrah [the capitol city of Edom], with his garments stained crimson? Who is this, robed in splendor, striding forward in the greatness of his strength?
>
> "It is I, proclaiming victory, mighty to save."
>
> Why are your garments red, like those of one treading the winepress?
>
> "I have trodden the winepress alone; from the nations no one was with me. I trampled them in my anger and trod them down in my wrath; their blood spattered my garments, and I stained all my clothing."[40]

Writes John,

> Then I saw heaven opened, and behold, a white horse! The one sitting on it is called Faithful and True, and in righteousness he judges and makes war. His eyes are like a flame of fire, and on his head are many diadems, and he has a name written that no one knows but himself. He is clothed in a robe dipped in blood, and the name by which he is called is The Word of

---

[40] Isaiah 63:1–3 (NIV).

God. And the armies of heaven, arrayed in fine linen, white and pure, were following him on white horses. From his mouth comes a sharp sword with which to strike down the nations, and he will rule them with a rod of iron. He will tread the winepress of the fury of the wrath of God the Almighty. On his robe and on his thigh he has a name written, King of kings and Lord of lords.[41]

It is not incidental that when the Lord returns to the earth at the battle of Armageddon, his robe is dipped in blood. The symbolism is clear: the King who drove the dragon from the field of Edom is coming to finish the job in the valley of Armageddon. Notice that the King's head is adorned with many diadems (crowns), which correspond to the title written on his thigh: King of kings and Lord of lords. These diadems and titles of regency imply a plurality of realms, terrestrial and extraterrestrial. The kingdom of heaven comprises many realms, and Jesus is King and Lord of all.

A closer look at Isaiah 63 forces us to contend with a perplexing scenario. Notice how the King is wroth with the nations because they did not support him in battle: "I have trodden the winepress alone; from the nations no one was with me."[42] The circumstance is emphasized in the verses that follow:

> "I looked, but there was no one to help, I was appalled that no one gave support; so my own arm achieved salvation for me, and my own wrath sustained me. I trampled the nations in my anger; in my wrath I made them drunk and poured their blood on the ground."[43]

Remarkably, the Song of Deborah identifies the faithless bystanders who declined to join the ranks of the King when he marched on the field of Edom:

---

[41] Revelation 19:11–16 (ESV).
[42] Isaiah 63:3 (NIV).
[43] Isaiah 63:5–6 (NIV).

Curse ye Meroz, said the angel of the Lord, curse ye bitterly the inhabitants thereof; because they came not to the help of the Lord, to the help of the Lord against the mighty.[44]

Two questions necessarily arise from this scenario: who are the mighty against whom the Lord requested support? And who or what is Meroz? The answer to the first question is apparent: *the forces of the dragon's confederacy.* And, according to ancient rabbinic tradition, the answer to the second question is *a planet.*

In his seminal work, *Cydonia: The Secret Chronicles of Mars*, the late researcher extraordinaire David Flynn explains,

> The Talmud (Moed Katan 16A) records that *Meroz* is the name of a planet. This planet Meroz was thought to be inhabited, as the verse literally explains, "curse ye bitterly the inhabitants thereof." The context in which the reference to Meroz is found defines it as a planet and not as a neighboring city. One verse earlier, Deborah stated, "From the heavens they fought, the stars from their orbits." The Zohar also follows the opinion that Meroz is a star, yet also states that "its inhabitants" refers to its "camp" (Zohar 3:269b).
>
> Additionally the Sefer HaBrit explains that the beings of Meroz are *ba'alei sekhel u'madah* (masters of intelligence and science) but they lack the human component of *behirah* which means, "Free Will."
>
> The Midrash teaches that there were seven worlds. The Zohar states that the seven worlds were separated by a firmament and were inhabited. Although not inhabited by man, they were the domain of intelligent creatures.[45]

Known in the esoteric tradition as *the shattered vessels of Edom,* seven primordial worlds, once inhabited by advanced civilizations, were thought

---

[44] Judges 5:23 (KJV).

[45] David Flynn, *The David Flynn Collection - Cydonia: The Secret Chronicles of Mars* (Crane, MO: Defense Publishing, 2012), 369–70.

to have been created and destroyed in the pre-Adamic age. The fate of these worlds is characterized in the appellative expression *olamim hatohu*, meaning *"the worlds of tohu"* (or *"the worlds of desolation"*). As we have seen, the word *tohu* is imbued with connotations of retributive destruction. Like the seven heads of the red dragon, the seven shattered vessels of Edom are symbolic of the seven apostate princes and their respective principalities, each one of which was laid waste in the wrath of God.

Flynn postulates that these desolated planets (and their princes) are personified in the fallen kings of Edom:

> The secrets regarding these seven worlds are hidden in the Torah within the genealogy of the family of Esau in Genesis 36:31–39. It speaks of "kings who reigned in the land of Edom, before there was a king in Israel." These Edomite kings are an esoteric reference to those primordial worlds of old.[46]

The postulation is affirmed by Rabbi Geoff Dennis, a teacher of Kabbalah and rabbinic literature in the Jewish Studies Program at the University of North Texas:

> This elliptical passage, which summarizes the family line of Esau, is a narrative dead-end that inexplicably interrupts the continuing epic of the blessed son, Jacob. But its very oddity and obscurity invites occult explanation.
>
> In this case, the mystics read this not as an account of an ancestral branch-off from the tree of Israel, but as a cosmic revelation, an allegoric telling of what preceded creation (Zohar III: 128a; 135a-b; Sefer ha-Gilgulim 15). The hermeneutic key is the phrase, ". . . who reigned . . . before any king reigned over the Israelites." The "king" here is taken to refer to the God of Israel. Prior to this creation, then, there were forces that disrupted God's effective rule of the earlier worlds.[47]

---

[46] Flynn, *Cydonia*, 368.
[47] Rabbi Geoffrey Dennis, "First Edom, Then Eden: The Primordial Kings of Strict Justice," *Jewish Myth, Magic, and Mysticism* (blog), December 16, 2008, http://ejmmm2007.blogspot.com/2008/12/first-edom-then-eden-primordial-kings.html.

Of the eight kings who reigned in the land of Edom, the deaths of only seven are recorded; the eighth corresponds to a forthcoming "king of fierce countenance" described by the prophet Daniel (of whom we shall have much to say later on).[48]

It is the author's own postulation that the planets in our solar system were once inhabited by nonhuman civilizations before they were reduced to rubble in the war of insurrection.

The question of whether life could have existed on the other planets in our solar system is almost always considered in comparison to the present conditions on Planet Earth. It is commonly assumed that in order for life to exist on another planet, Earth-like conditions must be met. A life-sustaining planet, it is thought, must necessarily be located in a circumstellar habitable zone, a so-called Goldilocks Zone. Like the favored bowl of porridge in the fairy tale from which its name is derived, a Goldilocks Zone is in just the right position from the sun to support the prerequisites for life (especially liquid water)—not too hot and not too cold. Mercury and Venus are too hot. Mars and the outer planets are too cold.

At face value, this simple proposition seems cogent enough. How can life exist on Venus, for example, where the median surface temperature is a blistering 872°F? Or on the frozen landscape of Jupiter, where temperatures hover just below –230°F? However, when the question is properly framed and unfettered from comparison to the earth, new possibilities emerge. We should not be asking whether these planets are *presently* capable of supporting life but whether they might have been inhabitable under different conditions in the distant past. Were the planets in our solar system once uniquely conditioned to support particular kinds of life before they became the hostile wastelands they are today?

According to the findings of a recent study at the Goddard Institute for Space Science, the answer is *yes*—at least as it pertains to Venus.

The study, conducted by Michael Way and Anthony Del Genio, ran a series of computer simulations on the topography of Venus. Surprisingly, the simulations indicated that the second planet from the sun was once covered in oceans and likely maintained stable temperatures, ranging between 122°F to 68°F, until a cataclysmic event precipitated its current

---

[48] See Genesis 36; Daniel 8.

life-prohibitive conditions. "Our hypothesis," writes Way, "is that Venus may have had a stable climate for billions of years. It is possible that the near-global resurfacing event [catastrophic volcanism] is responsible for its transformation from an Earth-like climate to the hellish hot-house we see today."[49] If this can be said of Venus, might it not also be said of the other planets in our solar system?

When considering the possibility of life on other planets, we should resist the temptation to compare them with the "Goldilocks" condition of Planet Earth. Distance from the sun is not the only determining factor for a planet's habitability; it may be that the composition of a planet's atmosphere is just as critical as its orbital position around a star. For example, if a planet closer to its sun than the earth, such as Venus, happens to be covered in a thick atmosphere densely composed of light-refracting particles to shield it from solar emissions, then it might, in theory, maintain an agreeable climate conducive to the propagation of life. Conversely, if a planet is farther from its sun than the earth but has an insulative atmosphere composed of light-absorbing particles, it might also maintain an agreeable climate. Moreover, the size and intensity of a planet's molten core must be taken into account. Perhaps there are planets whose cores are much hotter than the earth's, producing a natural greenhouse effect through the effusion of heat rising into the atmosphere.

It is possible, then, that although barren and lifeless today, the other planets in our solar system were once intentionally designed with habitable conditions uniquely tailored to their orbital positions around the sun. There is also the possibility that these planets were in fact situated in the Goldilocks Zone before being knocked out of orbit by an immensely powerful explosion. Whatever the case, one thing is certain—the planets orbiting our sun were thoroughly pulverized in the distant past.

The desolated topography of Earth's neighboring planets, marred by the gaping craters of intense meteoric bombardment, implies that some cataclysmic event rocked the solar system. The asteroid belt between Mars and Jupiter is likely the debris of an obliterated planet called Rahab, one of the seven shattered vessels of Edom. The connotations of the word *Rahab*

[49] "Could Venus Have Been Habitable?" Euro Planet Society, September 20, 2019, https://www.europlanet-society.org/could-venus-have-been-habitable.

("fierce, insolent, proud, boaster") are the calling cards of its renegade prince. References to Rahab in the biblical text are distinctly bellicose and directly associated with the dragon's rebellion and the triumph of the King who vanquished him:

> The pillars of heaven tremble and are astounded at his rebuke. By his power he stilled the sea; by his understanding he shattered Rahab.[50]

> Awake, awake, put on strength, O arm of the Lord [Son of God]; awake, as in days of old, the generations of long ago. Was it not you who cut Rahab in pieces, who pierced the dragon?[51]

> You rule the raging of the sea; when its waves rise, you still them. You have broken Rahab in pieces, as one who is slain; you have scattered your enemies with your mighty arm.[52]

Stilling and ruling the raging sea are metaphors for quelling and subduing insurrection. The shattering of Rahab was the decisive blow that pierced the dragon and brought his rebellion to an abrupt and devastating end.

When Rahab exploded, its smoldering shards rained down on the planets in its vicinity, each one striking with a force many thousands of times more powerful than a nuclear bomb, igniting their atmospheres with a firestorm hot enough to liquefy solid rock and vaporize everything else. The impacts would have triggered chains of volcanic eruptions and mile-high tidal waves, melting and washing away every vestige of the rebel kingdoms so that nothing would be left to posterity.

Personified as a spectator to this cataclysmic event, the earth saw and trembled as the insurgent forces of the apostate princes (the gods) were incinerated before the Lord, his garments stained crimson, striding forward in the greatness of his strength:

---

[50] Job 26:11–12 (ESV).
[51] Isaiah 51:9 (ESV).
[52] Psalm 89:9–10 (NKJV).

Fire goes before him and burns up his adversaries round about. His lightnings lit up the world; the earth saw and trembled. The mountains melted like wax at the presence of the Lord ... Worship Him, all you gods. Zion heard this and was glad, and the daughters of Judah have rejoiced because of your judgments, O Lord. For you are the Lord Most High over all the earth; you are exalted far above all gods.[53]

Psalm 89 provides a fitting synopsis of the concepts presented thus far. Written in memoriam of the dragon's rebellion, the psalm proclaims a solemn warning to all those who would dare to defy the King of heaven and rise up against him:

For who in the skies [cosmos] can be compared to the Lord? Who among the heavenly beings is like the Lord, a God greatly to be feared in the council of the holy ones [cherubim], and awesome above all who are around him? O Lord God of hosts [armies], who is mighty as you are, O Lord, with your faithfulness [faithful] all around you? You rule the raging of the sea [insurrection]; when its waves rise, you still them. You crushed Rahab like a carcass; you scattered your enemies with your mighty arm [the Son of God]. The heavens are yours; the earth also is yours; the world and all that is in it, you have founded them.[54]

A living illustration of these verses is recorded in the synoptic gospels, where Jesus and his disciples (his faithful all around him) set off in a boat to cross the Sea of Galilee, when suddenly they are caught in a great windstorm. As the waves beat against the boat, the disciples, fearing for their lives, awaken Jesus, who is asleep in the stern:

And a great windstorm arose, and the waves beat into the boat, so that it was already filling. But he was in the stern, asleep

---

[53] Psalm 97:3–5, 7–9 (NASB).
[54] Psalm 89:6–11 (ESV).

on a pillow. And they awoke him and said to him, "Teacher, do you not care that we are perishing?"

Then he arose and rebuked the wind, and said to the sea, "Peace, be still!" And the wind ceased and there was a great calm. But he said to them, "Why are you so fearful? How is it that you have no faith?"

And they feared exceedingly, and said to one another, "Who can this be, that even the wind and the sea obey him!"[55]

The disciples had not yet recognized who Jesus was, even though the powers of darkness shrieked and cowered in his presence. After disembarking on the shore of Gadara, Jesus was immediately confronted by a legion of demons dwelling in the body of an unfortunate man.[56] As soon as they saw him, they threw the man at his feet and begged for mercy. They knew who it was that stood before them; this was the very Word of God, the King of old who pierced the dragon and broke Rahab in pieces like a vessel of clay.

Is not my word [the Son of God] like fire, declares the Lord, and like a hammer that breaks the rock [Rahab] in pieces?[57]

The dragon's insurrection was an unmitigated disaster that reaped unimaginable destruction in the solar system. By the end of the war, the planetary domains of the seven apostate princes were laid waste and left to career in their orbits, *tohu va-bohu*. Only the earth would ever be inhabited again. The others were condemned to lie in ruin forever:

I will stretch out my hand against you and make you a desolate waste. I will turn your towns into ruins and you will be desolate. . . . I will make you desolate forever; your towns will not be inhabited. . . . You boasted against me and spoke against me without restraint, and I heard it. This is what the

---

[55] Mark 4:37–41 (NKJV).
[56] Or *men*, according to Matthew.
[57] Jeremiah 23:29 (ESV).

Sovereign Lord says: While the whole earth rejoices, I will make you desolate. . . . You will be desolate, Mount Seir, you and all of Edom. Then they will know that I am the Lord.[58]

Mount Seir was Esau's abode in Edom and the command center in his campaign against the nation of Israel. In addition to symbolizing the insurgency at large, Edom, like Mount Seir, may also be emblematic of the dragon's own planetary abode, which served as the command center in his campaign against the kingdom of heaven. The clue to identifying *Planet Edom* is likely encoded in the meaning of its name—"red."

I am persuaded that Edom is emblematic of the red planet, Mars. Throughout the ages, Mars has always evoked a sentiment of foreboding. The ancients regarded it as an omen of war and destruction. Adepts of the mysteries have long considered the red planet to be the source of great power, where the secrets of the gods reside. Man's obsession with Mars is not incidental. Even now, something beckons us to the forbidden gates of its ruined cities.

Mars was likely the seat of the dragon's dominion and the high command of his confederacy until it was reduced to a wilderness of rubble in the bombardment of Rahab. Since the day he was deposed from his lofty throne and exiled to the earth, the dragon has been brooding over his revenge and conspiring to rebuild the ruins of his ancient habitation.

A shadow of this contingency may be discerned in an obscure oracle of Malachi:

I hated Esau [*Satan*], and made his mountains waste, and his heritage a wilderness for dragons.

Edom may say, "Though we have been crushed, we will rebuild the ruins."

Thus says the Lord of hosts: "They may build, but I will throw down; they shall be called the Territory of Wickedness, and the people against whom the Lord will have indignation forever."[59]

---

[58] Ezekiel 35:3–4, 9, 13–14, 15 (NIV).
[59] Malachi 1:3 (1599 Geneva Bible), 4 (NIV/NKJV).

Paul warns the brethren in Ephesus to be "strong in the Lord and in the strength of his might. Put on the whole armor of God, that you may be able to stand against the schemes of the devil. For we do not wrestle against flesh and blood [human beings], but against the rulers, against the authorities, against the cosmic powers over this present darkness, against the spiritual forces of evil in the heavenly places."[60] It is perhaps redundant, at this point, to emphasize the plurality of realms implied in this admonition. We, like the Ephesians, should also take heed: cosmic powers operating on—and off—Planet Earth are conspiring to reignite the insurrectionary fires that led to the destruction of many worlds.

There is reason to believe that the dragon is mobilizing an extra-terrestrial army on the planetary bodies in our solar system (and perhaps other star systems) in preparation for a final assault on the kingdom of heaven. It appears that Michael will launch a preemptive strike against the enemy's forward operating bases before the return of Christ.

John gets a glimpse of the battle that ensues:

> Then war broke out in heaven: Michael and his angels fought against the dragon. The dragon and his angels also fought, but he could not prevail, and there was no place for them in heaven any longer. So the great dragon was thrown out—the ancient serpent, who is called the devil and Satan, the one who deceives the whole world. He was thrown to earth, and his angels with him.[61]

This war clearly occurs in an eschatological context, as it preludes the rise of the beast, the tribulation of the saints, and the battle of Armageddon. But before we can survey the battlefield of the future, we must look back to the dismal scene where our story begins.

After Rahab's destruction, the earth became a watery grave enveloped in the impenetrable gloom of an atmosphere laden with volcanic ash. And thus it would have remained forever, had the Lord not sworn in his wrath, "The whole land shall be desolate; yet will I not make a full end."

---

[60] Ephesians 6:10–12 (ESV).
[61] Revelation 12:7–9 (Christian Standard Bible).

Chapter 4

MANKIND

A bleak interval of inundated oblivion had likely befallen Planet Earth before the Spirit of God began to move over the face of the waters. The time had come, at last, to renew the terrestrial realm and appoint a regent to govern it.

We may imagine the scene:

Black clouds billow above a cold, turbid sea haunting the eternal night with the foaming of its barren waves, when suddenly, a voice thunders in the dark, *"Let there be light!"*

All at once, a torrent of wind rips through the atmosphere, rending the clouds asunder and revealing the long-forgotten sun, whose golden rays plunge into the water like shimmering spears.

The psalmist describes what happens next:

> The waters stood above the mountains. At your rebuke they fled; at the voice of your thunder they hastened away. They went up over the mountains; they went down into the valleys, to the place which you founded for them. You have set a boundary that they may not pass over, that they may not return to cover the earth. . . . O Lord, how manifold are your works! In wisdom you have made them all. . . . You send forth your Spirit, they are created; and you renew the face of the earth.[1]

[1] Psalm 104:6–9, 24, 30 (NKJV).

The six-day work chronicled in the first chapter of Genesis does not describe the initial formation of a planet but the renewal of a world shrouded in darkness and covered in the waters of divine wrath. Note the line that precedes the passage above:

You covered [the earth] with the deep as with a garment.[2]

This dismal picture of a dead planet inundated in water before being resurrected to life is a prefiguration of baptism in Christ Jesus.[3] Baptism is symbolic of the faith and hope of a believer. The water into which a convert is submerged represents wrath, judgment, and condemnation with the dragon. The old man, bearing the wrath of God because of sin, is submerged in the water, identifying with Christ's atoning death; a renewed man emerges from the water, identifying with Christ's righteousness and resurrection to eternal life. Those who die in their sins are condemned with the dragon. Those who die in Christ are reconciled to the Father and restored to the Edenic mandate of mankind:

For if we died with him, we shall also live with him. If we endure, we shall also reign with him.[4]

After five days (or perhaps, epochs) of renewal, the earth was radiant with life. The gloom of desolation and death was displaced by the glory of God. A new realm had been inaugurated in the cosmos, and it was very good, but one thing lacked.

The King's council was convened. The mightiest of the morning stars, princes and potentates all, took their places around his throne. To whom would the deed of Earth's dominion be given?

---

[2] Psalm 104:6 (NKJV).

[3] Theologians throughout history have viewed the pre-Adamic and Noahic deluges as baptismal cleansings of the planet necessary for the life-renewing process of regeneration. "A flood is an overflow of water, covering all that is under it, and purifying every defilement," wrote Basil of Caesarea in the fourth century AD. "Therefore he calls the grace of baptism a flood; so that the soul washed from sin, and cleansed from the old man, may be, afterwards, a fit habitation for God, by His Spirit" (Basil, I, 304).

[4] 2 Timothy 2:11–12 (NKJV).

The writer of Job describes the King's disposition:

> Behold, God puts no trust in his holy ones, and the heavens are not pure in his sight.[5] . . . Even in his servants he puts no trust, and his angels he charges with error.[6]

Who among the host of heaven could be trusted to rule and not rebel? The council deliberated. What they needed was a servant whose heart and mind was uncontaminated by the affairs of the past. Indeed, more than a servant—a sibling in the royal family, invested with the authority of a son. The resolution came forth:

> "Let us make man in our image, according to our likeness; let them have dominion over the fish of the sea, over the birds of the air, and over the cattle, over all the earth and over every creeping thing that creeps on the earth."[7]

This extraordinary pronouncement has vexed theologians for centuries and has supplied fodder for endless speculation. The problem is in the plurals. "Many Bible readers note the *plural* pronouns (us; our) with curiosity," remarks Michael Heiser, a scholar-in-residence for Logos Bible Software. "They might suggest that the plurals refer to the Trinity, but technical research in Hebrew grammar and exegesis has shown that the Trinity is not a coherent explanation. The solution is much more straightforward, one that an ancient Israelite would have readily discerned. What we have is a single person (God) addressing a group—the members of his divine council."[8]

That Yahweh sits enthroned above lesser gods, the *Elohim*, is not a controversy among scholars. Gerald McDermott, professor of religion at Roanoke College, explains,

---

[5] Job 15:15 (ESV).
[6] Job 4:18 (ESV).
[7] Genesis 1:26 (NKJV).
[8] Michael S. Heiser, *The Unseen Realm: Recovering the Supernatural Worldview of the Bible* (Bellingham, WA: Lexham Press, 2015), 39.

The idea that there are other "gods" who exist as real supernatural beings, albeit infinitely inferior to the only Creator and Redeemer, pervades the Bible. The Psalms fairly explode with evidence. "There is none like you among the gods, O Lord" (86:8); "For great is the Lord, and greatly to be praised; he is to be revered above all gods" (96:4); "Our Lord is above all gods" (135:5); "Ascribe to Yahweh, [you] gods, ascribe to Yahweh glory and strength" (29:1, my trans.); "He is exalted above all gods" (97:7); "For Yahweh is a great god, and a great king above all gods" (95:3, my trans.). And so on.[9]

In a setting suffused with the air of empire, Psalm 82 depicts the King of heaven presiding in judgment over a company of derelict princes who have failed to perform their duties:

> God has taken his place in the divine council; in the midst of the gods [*Elohim*] he holds judgment:
> "How long will you judge unjustly and show partiality to the wicked? *Selah*. Give justice to the weak and the fatherless; maintain the right of the afflicted and the destitute. Rescue the weak and the needy; deliver them from the hand of the wicked." . . .
> I said, "You are gods, sons of the Most High, all of you; nevertheless, like men you shall die, and fall like any prince."[10]

Other such scenes could be cited, but in the interest of brevity we shall return to the one at hand. The decision to give life to mankind and appoint him regent of Planet Earth was the consensus of the divine council, but the act of creating him was the sole prerogative and power of the King who presided over it.

And so it was. The King fashioned the anatomy of man from the very soil of the realm he was meant to rule and molded him in his own image,

---

[9] Gerald McDermott, "The Bible's Many Gods," *First Things* (blog), January 20, 2014, https://www.firstthings.com/web-exclusives/2014/01/the-bibles-many-gods.
[10] Psalm 82:1–4, 6–7 (ESV).

the seal of his royal house. The question of what it means to be made in the image of God is rarely resolved with a satisfying answer. Even in the hands of the most competent theologians, the matter seems to have the consistency of pudding. There does appear to be a general consensus, however, that whatever the meaning of the *imago dei*, mankind is its sole bearer. Popular as this presumption may be, it is not derived from the scriptures. Rather, it follows from the anthropocentric perspective of the universe, which elevates man above all creation and assigns to him an exclusivity on the trademark likeness of the Creator.

The argument in favor of the presumption is usually framed in the following way: Of all the creatures in the universe, only man possesses the emotional, imaginative, and cognitive qualities of the Creator himself. Other intelligent beings (such as angels) somehow lack that special *something* that makes mankind uniquely God-like.

The proposition is neither biblical nor logical.

Whether you believe that the image of God represents man's self-awareness, his higher intellect, his rationality, his physical anatomy, his emotional complexity, his creativity, or the combination of all these attributes, you cannot reasonably argue—not from the scriptures, at any rate—that he is the only being in the cosmos endowed with such. It is apparent in the biblical text that mankind resembles the morning stars, who not only display the very same attributes but seem to possess them to a greater extent.

The breathtaking arrogance of the fallen sons of God and the exuberance exhibited by the faithful sons in heaven demonstrate beyond doubt that they, too, are emotionally complex creatures. The simple fact that they sing and compose music should suffice to evince their creativity. And I think we can say with some degree of confidence that human beings have not cornered the market on intelligence.

So manifold are the similarities between men and morning stars that, if not for the testimony of scripture, one might be tempted to conclude that we are in fact the same race. It is clear, however, that the divine council resolved to create a new kind of creature to govern the earth, one that did not previously exist in the cosmos, man*kind*. Whereas mankind was fashioned from terrestrial clay, the physiology of the morning stars is of a different nature—a higher nature. Perhaps, in the same way that we were created from the substance of a planet, they were created from the substance of a star. Who can say?

While we are not members of the same race, we are, nevertheless, siblings in the same family, and as such, we bear the same likeness, the image of our Father.

That Adam was created to be a son of God is evidenced in the genealogy of Jesus of Nazareth, "the son of Joseph . . . the son of Noah, the son of Lamech, the son of Methuselah, the son of Enoch, the son of Jared, the son of Mahalalel, the son of Cainan, the son of Enos, the son of Seth, the son of Adam, *the son of God.*"[11]

The designation *son of God* is not incidental; it denotes family and delineates between the creatures of created order. For instance, it delineates between men and apes. Although apes, such as chimpanzees and bonobos, display a degree of higher sentience, they were not created to be sons of God. They're not part of the family.

Although mankind is not the only image-bearer on the block, he is afforded a unique privilege—he is permitted, indeed mandated, to replicate the image through reproduction. The chromosomes of the human species are encoded with the image of God, the seal of man's authority on Earth.

Notice how the genealogy of Adam begins:

> This is the book of the genealogy of Adam. In the day that God created man, he made him in the likeness of God [the *Elohim*]. He created them male and female, and blessed them and called them mankind in the day they were created. And Adam lived one hundred and thirty years, and begot a son in his own likeness, after his image, and named him Seth.[12]

The writer of Genesis is careful to emphasize that the offspring of Adam are born in his likeness and bear his image, the seal of the royal house, which endows them with the authority to govern the terrestrial realm.

---

[11] Luke 3:23, 36–38 (NKJV, emphasis added).
[12] Genesis 5:1–3 (NKJV).

Dominion of Planet Earth is the birthright of mankind.

After fashioning man in his own image, the King breathed life into his new regent, and Adam became a living being. Though the text does not expatiate the circumstance, we may imagine Adam kneeling before the King in the sight of his elder siblings when the deed of dominion was conferred:

> "Be fruitful and multiply; fill the earth and subdue it; have dominion over the fish of the sea, over the birds of the air, and over every living thing that moves on the earth."[13]

We should not pass too casually over this momentous occasion. The appointment of a new regent in the kingdom was no small affair, especially considering that mankind was an infant species, the youngest sibling in the family of God. Certain extraterrestrial beings of ancient provenance (and superior qualification) would surely have looked upon Adam's endowment with eyes full of envy and loathing.

An allegory of the scenario is presented in the story of Joseph. The youngest of Jacob's eleven sons (Benjamin had yet to be born), Joseph enjoyed the special affection of his father, who demonstrated his partiality by gifting him with a beautiful tunic:

> But when his brothers saw that their father loved him more than all his brothers, they hated him and could not speak peaceably to him.
>
> Now Joseph had a dream, and he told it to his brothers; and they hated him even more. So he said to them, "Please hear this dream which I have dreamed: There we were, binding sheaves in the field. Then behold, my sheaf arose and also stood upright; and indeed your sheaves stood all around and bowed down to my sheaf."
>
> And his brothers said to him, "Shall you indeed reign over us? Or shall you indeed have dominion over us?"[14]

---

[13] Genesis 1:28 (NKJV).
[14] Genesis 37:4–8 (NKJV).

Like Joseph, Adam, the youngest son of the Father, was endowed with a magnificent gift in the sight of his older brothers. Mankind was to be the regent of the renewed terrestrial realm. The proclamation must have been truly shocking to the citizens of the kingdom (and especially to the disenthroned dragon princes exiled on Earth). How could man, a mere babe in the order of creation, be awarded so great an honor? King David seems to have been perplexed by the same question:

> When I look at your heavens, the work of your fingers, the moon and the stars, which you have set in place, what is man that you are mindful of him, and the son of man that you care for him? Yet you have made him a little lower than the heavenly beings and crowned him with glory and honor. You have given him dominion over the works of your hands; you have put all things under his feet.[15]

The hierarchical position of the human race is clearly defined. Man was not made to be a little higher than the beasts of the earth but a little lower than the beings of heaven. As a son of God, Adam was equipped with the same sentient faculties of his elder siblings in order to fulfill a function analogous to their own. He was specifically designed for fellowship in the divine family and for the exercise of authority in the kingdom.

While instructing the Corinthians in regard to how they ought to judge one another, Paul alludes to the remarkable authority invested in mankind: "Do you not know," he writes, "that we are to judge angels? How much more, then, matters pertaining to this life!"[16]

The angels to whom Paul refers are likely the *watchers*, who unlawfully interloped into man's domain (an incident we will analyze at length). As the regents of Planet Earth, it is appropriate that we judge the offenders of our realm, be they men or angels. We are all familiar with the concept of sovereign jurisdiction. If a foreigner breaks the law in, say, Iran, he will be subject to the jurisdiction of the Iranian government and the penalties imposed thereby, even if the violation is permissible in his country of

---

[15] Psalm 8:3–8 (ESV).
[16] 1 Corinthians 6:3 (ESV).

origin. Foreigners are always subject to the governing authorities of the nations into which they travel.

Authority is the key to understanding the hierarchical architecture of the kingdom. The conferral and exercise of authority is the lever that moves the gears of government. Like civilization itself, government is not a human invention but the extension of an order implicit in the cosmos. When properly administered, civic institutions (law enforcement, judicial arbitration, provision for public goods and services, etc.) are the instruments of a just society. Government is not an option; it is an ordinance of God for the good of mankind and the suppression of evil. Even a ruthless regime, when not entirely corrupt, keeps evildoers in check. It was during the height of Roman power that Paul wrote to the church in Rome:

> Let every soul be subject to the governing authorities. For there is no authority except from God, and the authorities that exist are appointed by God.
>
> Therefore whoever resists the authority resists the ordinance of God, and those who resist will bring judgment on themselves. For rulers are not a terror to good works, but to evil. Do you want to be unafraid of the authority? Do what is good, and you will have praise from the same. For he is God's minister to you for good. But if you do evil, be afraid; for he does not bear the sword in vain; for he is God's minister, an avenger to execute wrath on him who practices evil.
>
> Therefore you must be subject, not only because of wrath but also for conscience' sake. For because of this you also pay taxes, for they are God's ministers attending continually to this very thing. Render therefore to all their due: taxes to whom taxes are due, customs to whom customs, fear to whom fear, honor to whom honor.[17]

It is no wonder that a centurion of the empire was able to recognize the authority of the Son of God, a revelation that eluded the custodians of the Mosaic law, who should have been the first to realize that the

---

[17] Romans 13:1–7 (NKJV).

Law-Giver and great Judge was in their midst. The exchange is worth recounting in full:

> Now when Jesus had entered Capernaum, a centurion came to him, pleading with him, saying, "Lord, my servant is lying at home paralyzed, dreadfully tormented."
>
> And Jesus said to him, "I will come and heal him."
>
> The centurion answered and said, "Lord, I am not worthy that you should come under my roof. But only speak a word, and my servant will be healed. For I also am a man under authority, having soldiers under me. And I say to this one, 'Go,' and he goes; and to another, 'Come,' and he comes; and to my servant, 'Do this,' and he does it."
>
> When Jesus heard it, he marveled, and said to those who followed, "Assuredly, I say to you, I have not found such great faith, not even in Israel! And I say to you that many will come from east and west, and sit down with Abraham, Isaac, and Jacob in the kingdom of heaven. But the sons of the kingdom will be cast out into outer darkness. There will be weeping and gnashing of teeth."
>
> Then Jesus said to the centurion, "Go your way; and as you have believed, so let it be done for you." And his servant was healed that same hour.[18]

As an officer exercising his command in Judea, having been conferred with authority from the emperor in Rome, the centurion recognized that Jesus was exercising his command on Earth, having been conferred with the authority from his Father in heaven (of whom he plainly spoke). This simple recognition of Christ's authority is counted as saving faith for the Roman soldier, who will "sit down with Abraham, Isaac, and Jacob in the kingdom of heaven." Faith in the Son of God is recognizing who he is and believing in him.

The recognition of authority is essential to the effective rule of any governing body, be it terrestrial or extraterrestrial. When a person is

---

[18] Matthew 8:5–13 (NKJV).

appointed, or elected, to a position of great authority, the office he holds is represented by a token of authentication, such as a badge, a certificate, or a seal. For instance, the Seal of the President of the United States is a symbol of the office and authority of the presidency. Official documents published under the president's name, such as presidential orders and commissions, are always authenticated with his seal, and the president is always accompanied by his seal when in public—it is emblazoned on the vehicles that transport him and on the lecterns from which he speaks. The presidential seal imbues its bearer with the honor and authority befitting the office, regardless of whether he merits them personally. It is also a reminder that the president commands the armed forces of the nation and is protected by the same. Everyone knows what would happen if they attempted to storm the podium while the president is speaking; they would be quickly neutralized by the agents of the Secret Service, the guardians of those who bear the presidential seal. Without the threat of force, and the power to enact it, governmental authority is entirely ineffectual.

Since the beginning of recorded history, seals have been utilized to endorse and authenticate the authority of the documents and persons that bore them. The ancient Mesopotamians made wide use of the cylinder seal—a small cylindrical object typically made of stone (though also of copper, bronze, and gold) that was engraved with the insignia of its owner. When rolled into moist clay, the cylinder would imprint a three-dimensional impression of its engravement, like a stamp. The cylinder seal was employed by every strata of Mesopotamian society as an instrument of personal identification to endorse transactions and agreements or to mark property. But the most significant application of the seal was in governmental affairs, where it was used to authenticate and exercise the king's authority.

When a king dispatched a regent to govern a province in his kingdom, the regent would necessarily bear the king's seal as authentication of his appointment. The seal signified that the regent was authorized to act on behalf of the king and that his policies would be enforced, and offenders punished, by the soldiery of the kingdom. To disobey the king's regent was to disobey the king himself. To attack the king's regent was to declare war on the kingdom and provoke the swift retribution of its armies.

Throughout the ages, kings, oligarchs, emperors, and monarchs wore signet rings engraved with the regalia of their royal house, which frequently included a facsimile of their own likeness. When written endorsement of their authority was required (e.g., a papal bull), they would imprint their seal onto the document by pressing the face of the signet ring into a softened solution of resin and wax. If the contents of the document were confidential, the seal would be used to glue it shut. It was unlawful for anyone but the intended recipient to break the royal seal and open the document.[19]

The practice of the seal in earthly affairs is the temporal iteration of a transcendent principle at work in the design of living creatures. The seal of authentication in the kingdom of heaven is bound within the biology of the beings that are created to exercise authority. The hierarchy is pre-ordained. Beings are not created *and then* provided with a purpose; they are explicitly created *for* a purpose. If a being is preordained to govern, he is created in the likeness of the sons of God, the ruling class.

When the King of heaven determined to bestow the deed of Earth's dominion to mankind, he authenticated the appointment with the seal of his royal house, bearing the facsimile of his own likeness. As with the cylinder seal and the signet ring, the image of the King was imprinted into earthen clay. Adam's very anatomy is the authorization of his authority. He bears the likeness of a son, signaling to all would-be contenders that he is a sibling in the royal house and a member of the ruling class. Mankind was not merely granted dominion of Planet Earth; he was explicitly created for it.

Dominion is the right to rule within the boundaries of an established domain. The principle presumes a multiplicity of factions and a plurality of realms. If a man is shipwrecked alone on a solitary, uninhabited island in the middle of the Pacific Ocean, it would be unnecessary for him to plant his flag in the sand and lay claim, as there would be no one else

---

[19] The archives at King's College, Cambridge, confirm the practice: "Seals typically bear their owners' likeness, emblem, or coat of arms and were used to endorse documents, just as the signature is today. They were also used to literally seal documents, fulfilling the same role as glue on envelopes now" (King's College Cambridge, "Seals: Stamps of Authority," Online Exhibitions, January 2010, http://www.kings.cam.ac.uk/archive-centre/archive-month/january-2010.html).

around to challenge his dominion. If, however, his island were surrounded by other inhabited islands whose populations were intent on expansion, he would be forced to either assert his dominion and defend his domain or abdicate to the first assailant.

Let's modify the scenario. Rather than being shipwrecked on the island, the man is sent there by a monarch in order to conquer and rule it. When he arrives, he plants the flag of his nation in the sand, claiming it for king and country. The factions inhabiting the surrounding islands regard him with disdain, but they dare not dispute his dominion. To do so would be to challenge the nation he represents and provoke the fury of its armies.

Because man's authority on Earth is authorized by the King of heaven, his dominion is enforced by the armies of the kingdom. If it were not so, the alien enemies of mankind, numerous and powerful as they are, would have seized control of his domain long ago. (Indeed, the scriptures record an antediluvian episode in which dominion of Earth was usurped by extraterrestrial agencies under specific circumstances. But this is the subject of another chapter.)

The authority of mankind cannot be wrested from him by force, but it can be abdicated, even usurped, under the right conditions.

The game of thrones has rules. Some are inclined to argue that Adam lost or forfeited dominion of the earth after he fell from grace in Eden. A simple glance at history disproves the notion beyond doubt. There has never been a time when anything other than a human being (or a human hybrid) has physically occupied the throne of an earthly kingdom. For better or for worse, only mankind is authorized to govern in his realm. "When the righteous are in authority, the people rejoice; but when the wicked rule, the people groan."[20] Whether righteous or wicked, the kings, lords, princes, presidents, and prime ministers of Planet Earth are, and have ever been, the sons and daughters of Adam. Human beings have never benefited from the benevolent rule of an angel nor suffered the tyranny of a demon. Men are the only monsters responsible for the reigns of terror in their realm.

Man's dominion is not contingent on how much he transgresses or

---

[20] Proverbs 29:2 (RSV).

how well he governs—it is a gift of God that will never be rescinded, for "the gifts and the calling of God," affirms Paul, "are irrevocable."[21] Although sin does not annul the authority of mankind, it does enable the agents of the insurgency to influence the affairs of nations through human proxies.

Satan's authority on Earth has been the subject of much debate and much conflation. Many assume that he actively rules the world from some hidden throne, or at least, he did until Christ stripped him of his power. These notions are not entirely true and not entirely false. The devil, as they say, is in the details.

After the epic failure of their cosmic coup d'état and the destruction of their planetary domains, the defected sons of God were banished from the kingdom and sealed within the bowels of the earth by the boundless waters that encompassed it. When the waters receded, the dragon and his cohorts, now shadows of their former selves, were released from confinement and subjugated to the dominion of Adam, the newly appointed regent of Planet Earth.

That the dragon is subject to the terrestrial dominion of mankind is evidenced in the fact that he has no practical authority in the world; his power is *perceived* through the actions of evil men.

Satan does not wield temporal power on Earth but rather the power to tempt those who do. It is precisely because he cannot force men to accomplish his will that he must persuade them to become his willing accomplices. Like wild beasts baited with the pheromones of carnal desire, wicked men are drawn to political power and harnessed for satanic purposes. Motivated by their own selfish ambition, they become unwitting pawns in the devil's game, moving themselves across the board. When his proxies advance into positions of governmental authority, entire nations may be brought under the sway of the evil one.

Human society at large is also susceptible to the widespread infusion of satanic influences through the practice of idolatry. When men spurn their Maker and venerate the powers that oppose him, they authorize the insurgency to exercise a manifest influence in the world that is otherwise prohibited. Pagan kings were prone to seek the counsel of the gods when

---

[21] Romans 11:29 (ESV).

pressing matters were at hand and relied on the divinations of their oracles to guide their decisions. Rather than obey the one who gave them dominion on Earth, they pledged their fealty to his enemies and abdicated their authority to alien agencies.

The fallen morning stars do not sit idly by, waiting for the day of judgment. They continuously oppose the kingdom of heaven by leading the sons of Adam into lawlessness and idolatry, pitting them against the King. Like proverbial puppet masters, the dragon princes manipulate the affairs of the world from behind the thrones of men, accruing terrestrial authority through their human proxies.

In a popular anecdote from the biblical narrative, an angel is dispatched to deliver a message to the prophet Daniel concerning the unfolding of future events. During the course of his journey, he is met with a blockade of enemy forces and requires military intervention to complete his mission:

> The prince of the kingdom of Persia withstood me twenty-one days, but Michael, one of the chief princes, came to help me, for I was left there with the kings of Persia, and came to make you understand what is to happen to your people in the latter days.[22]

This incident is highly intriguing for several reasons. First, in order to dispatch the message, the angel had to traverse an unknown distance by means of an undisclosed technology. This implies a vehicle of conveyance. Second, the fact that he was blockaded in the course of his journey indicates that the insurgency is also in possession of such vehicles, which they must have deployed to intercept him. Third, it is evident that this prince of Persia was able to oppose the kingdom of heaven but not to harm the man Daniel nor destroy the Hebrews who were captive in Babylon. What we have in this story is a demonstration of human dominion at work and the sovereignty of God.

A dragon prince had gained proximal authority through the king of Babylon, Darius the son of Ahasuerus, and was therefore legally authorized

---

[22] Daniel 10:13–14 (ESV).

to resist the angelic emissary dispatched to the region under his dominion. The Babylonians practiced idolatry in the extreme and worshipped the fallen princes, thereby empowering them to operate in their realm. Nevertheless, the King of heaven reserves the right to intervene in the affairs of men, his regents on Earth, whenever and wherever he sees fit. Hence, Michael was sent to break the blockade and ensure the execution of the King's command.

This rule-by-proxy modus operandi is further manifest in the temptations of Christ. By the time Jesus of Nazareth was born at the turn of the first century, the whole world was in thrall to the influence of Satan. Knowing full well that this Son of Man—born of a virgin, according to the Dragon Slayer Prophecy—was destined to rule the nations, the old serpent attempted to beguile him with a cunning proposition:

> And the devil took him up and showed him all the kingdoms of the world in a moment of time, and said to him, "To you I will give all this authority and their glory, for *it has been delivered to me*, and I give it to whom I will."[23]

Note that authority over the kingdoms had been *delivered to* the devil. Nowhere in the biblical narrative is he granted such an endowment by God. Instead, he had gradually accumulated his authority through the willful abdication of human kings.

It is a matter of history, and no coincidence, that the first and greatest Roman emperor, Caesar Augustus, reigned at the time of Christ's birth. All the power of the empire, which governed the known world, was invested in its emperors, who claimed to have received their divine authority from Jupiter, king of the gods and patron of the Roman state, in whose image they were often portrayed.[24] Jupiter (or *Jove*) was the Roman adaptation of Zeus, whom Jesus, in his admonition to the church of Pergamon, identifies as Satan. Pergamon was home to the famed Altar of Zeus, which was no doubt smoldering with burnt offerings at the very

---

[23] Luke 4:5–6 (ESV, emphasis added).
[24] E.g., the marble statue of the Emperor Octavian Augustus as Jupiter, which was sculpted in the time of Christ.

moment John penned the Lord's words, "I know where you live—where Satan has his throne."[25]

Satan's throne as the Altar of Zeus is a fitting portrait of his rule by proxy. Like the Roman emperors, Greek kings were believed to receive their authority from Zeus and governed as his representatives—a brazen adulteration of Adam's original mandate to represent the true King of the gods on Earth. By worshipping Zeus and Jupiter, the Greeks and the Romans were willfully bowing their knees to Yahweh's archenemy, who made a lurid show of triumph through his proxies on two separate occasions. In 168 BC, the Greek king Antiochus Epiphanes, who regarded himself as a manifestation of Zeus (hence, *Epiphanes*, meaning "god manifest"), sacked the city of Jerusalem and, to the horror of the Jews, erected a statue of Zeus in the Temple of Yahweh before sacrificing a pig on the altar of incense and declaring himself to be God. Nearly two hundred years later, the Roman Emperor Hadrian raised a temple to Jupiter over the desecrated remains of Yahweh's Temple, which had lain in ruin since the destruction of Jerusalem in 70 AD. In both cases, the message was clear: Satan would be the god of this world.

And indeed, he was, insofar as men worshipped him, which they did with fervent enthusiasm in the age preceding the advent of Christ. The fabulously idolatrous Greco-Roman culture, which had spread its influence over the far reaches of the known world, ensured that Zeus/Jupiter was the supreme deity in the minds of men. It is for this reason that Satan is called the *god of this age* by Jesus and his apostles.

The Greek and Roman occupations of Israel amounted to more than the devil sticking his finger in the eye of Yahweh. We must not forget that the dragon's prime objective on Earth, previous to the resurrection of Christ, was to foil the Dragon Slayer Prophecy. It is likely that Satan knew the general timeframe in which the Christ would appear, according to the astronomical signs (the same that the magi followed with success), as well as the place of his birth, according to the scriptures:

> But you, O Bethlehem of Ephrathah, who are one of the little clans of Judah, from you shall come forth for me one who is to

---

[25] Revelation 2:13 (NIV).

rule in Israel, whose origin is from of old, from ancient days.

Therefore he shall give them up until the time when she who is in labor has brought forth; then the rest of his kindred shall return to the people of Israel.[26]

This oracle of Micah evokes John's vision of the pregnant woman and the red dragon poised to devour her child, which plays out in the campaign of infanticide that followed the birth of Jesus in Bethlehem.

Some historical context is necessary to properly frame the scene. When Pompey invaded Palestine in 63 BC, he was aided by a powerful political figure named Antipater the Idumaean, who, as his name suggests, was a man of Edomite descent. With the help of Antipater, Jerusalem fell to Pompey's legions, and Judea became a province of the Roman Empire. Adding insult to injury, Antipater would eventually be appointed procurator of Judea by Julius Caesar, effectively installing a son of Esau to rule over the sons of Jacob—an affront of the highest order. Antipater would go on to found the Herodian dynasty and to father Herod the Great. It was King Herod who attempted to kill the Christ child by ordering the execution of all the little boys in the vicinity of Bethlehem, a truly appalling ordeal and one that must be attributed not only to the Edomite king but to the red dragon behind his throne seeking to devour the seed of the woman destined to crush his head. But, in accord with John's vison, the Christ child evaded the jaws of the dragon and was carried away to Egypt by his parents until Herod's death, at which time they returned to Nazareth, where Jesus "grew and became strong in spirit, filled with wisdom; and the grace of God was upon him."[27]

With the scene thus set, let us now return to the confrontation between Jesus and Satan in the desert of Judea.

The dragon had failed to devour the Christ; his next move was to tempt him to defect from the kingdom. Here was a fortuitous moment that Satan could never have imagined in his wildest dreams. The Son of God stood before him, a frail human being, haggard and hungry after a forty-day fast. Surely he would succumb to the guile of the serpent. All men do.

---

[26] Micah 5:2–3 (New Revised Standard Version, Catholic Edition).
[27] Luke 2:40 (NKJV).

As Jesus beheld the vision of the Roman Empire and the glory of its vast dominion, Satan, leaning over his shoulder, whispered, "If you worship me, it will all be yours."[28]

The dragon's black heart throbbed with anticipation. His greatest desire was about to be fulfilled. Since the day he stood in the presence of God, salivating at the unceasing adoration lavished upon his preeminent Son, he had desperately longed for this moment. What was the worship of men and angels compared to this? *This* was the Son of God. To be worshipped by him was to be worshipped as the Most High.

But it was not to be so.

"It is written," said Jesus solemnly, turning his eyes from the vision and looking toward heaven, "'You shall worship the Lord your God, and him only shall you serve.'"[29]

Christ would indeed rule the nations, but not at the pleasure of the fallen cherub prince.

We must not underestimate the devil's offer. Jesus was well aware of the terrible suffering that awaited him on the path of obedience to the Father. Here were the nations set before him on a silver platter. Could he not avoid the suffering by bending his knee to Satan, and so gain the prize that rightfully belonged to him? Yes. But this would amount to rule without redemption. He had not yet come to rule over the sons of Adam but to redeem them.

It is worth pondering, in the context of our present theme, what would have happened if Jesus had acquiesced and bowed his knee? It is important to remember that Satan's temporal power is proximal. He is not himself authorized to occupy a human throne but only to influence those who do. Jesus, however, was a son of Adam in the line of David. Not only could he rightly claim the throne of his ancestor in Israel, he could don the purple[30] and occupy the seat of the emperor in Rome. (Indeed, he was draped in a purple robe by the Roman soldiers who savagely beat him and placed a crown of thorns on his head to mock him as a pretender king.) By submitting himself to Satan, Jesus would likely have become the

[28] Luke 4:7 (NIV).
[29] Luke 4:8 (NIV).
[30] As the emperors of Rome were often arrayed in purple togas, "donning the purple" was an expression used by the Romans to describe one's ascent to the imperial throne.

emperor of Rome and ruler of the known world.[31] Hence, the dragon would have evaded his fate, and mankind would have been left without a savior.

How scarcely we have fathomed the faithfulness of our kinsman redeemer.[32] If the Son of Man had been as faithless as Adam, or the author, or the reader, then we would all be hopelessly lost forever.

Although the dragon does not have the authority to wield temporal power on Earth, he does have a legal claim to his own spiritual *seed*, whom Christ called *serpents* and *vipers* and whom Paul denominates the *sons of disobedience* and *children of wrath*. Just as God is the Father of the righteous, who are made alive together with Christ because of his obedience, so Satan is the father of the unrighteous, who are dead in their trespasses and condemned together with him for disobedience. Writes Paul to the Ephesians:

> And you he made alive, who were dead in trespasses and sins, in which you once walked according to the course of this world, according to the prince of the power of the air, the spirit who now works in the sons of disobedience, among whom also we all once conducted ourselves in the lusts of our flesh, fulfilling the desires of the flesh and of the mind, and were by nature children of wrath, just as the others.[33]

The epithet *prince of the power of the air* has provoked more than a few peculiar ideas. Some have taken it to mean that Satan literally controls the gaseous atmosphere surrounding the planet, through which his demonic forces freely traffic. This concept, archaic and nonsensical as it is, should have been discarded the moment we took flight to navigate the

---

[31] In 314 AD, Pope Silvester received from Emperor Constantine the first vestiges of that which Christ had rejected from Satan—the temporal power, glory, and dominion of the Roman Empire. Silvester was coronated Bishop of Rome in his new dowry, the Lateran Palace, with all the pomp and circumstance of an exalted prince. Soon, Christ's "Vicar" would assume the title of *Pontifex Maximus* and rule not only in the place of the Roman emperors but in the place of Christ himself.

[32] According to the Hebrew custom, a kinsman redeemer was authorized to act on behalf of a relative who was in dire straits or in need of vindication. The kinsman acting in this role could redeem the property and community rights of a disadvantaged family member and restore them to their former estate. The function of the kinsman redeemer is beautifully illustrated in the Book of Ruth, and perfectly describes the work of Christ.

[33] Ephesians 2:1–3 (NKJV).

skies in the same way we navigate the oceans. We are no more subject to the power of Satan in the air than we are on land or at sea.

When viewed against the backdrop of the first century, it is evident that Paul is referring to the *spiritual atmosphere* of the age, which, as we have seen, was saturated with the prolific idolatry of the Greeks and Romans. The *power of the air* is the satanic influence that pervaded every strata of pre-Christian society like a sinister fog. Having anticipated the coming of Christ, Satan ensured that the minds of men were thoroughly blinded before Jesus of Nazareth was born into the world.[34]

The dragon's purchase on his spiritual progeny is one of mutual condemnation. He does not have the authority to override the free will of any human being, nor intervene directly in human affairs. We have five thousand years of recorded history in the rearview mirror. At no time has the human race been forcefully subjugated to an inhuman power.

As a closing remark on this chapter, it should be stated that the author is not a proponent of Dominion theology (also known as Dominionism). In brief, Dominionism propounds that Christians are mandated (often referred to as the "Dominion mandate" or "God's mandate") to take dominion of the earth in order to establish the kingdom of God. The doctrine has been utilized throughout the centuries to justify brutal military conquests of non-Christian peoples (especially during the crusades) and is predicated on the papal policy that only Christians have the right to rule.

Modern Dominionists have adopted a less violent, though no less erroneous, approach. Certain Protestant sects teach that they, as Christians, are the exclusive inheritors of Adam's dominion and are therefore mandated to conquer the so-called seven spheres, or mountains, of societal influence (religion, family, education, government, media, arts and entertainment, business). Most adherents of the doctrine believe that only when the church has accomplished this societal conquest will Christ return to establish his millennial kingdom.

The old ghost of Dominionism is quickly dispelled in the light of two biblical facts. First, Adam was never commanded to take dominion of the earth but was given dominion from the moment the Maker breathed life

---

[34] See 2 Corinthians 4:3.

into his nostrils (indeed, he was created for this very purpose). Second, dominion of the earth does not belong to one religious faction or another but to the whole of mankind. The Christian has no more claim to the throne than the heathen, and the righteous no more than the wicked; it belongs to all of Adam's descendants—good, bad, or indifferent. The corporate consignment is proclaimed in the psalms:

> The heavens are the Lord's heavens, but the earth he has given
> to the sons of men.[35]

The birthright of Adam is not merited but inherited through his genome. The seal of man's authority is the image he bears. As long as men remain human, they retain dominion of Planet Earth.

---

[35] Psalm 115:16 (RSV).

Chapter 5

EXILES OF EDEN

M an was created for a purpose. His physical and intellectual faculties were specifically selected to facilitate his function. All who looked upon him knew—this was a delegate of the King made in the image of the Elohim, a sibling in the royal house and a member of the ruling class.

Adam was the prototypical man, the perfect *homo sapien*. His genetic architecture was impeccable, enabling him to command the full spectrum of abilities inherent in the human species. Fashioned in the likeness of the elder race, he was endowed with many of their remarkable proficiencies. Extraordinary feats of mind and body—some, perhaps, resembling the superhuman powers of our comic book heroes—were doubtless performed with ease by our primordial parents.[1]

As a son of God and regent of Planet Earth, Adam enjoyed the rights and privileges of his estate, including a seat in the divine assembly. An echo of this Edenic arrangement may be heard in the ancient words of Eliphaz as he attempted to comfort his crestfallen friend:

> "Are you the first man who was born? Or were you brought
> forth before the hills? Have you listened in the council of God?"[2]

---

[1] Such as heightened cerebral function, enhanced strength, telepathy, telekinesis (the ability to manipulate objects with the mind), accelerated regeneration (fast healing), and extrasensory perception. The first and last of these, at the very least, were in operation.
[2] Job 15:7–8 (ESV).

There is no doubt that the first man communed with the Maker, who walked among the trees in the cool of the day. No doubt, moreover, that he communicated openly with his elder siblings, a liberty that would ultimately lead to his downfall and the degeneration of his descendants. It is probable, then, that Adam and Eve could perceive and delight in the dimensional totality of created order.

Eden means "delight." It is emblematic of the Father's house and represents fellowship in the divine family.[3] Far from a trivial Sunday school anecdote, the garden of Eden is a profound allegory pertaining to the transcendent patrimony and purpose of mankind. Embedded in this seemingly childish tale of innocence, temptation, and paradise lost are the explanations to the deepest yearnings of the human heart. The primal longing to return to paradise is deeply ingrained in the DNA of every son of Adam and daughter of Eve. Eden is the only place we truly belong.

In all religions of every culture on Earth, gardens are associated with the divine. The efflorescent loveliness of a well-kept garden, intoned with the effervescent melody of flowing water, is the essence of tranquility. Beautiful gardens evoke the recollection of Eden and reconjure, if for a fleeting moment, the excellence of what was lost.

But *what* and *where* exactly was Eden? Surely it was more than a simple garden. Adam was not created to till soil and grow vegetables but to govern the earth.

The answer lies in the cosmic mountain cosmology of the ancient Near East. According to Assyriologists, the Sumerians believed that their gods dwelt in a luxurious garden situated on the summit of Mount Hermon. The Canaanites imagined *El*, the supreme deity in their pantheon, holding court with his divine assembly on the same mountain "at the springs of the rivers, at the channels [or] meeting place of the two deeps," where the realms of heaven, Earth, and the underworld converged.[4] In the Hebrew tradition, the *garden of Elohim* (another appellation for the garden of Eden) is associated with the *mountain of Elohim* and the paradisaical

---

[3] Note that the author is using *royal* and *divine* as interchangeable terms. The royal family is synonymous with the divine family.
[4] Ryan Thomas, "The Mythological Background of the 'ēd in Gen 2:6: Chaoskampf, the Garden of Eden, and the Mountains of Lebanon," *Religion and Literature of Ancient Palestine* (blog), accessed on June 7, 2020, http://www.religionofancientpalestine.com/?page_id=592.

abode of Yahweh.[5] The motif of the cosmic mountain and garden paradise of the gods was famously modeled with brick and mortar in one of the seven wonders of the ancient world, the Hanging Gardens of Babylon. Legend has it that King Nebuchadnezzar built a great ziggurat in the city of Babylon and planted lush gardens on its broad terraces, replete with exotic animals. A ziggurat is a step pyramid constructed with a series of platform levels ascending to the zenith, typically culminating in a temple or shrine. Essentially, it is an artificial mountain designed to invoke the cosmic mountain of Hermon and communion with the gods that hold court on its summit.

The concept of communion with the gods on the summit of a cosmic mountain is woven into the fabric of human culture far and wide, a phenomenon that poses no mystery to those familiar with the Tower of Babel affair.[6] The fact that step pyramids can be found in every quarter of the planet testifies to the proliferation of the Mesopotamian motif and to man's profound—though misguided—longing for the divine fellowship of his original estate.

At first glance, cosmic mountain cosmology presents a contradiction: *Do the gods dwell on Earth or in heaven?* The nuance of the answer, which has eluded the grasp of secular anthropologists and biblical scholars alike, has always been comprehended by adepts of the occult. The gods dwell in heaven, but their abode is mystically conjoined to the earth at specific points of contact. The ancient sages believed that magical gates (*stargates* in the sci-fi vernacular) facilitated access to and from the immortal realms of their deities.[7] Naturally, primitive cultures assumed that these gates

---

[5] See Ezekiel 28.

[6] The kernels of Mesopotamian culture and mythology were carried throughout the earth in the aftermath of the Babel dispersion and germinated in the soils of distant lands with distinct but familiar forms. As all peoples originate from the same family, namely, Noah and his sons, and from the same culture, namely, the Sumerians, we should expect to find—and indeed, do find—residues of the Mesopotamian influence in each and every tribe regardless of its isolation from the rest of humanity.

[7] One of the most well-known examples of a magic gate is preserved in the mythology of the Norse, who believed that a mystical bridge called *Bivröst* joined Asgard, the realm of the gods, to Midgard, the realm of mortal men. Intriguingly, the ancient motif has been revivified in modern times by Hollywood screenwriters, who, having recognized its intrinsic appeal to the human psyche (and its convenient application as narrative duct tape), continue to avail themselves of the stargate in countless motion pictures.

must be located on the highest geographical positions of the landscape surrounding their domiciles, closest to the heavens. Having breached the stratosphere with airplanes and the exosphere with rockets, we are now quite conscious of the fact (most of us, at any rate) that climbing to the summit of a mountain, even Mount Everest, hardly puts one in proximity to the edge of space, let alone to the cosmic abode of the gods. The superstitious practice of seeking intercourse with the divine by way of the *high places* is the residue of a reality known to the progenitors of our race, who fellowshipped with their elder siblings (the gods) in the garden of Eden, the gate to which was likely located on Mount Hermon.

The Sumerian civilization, founded by Nimrod, was not far removed from the advent of the Flood; hence, the story of Eden was still fresh and close at hand. We sometimes err in ascribing too much ignorance to men of the ancient past.[8] It is improbable that Sumerian sages, perfectly capable of ascending the slopes of Hermon themselves, believed that there was a lush garden nestled atop its snowy peaks. Rather, they knew that what it concealed was a stargate (to use the vernacular), which, when opened, provided access to the confluence of cosmic waters through which man had once ascended to heaven and the gods had descended to Earth.

The metaphysical convergence of multiple realms at the center of the cosmos is known as the *axis mundi* (or cosmic axis). Commonly portrayed in the form of a world tree (or cosmic tree), with its branches reaching into the heavens, its trunk fixed on the earth, and its roots sinking into the underworld (often with the branches and roots connected in a circular configuration), the *axis mundi* functions as a crossroads between worlds—the axis of creation where the four cardinal directions come together or diverge, sometimes represented in the merging or dividing of four rivers. A thorough synopsis of the concept is supplied by the *Thomson Gale Encyclopedia of Religion*:

> Vivid images of the axis of the universe vary widely, since they
> depend on the particular worldview entertained by a specific

---

[8] Conversely, we also tend to ascribe to them too much knowledge. The ancients were neither as ignorant as conventional anthropologists have supposed nor as intelligent as alternative historians have suggested.

culture. Foremost among the images designated by the term *axis mundi* is the cosmic mountain, a sacred place deemed to be the highest point of the universe and perhaps identified with the center of the world and the place where creation first began. Well-known examples of the cosmic mountain are Mount Meru of South Asian cosmology, Haraberazaiti of Iranian tradition, and Himinbjorg of Scandinavian mythology.

The cosmic tree, at whose top abides the celestial divinity, is another frequent image standing for the axis of the world. The roots of such a tree may sink into the underworlds, while its branches traverse the multiple world planes. At the center of the classical Maya vision of the world stood Yaxche, the "first tree," the "green tree," whose place marked the center of all meaningful directions and colors of the universe.

A cosmic pillar may also serve as an *axis mundi*. Such is the case with the Delaware (Lenape) Indians and other Eastern Woodland peoples of North America. The center post of their ceremonial cult house supports the sky and passes into the very hand of the celestial deity. . . .

Many other images fall under the designation *axis mundi* because they share in the symbolic meaning represented by a cosmic mountain, tree, or pillar that joins heaven, earth, and underworld. This category includes cities, especially imperial capitals deemed "heavenly" sites by virtue of proximity to the divine realm; palaces or temples that continue the imagery of the cosmic mountain (e.g., the Babylonian ziggurat); vines or ropes that pass from heaven to earth; and sacred ladders such as the seven-rung ladder, described by Origen, that brings the candidate in the cult of Mithra through the seven heavens.

None of these images has a static function. They are all places of active passage and transition. . . .

Because the *axis mundi* serves as the locus where cosmic regions intersect and where the universe of being is accessible in all its dimensions, the hub of the universe is held to be a place sacred above all others. It defines reality, for it marks the place where being is most fully manifest. This connection of the *axis mundi* with the full manifestation of being is often expressed as an association with the supreme being to whom the axis provides access.[9]

The variegated depictions of the *axis mundi* in diverse cultures around the globe communicate the same universal principle: every world is connected to the axis of creation and sustained by the Creator enthroned above all (which is essentially an expression of the Singularity *through whom* all things were made and *in whom* all things consist). Hence, the function of the *axis mundi* is to conjoin all realms with paradise, the fountainhead of creation, and to facilitate fellowship with the Creator, who abides therein (a concept that is often portrayed in the symbology of the umbilicus [naval], through which the fetus is attached to and nourished by its mother). Additionally, the *axis mundi* operates as a concourse through which the various realms of the universe may be accessed. It should therefore not be thought of as a world in itself but the place between the worlds.

C. S. Lewis provides us with a creative illustration of the concept in *The Chronicles of Narnia*. Fans of the series will recall the Wood Between the Worlds featured in chapter 3 of *The Magician's Nephew*. The Wood Between the Worlds was a serene in-between place that served as a terminal to multiple worlds, accessible through pools of water distributed over the forest floor. The pools functioned like portals. When Digory and Polly (the young protagonists in the story) jumped into a particular pool, they were instantly transported to the world with which it was communicated. The Wood itself was not a world but a crossroads between the worlds—the *axis mundi*. Perhaps unbeknownst to Lewis, the medium he imagined as the tether that binds the worlds to the Wood, namely, pools of water, is remarkably harmonious with the Mesopotamian view of Mount Hermon and the confluence of cosmic waters where heaven, Earth, and the underworld converged.[10]

Not surprisingly, the biblical narrative affirms the view. The transfiguration of Christ, an event which most certainly transpired

---

[9] Lindsay Jones, ed., *Encyclopedia of Religion*, 2nd ed. (Detroit: Thomson Gale, 2005), 712–13.
[10] See Thomas, "The Mythological Background of the 'ēd in Gen 2:6."

on Hermon,[11] is a preview of the *axis mundi* in operation. Upon ascending the cosmic mountain, Jesus is met by Moses, who had died and descended to Abraham's bosom in the underworld, and by Elijah, who had not died but ascended into heaven aboard a fiery chariot. Jesus, Moses, and Elijah represent the convergence of three realms: the first, the land of the living; the second, the abode of the dead; and the third, the paradise of heaven.

It is not by happenstance that the watchers arrived from an extra-terrestrial realm on the summit of Hermon before going down into the plains to despoil our women and defile our race.[12] Nor is it coincidental that Christ, while standing in front of a cave called the "Gates of Hades" at the base of the same mountain near Caesarea Philippi, declared to his disciples that the gates of hell would not prevail against his church.[13] It is evident that the Hebrews, like the Sumerians, Akkadians, Babylonians, and Canaanites before them, believed there was a stargate on the cosmic mountain of Hermon.

Considering that the Pentateuch[14] was written by the hand of an ancient Hebrew (probably Moses) and that the father and founder of the Hebrew nation, namely, Abraham, migrated to the land of Canaan from Mesopotamia,[15] we are compelled to contemplate the garden of Eden within the context of cosmic mountain cosmology. As we have seen, the Mesopotamian motif of a lush garden in which the gods repose and hold court on the summit of the mount, modeled in the Hanging Gardens of Babylon, is a portrait of the heavenly abode once accessible to man.

Heaven and paradise are employed synonymously throughout the scriptures. Jesus, for example, tells the thief on the cross that he would be with him in paradise.[16] Since we know that after rising from the dead, Jesus

---

[11] Historically, two mountains have been considered as possible locations for the transfiguration of Christ: Mount Tabor and Mount Hermon. While some early church scholars, such as Origen, favored Tabor as the mount of transfiguration, most modern scholars favor Hermon.

[12] See 1 Enoch 6.

[13] See Matthew 16:18.

[14] The Pentateuch refers to the first five books of the Old Testament (Genesis, Exodus, Leviticus, Numbers, and Deuteronomy).

[15] Whereas Ur was a well-known city of Sumer in southern Mesopotamia, Ur of the Chaldeans, from whence Abraham migrated, was probably located in northern Mesopotamia. Hence, Abraham may have been of Akkadian descent rather than Sumerian. In any case, it is safe to assume that the roots of Hebrew culture are Sumero-Akkadian (see Genesis 11).

[16] See Luke 23:43.

ascended to his Father in heaven, we may infer that paradise *is* heaven. Indeed, Paul leaves no room for doubt when he refers to the *third heaven* (the location of Yahweh's throne) as paradise.[17] Several other passages in the Bible, as well as extrabiblical texts, confirm the equivalence.[18]

Whereas the synonymity of *heaven* and *paradise* is widely acknowledged by scholars, the same parallels pertaining to *heaven* and *Eden* are less frequently noted, though nonetheless apparent. Jesus, while admonishing the church of Ephesus in John's Revelation, makes the curious proclamation, "To the one who conquers I will grant to eat of the tree of life, which is in the paradise of God."[19] According to Genesis, the tree of life was in the midst of Eden; it follows, then, that the paradise of God *is* Eden. Given the seeming interchangeability of the terms, we may formulate the following equation: Eden *is* paradise *is* heaven.[20] Though difficult to parse in the Western mind, this equation comfortably conforms to the cosmic mountain cosmology of the ancient Near East.

Christians by and large assume that Eden was a garden proper, situated somewhere in the Middle East—that is to say, it had a precise terrestrial address. However, this most basic of assumptions may not be entirely true, nor entirely false.

Eden is described as the fountainhead of four rivers that flowed down through the surrounding provinces, a clear indication of its elevated position in the landscape.[21] As the writer of Genesis names the rivers and delineates their courses, it is commonly hypothesized that Eden must have been located somewhere in the vicinity of the fertile crescent, where at least one of the rivers, the Euphrates, still flows to this day, discharging, as

---

[17] See 2 Corinthians 12:2–4. Having studied in the Jerusalem school of Rabbi Gamaliel, one of the leading Jewish scholars at the time of Christ, Paul was well versed in Hebrew cosmology. His denomination of the third heaven as paradise reflects the tradition of Second Temple Judaism.

[18] See Don Stewart, "What Is Paradise?" Blue Letter Bible, accessed on June 7, 2020, https://www.blueletterbible.org/faq/don_stewart/don_stewart_149.cfm.

[19] Revelation 2:7 (ESV).

[20] There are only three possible ways to solve this equation: (1) Eden is still somewhere on Earth; (2) though originally on Earth, Eden was relocated to heaven; or (3) Eden was never on Earth. Unless one is willing to entertain the notion that the garden of Eden is still located on Earth but hidden within a hyperdimensional space imperceivable to human eyes, the first proposition is obviously false. The second is entirely speculative and highly unlikely, as there are no mentions of such a momentous event in the biblical text. The third proposition is the most cogent and harmonious with the full testimony of scripture.

[21] See Genesis 2:10–14.

always, into the Persian Gulf. The commentary on the minerals that can be found in the regions through which the rivers flow is taken as definitive proof that the location and story of the garden of Eden amount to literal geography and history (as opposed to metaphor).[22] However, pursuant to the ancient esoteric tradition, in conformance to which much of the Tanakh was penned, a thing can be both literal and metaphoric, veritable history and allegory.

The high place of Eden, the fount and confluence of four rivers (symbolic of the four cardinal directions), is evocative of the cosmic mountain and *axis mundi*. It is from Eden that the life-giving force of the Creator flows down from atop the axis of creation to water the earth. The terrestrial address provided by the writer of Genesis designates the location of the stargate through which Eden is accessed on the cosmic mountain. (Much like the gate at the beginning of a long driveway leading to a sprawling mansion, the gate, rather than the mansion itself, supplies the address point.) The Mesopotamians had preserved the memory of man's primordial access to paradise and communion with the gods on the summit of Mount Hermon.

The garden of Eden is more than a lovely place; it represents the privilege of Adam's original estate and the status of sonship in the divine family, to which we are restored in Christ, who reconciles us to the Father. "In my Father's house are many rooms," said Jesus, as he reclined at the table with the twelve the night before he would die to redeem them,

> "If it were not so, would I have told you that I go to prepare a place for you? And if I go and prepare a place for you, I will come again and will take you to myself, that where I am you may be also. And you know the way to where I am going." Thomas said to him, "Lord, we do not know where you are going. How can we know the way?" Jesus said to him, "I am the way, and the truth, and the life. No one comes to the Father except through me."[23]

---

[22] As the courses of all rivers were inexorably altered or eradicated by the deluge, it is an exercise in futility to try and locate the garden of Eden by way of the rivers named in Genesis 2.

[23] John 14:2–6 (ESV).

Though likely undiscerned by his disciples at the time, the Lord's reassurance was meant to reconjure the Parable of the Prodigal Son. Jesus would not leave his brothers to wallow in the pigpen. His mission was to redeem the long-lost sons and lead them back to the Father's house.

Adam's charge to tend and keep Eden was not an ordinance for gardening but for fellowship. (That is not to say that he did not plant and prune in the literal sense; he surely did, just as we do today. Life for Adam was much the same as life for us, sans the pain, suffering, hardship, and death. Eating, drinking, merrymaking, laboring, and resting were all integral parts of the human experience in Eden. There was serious business to be done, but enjoyment was just as important as employment.) Like the other sons of God, Adam was to steward his realm from the axis of Eden. The directive to subdue the earth was one of expansion—he was to advance the Edenic rule throughout his domain. As replicate image-bearers, his offspring were to multiply and fill the whole face of the earth, extending the kingdom of heaven from the paradise of God. The directive is affirmed in the Lord's prayer:

> "Our Father in heaven, hallowed be your name. Your kingdom come, your will be done, on earth as it is in heaven."[24]

In a show of extraordinary favor, Adam, like Joseph and his beautiful tunic, was endowed with a special gift from his Father—a female counterpart. Fashioned from his own genetic material and made in his likeness, Eve became Adam's helpmate and the means through which offspring could be procreated. The faculty of human procreation, though taken for granted today, is an unprecedented wonder among the sons of God.

The divine family is represented in the traditional hierarchy of the nuclear family: the father is the head of the house, followed by the firstborn son and then the other siblings. Adam was granted the exceptional privilege to procreate his own family on Earth as a reflection of the divine family in heaven. The benefaction of the family is a marvel of the Father's affection for mankind. It is precisely for this reason that the adversaries of our race work tirelessly to malign and destroy it. Familial neglect,

---

[24] Matthew 6:9–10 (ESV).

domestic abuse, divorce, and above all, abortion, are grave affronts to the awesome gift of family afforded to the offspring of Adam.

The Father's favor for mankind did not go unnoticed. Envy among the other sons in the cosmos would ultimately lead to the hijacking of human reproduction for the procreation of unsanctioned hybrid families. Reproduction is a powerful weapon in the hands of malevolent agencies seeking expansion through conquest, as conquest is unsustainable without occupation (more on this later).

Adam and Eve were not alone on Earth. Creatures of all kinds populated the prehistoric landscape with them. It is plausible that other sentient beings, subject to Adam's dominion, were also present from the beginning of his rule[25]—the fallen morning stars not least among them.

Perplexingly, the dragon was also in Eden.

It is obvious that the serpent in Eden was not of the ordinary garden variety. The word *serpent* in the Genesis account is derived from the Hebrew *nachash*. When used as a noun, *nachash* usually describes a snake of common breed. When employed as a verb, it means "deceiver." In adjective form it means "bright, burnished, and shining," as in Ezekiel's shining son of the morning, the signet of perfection, full of wisdom and perfect in beauty, who was in Eden, the garden of God.[26] Rather than depicting a legless reptile, *nachash* conveys the dual attributes of the being who beguiled Eve—he is extremely beautiful, like a shining star, and exceptionally cunning, like a slithering serpent.

We should not make too much of the anthropomorphizing of animals in the Bible, as the practice was prevalent in antiquity. It is not uncommon to find certain traits or personalities characterized by the same animals in diverse cultures around the world. Even today, the basic formula is generally followed. The wicked are likened to the lowly creatures of the animal kingdom that best portray their attributes, such as serpents, scorpions, locusts, carrion birds, dogs, jackals, swine, and so on, while the

---

[25] It is the author's postulation that a pre-Adamic indigenous reptilian race may have inhabited the interior of the planet during its long interval of dark inundation. It is also possible that the reptilians migrated to the earth in the aftermath of Rahab's destruction. Among all the desolated planets in the solar system, the earth, with its atmosphere intact, would have presented the most inhabitable environment.

[26] See Ezekiel 28.

righteous are often depicted by the nobler animals, such as eagles, lions, and oxen. Sometimes the same animals are used to embody the good and bad actors.[27] It is often overlooked that both Jesus and Satan are depicted by the serpent and compared to the lion.[28] As previously mentioned, when employed in the context of prophetic iconography, animals also represent the signs of the zodiac, the cardinal directions, and constellations.

Because Satan is associated with a serpent, many have assumed that he is serpentine in appearance. According to this logic, one ought to draw the same conclusion concerning Christ, who is often portrayed as a lamb, and yet the proposition that Jesus had the physical features of a sheep would certainly be considered ridiculous by all. In fact, the fallen dragon prince, as we have seen, is a morning star made in the likeness of the Son of God, which is to say that he looks very much like us but with the highborn complexion of the elder race.

Fallen angels are not the hideous demonic creatures portrayed in popular culture (as much as they might like you to believe otherwise). There may be a myriad of revolting entities in the cosmos that fit the classic depictions of demons, but not the sons of God. Satan is never depicted in the scriptures with grotesque features. On the contrary, he is always described as a being unrivaled in beauty—the most illustrious of the morning stars. Indeed, it is precisely his magnificence that led to his downfall: "Your heart was proud because of your beauty; you corrupted your wisdom for the sake of your splendor."[29] Some have contended—and contend still—that the resplendent nature of the defected morning stars was defiled and darkened when they were cast to the earth, but this is pure conjecture. When a son of God defects from the kingdom, it is not his *appearance* that changes but his *allegiance*.

Satan's propensity to disguise himself as an "angel of light" is often cited as proof that he has the power to shapeshift—after all, so the argument often goes, he transformed himself into a snake in the garden of Eden. A relic of the Middle Ages, the proposition that the devil and his minions can metamorphosize at will into different bodily forms, even

---

[27] E.g., the strong warriors of Yahweh are compared to oxen and those of his enemies to wild oxen.
[28] Jesus portrays himself as the serpent that was lifted up in the Sinai wilderness (John 3:14), and Peter depicts Satan as a roaring lion (1 Peter 5:8).
[29] Ezekiel 28:17 (ESV).

inanimate forms, seems to be generally adopted by Christians everywhere, even though it has no basis in the biblical text.[30] If we examine the primary passage from which the notion is derived, it becomes apparent that a misconception is at work. In 2 Corinthians 11, Paul is furious with the false apostles parading themselves as emissaries of Christ and servants of righteousness, when in reality they were ravening wolves preying on the undiscerning. "And no wonder," he remarks, "for even Satan disguises himself as an angel of light. So it is no surprise if his servants, also, disguise themselves as servants of righteousness."[31] Keep in mind that the world *angel* means "messenger." Clearly, Paul is drawing an analogy between false apostles who minister in the name of Christ and Satan, who masquerades as a messenger of light. To construe from this passage that the devil is a doppelganger is to miss the point.[32] Like the false apostles, Satan disguises his evil intentions behind a veil of cunning words and enchanting propositions, which is precisely how he seduced Eve.

Our regal mother was not deceived by a magical snake but by a majestic member of the elder race offering to illuminate her mind with the transcendental knowledge of the morning stars. Mesmerized by the cunning of the dragon prince, she hung on his every word, eyes wide with wonder, as he tempted her with promises of apotheotic glory.

> "If the Father truly loves you, why does he not make you wise like the others? Why does he withhold knowledge from you? He doesn't want you to be like them, to know what they know, because you were created to be their slaves. But I can break your chains! I can teach you the secrets that have been unjustly withheld from you. Listen to me. You will not surely die. No. You will become gods yourselves and live forever!"[33]

---

[30] There is a very real probability that the fallen morning stars are in possession of advanced technology that might enable them to alter their appearance through technological means, such as a holographic projection; however, to suggest that they are by nature biological *transformers* is beyond the bounds of reason. A being that can assume any form is a being without form.

[31] 2 Corinthians 11:14–15 (ESV).

[32] Those who argue that Satan is inherently hideous but has the power to change his appearance at will for the purpose of deception should contemplate the following question: Having transfigured into a being of superior beauty, why in the world would he ever reassume his hideous form?

[33] This is, of course, a paraphrase of the serpent's words to Eve (see Genesis 3:1–5).

As the serpent whispered into her ears, Eve's mind was filled with visions of grandeur. She and Adam could learn the forbidden secrets of the elder race and become like the gods. And why should they not? Were they not also sons and daughters? Why should they be inferior to the morning stars?

What happened next is a matter of speculation. Was Adam also seduced by the same visions of glory and apotheosis promised by the serpent? Did he find his wife in a state of sublime enlightenment and desired to be like her?

In the author's opinion, quite the opposite occurred. When Adam discovered that Eve had succumbed to the temptation of the dragon and disobeyed the commandment of God, he was greatly distraught and forced to make a terrible choice. Eve would now be banished from paradise and suffer the consequences of her actions. Adam knew he would be forever separated from his beloved wife, never to see her again. This he could not bear. In a fateful act of love, he chose to assume her condition and share in her condemnation, whatever should befall. Eden would be lost, but Eve was won.

Heaven took notice of Adam's love. A plan of redemption was set in motion. The Son of God would assume our condition and bear our sin in order to save us from condemnation. It is not incidental that we are called the Bride of Christ.

Mankind was created for fellowship in the family of God. The King desired more than a dutiful servant when he breathed life into Adam's earthen frame; he wanted a faithful son who would love without compulsion. Love is only truly tested through choice and expressed in action. When a man chooses to marry a woman, he dedicates himself to her alone, shunning all others. His faithfulness to her, or lack thereof, is an expression of his love. In the same way, a son who loves his father will choose to be obedient to him and submit to his authority.

Love is the most precious commodity in the universe.

It is for the sake of love that man was given a choice in the garden of Eden. He could freely choose to be faithful to the King or join in the rebellion of his enemies. The dragon was permitted to fraternize with Adam and Eve in order to test their allegiance.

The scriptures paint the portraits of two antithetical sons: the faithful son and the faithless son. The faithful son loves his Father and is perfectly submitted to his authority. The faithless son hates his Father and is entirely insubordinate. Both sons are represented by the two trees in the garden of Eden. Jesus is the tree of life: obedience to the Father leads to divine fellowship and eternal life in the paradise of God. Satan is the tree of knowledge: disobedience leads to alienation, eviction, and death.

That Jesus chose to wait for Judas, his betrayer, in a garden was not a matter of happenstance.

It was in the garden of Gethsemane on the Mount of Olives that the Son of Man, the second Adam, was confronted with the choice to be faithful to his Father and endure the unspeakable suffering of the crucifixion or to forsake his mission and forgo the gruesome ordeal altogether. The redemption of mankind would exact a terrible toll. The crushing weight of our sin was placed upon the shoulders of the faithful son who knew no sin. He fell to his knees, heavy with his affliction, and watered the Edenic soil with the bloodstained sweat dripping from his brow. "Father, if you are willing, remove this cup from me. Nevertheless, not my will, but yours, be done."[34]

Man's reconciliation to the family of God would be long in the coming. It would begin at the cross thousands of years after the gate of Eden was closed and would not be fully consummated until the end of the age, at the advent of the resurrection, the hope of every believer, when the gate will be open again.

In the meantime, all men must suffer the grim consequence of Adam's disobedience. Although exiled from Eden, Adam and his offspring were still the regents of Planet Earth, but they would now persist in a hostile world, sundered from the family of God, subject to degeneration, and shackled to the grave.

Such are the wages of sin.

---

[34] Luke 22:42 (ESV).

Chapter 6

THE ATROPHY OF ADAM

Contrary to the popular conception, our prehistoric ancestors were not Fred Flintstone and Barney Rubble. We have been deliberately misinformed concerning the nature of the antediluvian age and the caliber of men that inhabited it.

All of us have been subjected throughout our lives to the Darwinian portraiture of pucker-lipped Neanderthals clasping spears or pounding stones together. The wax-sculpted physiques of our apish ancestors pose defiantly in every natural history museum of the civilized world, despite the incontrovertible fact that no hard evidence has ever been furnished to verify human evolution. Unencumbered by the burden of proof, evolutionary anthropologists freely advance the preposterous notion that our predecessors were little more than chimpanzees with better brains, the winners of Darwin's pointless lottery.

In the evolutionary sweepstakes, man is a stroke of sheer luck, a fluke, an unintentional accident that could have just as easily resulted in another species of baboon or orangutan. His origin is insignificant, his existence meaningless, his destiny irrelevant. With one fell hammer blow, Darwin vandalized the noble figure of mankind's ancient forebearer, reducing him to a faceless primate—just another animal in the zoo.

Darwin orphaned mankind, in a manner of speaking, leaving him at the doorstep of a cold and hostile world without a certificate of pedigree to enlighten his past or a purpose to guide his future. As a result, modern man has adopted a condescending view of his primordial ancestors, believing himself to be the apex of the human species. He perches, as it were, upon the pinnacle of evolution's highest peak, peering down at his predecessors with a wry smirk. Surely, *he* is the most wondrous specimen of *homo sapien* ever to walk the earth!

Nothing could be further from the truth.

Charles Darwin managed to distill from nature the very antithesis of nature's condition. The premise of his theory necessitates the perpetual aggregation of beneficial mutations over time amounting to an increase of order and complexity in the biological matrix of life, which is a clear contradiction of the entropic mechanism at work in the universe.

Pursuant to the Darwinian paradigm, all higher animals began their evolutionary ascent from the very same single-celled organism, which over billions of years gradually mutated into exceedingly intricate forms. This profusion of biodiversity represents a tremendous increase in the information, organization, and diversification of the genome into a living library of incomprehensibly voluminous "books of life."

Consider the complexity of the human genome. If published in book form, our genetic code would fill two hundred New York City telephone directories, each one containing over one thousand pages. It would take a person typing sixty words per minute for eight hours a day more than fifty years to inscribe it in its entirety. Despite being composed of only four letters (A, C, G, T), the sequence of the human genome requires three gigabytes of hard-drive space to store on a computer. If unwound and tied together, the strands of DNA in one cell would stretch approximately six feet (but would be only fifty trillionths of an inch wide). If all the DNA in the human body were put end to end, it would reach to the sun and back over six hundred times. If all three billion letters in the human genome were stacked one millimeter apart, they would soar to a height seven thousand times that of the Empire State Building.[1]

The composition and organization of such an enormous volume of genetic information simply cannot happen by chance, no matter how many billions of years are afforded the process.

[1] Public Broadcasting Service, "Genome Facts," *NOVA Online*, April 2001, https://www.pbs.org/wgbh/nova/genome/facts.html.

Imagine a time traveler exploring the primordial landscapes of the planets in our solar system. While wading through the miry froth of Earth's prebiotic soup, he happens upon a sheet of paper lightly floating on the surface. When he examines the paper, he is astonished to find that it is inscribed with a single legible sentence: *It was a dark and stormy night.* The paper and sentence were apparently spontaneously generated from the chemical compounds contained in the mire. Baffled by the enormous improbability of the phenomenon, he places the paper back where he found it and departs to explore another planet.

After a while, he decides to return to Earth, but he sets his time machine to take him four billion years into the future from the date of his initial visit. When he arrives, he cannot believe his eyes. Where there was once a solitary sheet of paper, there are now billions of gigantic leather-bound books scattered about, each one containing many thousands of pages. As he flips through the pages, perusing one book after another, he discovers that they are all unique, elegantly written novels. What's more, every volume has been meticulously edited, with little to no errors.

Preposterous as this simple thought experiment may seem, it is a fitting parable for the theory of evolution. In Darwin's universe, vast periods of time produce order and complexity, and yet, nowhere is this principle observed in nature. Time is always the agent of disorder and chaos. Indeed, in the real universe, the opposite of our thought experiment would be true. The time traveler would discover a beautifully written book with no spelling errors during his first visit to primordial Earth. Upon his second visit, he would find the ground littered with disheveled and disintegrating pieces of paper scribbled with incomplete sentences, mere fragments of a once great novel.

Nature is not undergoing a perpetual increase of order and organization over time but, to the contrary, is languishing in the inexorable corrosion of entropy's slow grind. Simply defined, *entropy* is the increase of disorder and chaos in a system. According to the second law of thermodynamics, matter and energy are ever inclined toward disorganization and uniform chaos. In the words of the psalmist, the fabric of the material world is wearing out like a garment.[2]

---

[2] See Psalm 102:26; Isaiah 51:6.

This presents a serious conundrum for evolutionists. If the universe is subject to entropy, why is evolution not also subject to the same? How can certain organisms, such as the human species, be undergoing a continual evolutionary upgrade of ever-increasing order and complexity over time, while the inorganic world around them is perpetually decaying? The problem, though evaded by most, has been acknowledged by a few introspective evolutionists, including syndicated columnist Sydney Harris, who published the following in the *San Francisco Examiner*:

> There is a factor called "entropy" in physics, indicating that the whole universe of matter is running down, and ultimately will reduce itself to uniform chaos. This follows from the Second Law of Thermodynamics, which seems about as basic and unquestionable to modern scientific minds as any truth can be. At the same time that this is happening on the physical level of existence, something quite different seems to be happening on the biological level: structure and species are becoming more complex, more sophisticated, more organized, with higher degrees of performance and consciousness. . . . How can the forces of biological development and the forces of physical degeneration be operating at cross purposes? It would take, of course, a far greater mind than mine even to attempt to penetrate this riddle. I can only pose the question—because it seems to me the question most worth asking and working upon with all our intellectual and scientific resources.[3]

The entropy riddle does not require the full muster of our intellectual and scientific resources to solve. The solution is readily apparent to the mind unfettered by Darwinism: evolution is running in reverse—nature is *devolving*. Entropy implies a beginning and an end. Like the whole universe of matter, life had a sudden beginning and is gradually winding down to an ultimate end.

---

[3] Sydney Harris, "Second Law of Thermodynamics," Field Enterprise Syndicate, *San Francisco Examiner*, January 27, 1984.

This scenario poses an important question as much for the Darwinist as for the Christian: what is the nature of mortality? The query is not inconsequential to either camp. Those in the former are earnestly seeking a way to forestall or reverse the entropic force that will inevitably lead to their demise. Those in the latter must formulate a theological response or else get ready to pass the cup from the Fountain of Youth.

For our purposes, we will inverse the question: *What is the nature of immortality?*

There are two ways to think about immortality: (a) it is a property intrinsic[4] in the anatomy of a living thing or (b) it is the product of an extrinsic[5] force acting upon the anatomy of a living thing. In the first case, a creature is immortal by nature, possessing an indestructible body and thus unable to die. In the second, a creature is immortal by virtue of a stimulant that rejuvenates the body when absorbed or consumed and without which the body begins to atrophy. Although space does not permit an exhaustive review of the many biblical references pertaining to eternal life, the second proposition is sufficiently affirmed by the writer of Genesis, who informs us that Adam was expelled from Eden "lest he reach out his hand and take also of the tree of life and eat, and live forever."[6]

Adam's immortality, therefore, was contingent on the consumption of a rejuvenating stimulant[7]—that is to say, he was *not* intrinsically immortal but *could* have continued to live forever, even in his fallen condition, had he access to Eden. As mentioned in the previous chapter, the gate of Eden will be open once again to those who, through Christ, are granted to eat of the tree of life. Immortality, then, is a gift of God to mortal men. Indeed, Paul reveals to Timothy that God alone has *intrinsic* immortality.[8] In light of this remarkable disclosure, one could make the case that all life, terrestrial and otherwise, is subject to death unless supplemented by

---

[4] Belonging to the essential nature or constitution of a thing (Merriam-Webster, s.v. "intrinsic," accessed on July 1, 2020, http://www.merriam-webster.com/dictionary/intrinsic).

[5] Not forming part of or belonging to a thing; originating from or on the outside (Merriam-Webster, s.v. "extrinsic," accessed on July 1, 2020, http://www.merriam-webster.com/dictionary/extrinsic).

[6] Genesis 3:22 (ESV).

[7] As the story of the Garden of Eden is most certainly allegorical, the stimulant may not have actually been a piece of fruit from the tree of life. The very atmosphere of paradise might contain some invigorating element that rejuvenates the cells and preserves the body in peak condition.

[8] See 1 Timothy 6:15–16.

the rejuvenating stimulant available exclusively in the paradise of God.[9]

Notice the way in which God's decision to expel Adam from the garden of Eden is phrased:

> "Behold, the man has become like one of us in knowing good and evil. Now, lest he reach out his hand and *take also* of the tree of life and eat, and live forever—"[10]

This passage paints a panorama of the divine assembly holding court in paradise to deliberate the matter of man's transgression, exactly as the Mesopotamians would have imagined it. There is a fascinating detail here that has gone largely unnoticed. The concern of the Elohim is that Adam has now become like them, knowing good and evil, and like them would *take also* of the tree of life and eat and live forever if not prevented from doing so. The phrase "take also" intimates that they, too, were partaking of the tree of life and, by extension, were dependent on it for immortality. This does not in any way impugn the eternal nature of God but rather upholds Paul's assertion that only he is intrinsically immortal. Ergo, the immortality of all other creatures is extrinsically contingent on the fruit from the tree of life and the charity of God, who grants or denies access to it according to the counsel of his will.

Now, continuing along this train of thought—the reader will decide if it has merit—we may entertain a fascinating possibility concerning the defected sons of God, who were likely also banished from paradise. If it is true that all divine beings are dependent on the tree of life for immortality, then it would follow that the dragon princes, having been deprived of its rejuvenating fruit, are presently dying like men. The postulation, though certainly foreign to most Christians, is not without biblical precedent. In a scene we have already surveyed, Psalm 82 depicts a company of angelic princes who have been summoned before the King and his council to

---

[9] Despite the fervent hope of pet owners everywhere, there is no reason to assume that animals are afforded the gift of immortality. However, considering that the biology of every organism indigenous to Planet Earth is composed of the same macromolecule building blocks (carbohydrates, lipids, proteins, and nucleic acids) and constructed from the same basic genetic architecture (double-helix DNA), it is plausible that were an animal to eat of the tree of life, it, too, would live forever.

[10] Genesis 3:22 (ESV, emphasis added).

answer for their dereliction of duty: "You are gods, sons of the Most High, all of you; nevertheless, like men you shall die, and fall like any prince."[11]

If the pronouncement is to be taken at face value, then it would seem that even the princes of the elder race may be condemned to death. The simplest way to enact this judgment would be to deny them access to the tree of life in paradise, which was precisely the penalty for Adam and Eve's transgression; it may also have been the penalty for the serpent who deceived them. After the Eden affair, cherubim and a flaming sword were placed at the gate of paradise to guard the way to the tree of life—a rather excessive measure if the sole objective were to prohibit lowly men from gaining entry. It is likely that the principal purpose of the guardians was not to prevent Adam and his descendants from entering, but the dragon and his cohorts.

Credence may be lent to this theory in the language of the serpent's curse, whereby he is consigned to crawl on his belly and eat dust. It is conceivable that the eating of dust and crawling on one's belly is a metaphor for the mortal condition to which the serpent would now be subject due to his exclusion from paradise.[12] If so, then, like all mortal creatures, the dragon princes must now eat, drink, and metabolize in order to maintain the biological mechanisms that sustain life. This potential scenario could provide insight into the seemingly insatiable appetite of the gods, who demand the continual sacrifice of animal and human flesh, which must be willingly offered. Perhaps there is a modicum of truth to the mythos of the vampire, who is condemned to drink the blood (eat the dust) of other creatures in order to sustain his own life and satisfy the thirst driving him to madness.

If the defected sons of God are indeed dying, then it follows that their bodies, like ours, are growing increasingly decrepit over the course of time; in other words, they are aging. It would be illogical to assume, however, that elder beings age at the same rate as human beings. Considering that Adam had a lifespan of nearly a thousand years and that the morning stars possess a biology far superior to man's, it is likely that they would live

---

[11] Psalm 82:6–7 (ESV).

[12] God himself employs the metaphor of dust in reference to mortality: "For dust you are, and to dust you shall return" (Genesis 3:19, NKJV).

many thousands if not hundreds of thousands of years before succumbing to death (another parallel to the vampire mythos). Of course, this is all hypothetical and should be taken with a grain of salt.

With extrinsic immortality in mind, let us now return to the question of entropy in the universe of matter. Here, we may find some accord with the deist of the seventeenth century, who maintained that creation was like a grand clock wound up at the beginning of time, the hands of which ever advance mechanistically toward the midnight hour of their final stroke. It appears that the Creator has determined to subject all of creation to the indomitable power of entropy so that every living thing, and the material world itself, would come to an appointed end in time, *except* those beings to whom the gift of eternal life is bestowed. Entropy and death, therefore, are natural and necessary components in the current design of the cosmos.[13]

The primordial condition of Adam's extrinsic immortality allows us to answer two contradictory questions in the affirmative:

Was man designed to die? *Yes.*
Was man intended to live forever? *Yes.*

As a biological creature, man was designed with a mortal body subject to entropy. As a son of God, he was intended to eat of the tree of life and live forever as a member of the divine family.

Sin, however, changed the equation. Adam's eviction from paradise was a death sentence for him and his descendants. When fellowship with the Father was broken and the gate to Eden closed, all of mankind was doomed to die. Subjection to the law of entropy and death was not a curse but a consequence of Adam's sin. The curse was corruption.

Death and corruption are different mechanisms. Death is the product of natural causes, while corruption is the perversion of nature itself. Adam was not only a son but a regent, responsible for the governance of a realm. Consequently, the penalty of his sin would not only be reflected in the

---

[13] I say "current" because the scriptures foretell of a new heaven and Earth that will be created at the end of time. It is possible that this new universe will function on a different set of laws that preclude the necessity of entropy and death.

decay of his body but in the perversion of the world under his dominion. Nature itself was inextricably bound to the atrophy of Adam. But just as creation groans in the bondage of man's corruption, so also will it glory in the liberty of his redemption:

> For the creation waits with eager longing for the revealing of the sons of God. For the creation was subjected to futility, not willingly, but because of him who subjected it, in hope that the creation itself will be set free from its bondage to corruption and obtain the freedom of the glory of the children of God. For we know that the whole creation has been groaning together in the pains of childbirth until now. And not only the creation, but we ourselves, who have the firstfruits of the Spirit, groan inwardly as we wait eagerly for adoption as sons, the redemption of our bodies. For in this hope we were saved.[14]

Symbolized in thistles and thorns, the precise nature of the blight that afflicted the earth in the aftermath of Adam's fall is a matter of controversy among scholars and extraneous to the focus of the present work. We will only venture to theorize that the closing of Eden's gate could have cut the planet off from the vein of paradise and life-imbuing blood that was supposed to circulate throughout Adam's realm—no doubt an integral facet of his stewardship. This is not to suggest that all creatures would have become immortal; rather, it might have assured a condition of maximal flourishment in nature and the mitigation of suffering. One of the ramifications of Adam and Eve's transgression was a pronounced *increase* in the hardship and suffering already experienced on the planet; work became *more* laborious due to a decline in soil fertility, childbearing became *more* painful, and organisms became *more* hostile (evinced in the proliferation of thorns and thistles). Rather than flourish in the light streaming through Adam's open access to paradise, the earth would now languish in the shadow of the forbidden gate that shut him out.

Whereas the effect of Adam's fall has not been fully comprehended in nature, the calamity it wreaked upon his offspring is woefully apparent.

---

[14] Romans 8:19–24 (ESV).

Once a magnificent being comparable even to the morning stars, mankind was disrobed of his immortal raiment and exposed to the bitter winds of entropy. He would now suffer the decrepitude of old age, bear the sorrow of death, and witness the gradual decline of his progeny.

One cannot truly appreciate the scandal of Darwinism without Eden in view. No more perfect a contradiction of the truth could ever have been concocted. Far from evolving into superior specimens of *homo sapiens*, our species has been successively degenerating into increasingly inferior copies of Adam.

In brief, genetic degeneration results from the corruption of information encoded in the genome. As the blueprint of Adam's DNA is copied from one generation to the next, it gradually accumulates deleterious (harmful) mutations—essentially, it devolves. Quite contrary to what we've been led to believe in textbooks and movies, we are pathetically inferior to our antediluvian antecedents, and the proof is in the genetic pudding.

Modern man is a mutant, and not in the *X-Men* way. Far from enhancing our abilities, the mutations in our genome are strictly debilitating and, in many cases, fatal. In other words, we are not gaining any superpowers by way of mutation but gradually losing the capabilities inherent in the human species. A genetic mutation is similar to a missing word or spelling error in a sentence, which renders it incomplete and incoherent. In computing terms, it may be compared to the loss or corruption of a file that leads to program errors and system crashes. The more our genome mutates, the less functional we become. Mutations are supposed to be the building blocks of biological evolution, but in reality, all they do is break things down. The real-life "X-Men" are broken human beings, frail and decrepit—mere shadows of Adam.

The mutational load accumulated over thousands of years of degeneration is manifest in the myriad genetic disorders afflicting modern man. According to the CDC, half of all adults in the United States have at least one chronic disease, such as heart disease, diabetes, or cancer, and many of our elderly now suffer from a condition of multimorbidity, which is the co-occurrence of two or more chronic diseases. Nearly 70 percent of Americans are on at least one prescription drug, and more than half take two. The greed of pharmaceutical companies is partly responsible for this egregious figure, but it reveals a sobering reality—we are not feeling very well, and for good reason. There are now over six thousand human genetic disorders, many of which are fatal or severely debilitating, and the number is growing every day.[15]

In the 1950s, geneticists were growing increasingly concerned about the accumulation of deleterious mutations in the human gene pool, which they estimated to be occurring at a rate of approximately 0.1 to 0.3 nucleotide mutations per person per generation. Among these men, renowned geneticist Hermann Muller projected that just one deleterious mutation per person per generation would inevitably lead to a critical mass scenario called *error catastrophe*, which is a technical way of saying extinction by genetic mutation.[16]

We now know that there are over one thousand deleterious nucleotide mutations per person per generation, and that is by some accounts a conservative estimate.[17] We also know that human fitness (the overall vitality and reproductive quality of our species) is declining at an alarming rate. In 2009, geneticist Michael Lynch published a research paper in which he concluded that the current rate of decline in human fitness could be as high as 5 percent per generation.[18] Others have been warning that the pace of fitness decline is quickening due to an increase of chemical and waveform mutagens in the environment. What we are witnessing, according to the quiet consensus of population geneticists around the world, is the beginning stages of a mutational meltdown that could ultimately render large communities reproductively unviable and precipitate error catastrophe. Unbelievable as this grim prognosis may seem, the evidence is all too abundant and close to home.

All of us have been touched, to one degree or another, by the cancer epidemic ravaging the human species, and all other species on Earth. Cancer is fundamentally the result of genetic mutation. There are many

---

[15] See Liat Ben-Senior, "10 Most Common Genetic Diseases," *Labroots.com*, May 22, 2018, https://www.labroots.com/trending/infographics/8833/10-common-genetic-diseases.

[16] See Hermann J. Muller, "The Relation of Recombination to Mutational Advance," *Mutation Research* 1, no. 1 (May 1964): 2–9.

[17] See John C. Sanford, *Genetic Entropy and the Mystery of the Genome* (n.p.: FMS Publishing, 2008), 37.

[18] See Michael Lynch, "Rate, Molecular Spectrum, and Consequences of Spontaneous Mutations in Man," *PNAS* 107, no. 3 (December 2009): 961–68.

factors that can trigger or accelerate cancer-causing mutations in particular genes (e.g., nuclear radiation, exposure to hazardous chemicals, consumption of carcinogens, etc.), but these are all ancillary to the underlying condition—genetic degeneration. The American Cancer Society has projected that by the end of the year 2020, nearly 1.8 million new cases of cancer will have been diagnosed in the United States alone. Over six hundred thousand people will have died. One out of every two men and one out of every three women will develop cancer in their lifetime.[19] These shocking statistics are a clear indication that our genetic clock is expiring. In his eye-opening book, *Genetic Entropy and the Mystery of the Genome*, Cornell University geneticist Dr. John Sanford presents a bleak prognosis for the human species:

> Unless selection [natural selection] can somehow stop the erosion in the human genome [and Sanford argues that it cannot], mutations will not only lead to our personal death, they will lead to the death of our species. . . . The extinction of the human genome appears to be just as certain and deterministic as the extinction of stars, the death of organisms, and the heat death of the universe.[20]

The gathering storm of error catastrophe looming on the horizon of humanity's future has yet to dawn on the masses, who have grown strangely accustomed to the cancer epidemic and have learned to accommodate it into their lives as if its occurrence were perfectly natural. Instead of evacuating the apartment when the fire alarm sounds, we've simply gotten used to the noise and carry on as if the building were not burning to the ground. Our apathy may be blamed in part on a false sense of security supplied by the crutch of our technology. We have a façade of fitness sustained by technological props.

Before the pivotal advances in medical science during the twentieth century, mankind had no way to buttress his genetic weakness, and as

---

[19] American Cancer Society, *Cancer Facts and Figures 2020* (Atlanta: American Cancer Society, 2020), https://www.cancer.org/research/cancer-facts-statistics/all-cancer-facts-figures/cancer-facts-figures-2020.html.

[20] Sanford, *Genetic Entropy and the Mystery of the Genome*, 27, 83.

a result, minor maladies were wiping out millions of people all over the earth. The average life expectancy in the nineteenth century—and for most of recorded history—was fifty years, a figure which would not have risen in the absence of certain technological breakthroughs (such as antibiotics and vaccines). The truth is, our technology is keeping us alive beyond the diminishing limitations of our biology. If the crutches of technology were suddenly kicked out from under us, we would quickly realize the crisis of our degenerate condition—the rate of life expectancy would plummet overnight, and a significant percentage of the global population would die in a matter of weeks, if not days.[21]

The equation is simple: the more we degenerate, the easier it is to kill us. If we were as genetically unadulterated as our antediluvian ancestors, our bodies would operate much more efficiently and require less medical intervention to maintain our well-being. We may be technologically superior to our predecessors, but we are, in every way, biologically inferior.

The genetic entropy of the human species is clearly charted in the diminishing lifespans of the biblical patriarchs: Adam lived 930 years; Lamech, the father of Noah, 753 years; Shem, the son of Noah, 435 years; Abraham, 175 years; Moses, 120 years; and David, 70 years.[22] Notice that the rate of degeneration was accelerated after the Flood, to such an extent that men were living only half as long as their pre-Flood predecessors. There are many speculations as to why this was the case, but the answer seems to be provided for us in Genesis 6, where God initiates the acceleration himself. The Septuagint records an intriguing rendering of the incident:

> "My Spirit shall certainly not remain among *these men* for ever, because they are flesh, but their days shall be an hundred and twenty years."[23]

"These men" may refer to the genetically compromised human hybrids that were propagating on Earth before the deluge, a situation we will

---

[21] Without access to insulin, diabetes alone would kill many millions within seven to ten days.
[22] As reckoned in the Septuagint (LXX).
[23] Genesis 6:3 (LXX, emphasis added).

examine at length in following chapters. Some have concluded that the above passage is an example of contradiction in the Genesis account, because the lifespans of the post-Flood patriarchs continued to exceed 120 years. In fact, what the biblical narrative demonstrates is not a contradiction but a confirmation of its historical veracity. When the full arc of the curve is plotted, the exponentially diminishing lifespans of the biblical patriarchs, both pre- and post-Flood, correlate precisely with the estimated rate of genetic degeneration due to mutation as calculated by modern geneticists.[24] Moreover, the consensus among many scientists is that 120 years is likely the maximum amount of time a human being can live, even under the most favorable conditions.

In summation, mankind has been progressively degenerating from his primordial ancestors and becoming genetically inferior over time. The human genome is decaying. Even if we find a cure for cancer in the next decade, new genetic disorders will continue to outpace our medical advances. We simply cannot escape the gravitational drag of entropy. To the degree that our technology develops, the quality of our genome declines. In the end, all we can really do is build better crutches for broken legs.

The late author and prominent atheist Christopher Hitchens was renowned for his acerbic wit and scathing polemics on the character of God. "Once you assume a creator and a plan," he was fond of saying, "it makes us objects in a cruel experiment whereby we are created sick and commanded to be well." I have observed Hitchens brandishing this argument on many occasions while debating eminent Christians in the course of his career, and to my dismay, very few of them ever rejoined with the appropriate response, "No, Mr. Hitchens, to the contrary; we were created well but because of sin were condemned to sickness and death." Such a reply might be followed with a summary of the gospel (the "good news"), which promises the rectification of the human condition and reconciliation in the family of God.

While we "wait eagerly for adoption as sons, the redemption of our

---

[24] See Philip M. Holladay, "An Exponential Decay Curve in Old Testament Genealogies," *Answers in Genesis Research Journal* (blog), October 19, 2016, https://answersingenesis.org/bible-timeline/genealogy/exponential-decay-curve-old-testament-genealogies.

bodies,"[25] we must endure the atrophy of Adam, the blight of corruption, and the bane of death.

Every human being born into the world bemoans the misery of his mortal condition. We all lament the corrosive gears of entropy grinding away at our bodies, reducing us to old and broken facsimiles of our former selves. Which of us does not loathe the cold-blooded indifference of disease, afflicting even the innocent babe with gross deformities, bone cancer, and sickle-cell anemia? Sickness and death are an affront to mankind—we were not supposed to suffer and die. But here we waste, shackled to the grave, longing desperately to be Adam again.

And this explains our fascination with superheroes. We desire to be more than what we are because we are less than what we should be. We are subconsciously dreaming of Eden.

"How inadequately which of us does not feel?" writes Pember in his elegant nineteenth-century prose. "For when at length we awake from the dream of this world; when our eyes are opened to a contemplation of realities, and a startling conviction of the ever decaying and quickly passing nature of all that is visible flashes upon our mind, from that moment we are possessed by one absorbing desire, that of attaining to life eternal. But to this end what guidance can we expect from the bodily senses, whose ceaseless march is ever to the grave?"[26]

The absorbing desire for life eternal is deeply embedded in the soul of every human being. We all pine for the amaranthine bliss of paradise and relentlessly pursue happiness in the hope that we might recover some relic of what was lost. Such a pursuit ought to impel us to the cross of Christ, through which we are restored to the glory of our original estate.

By divorcing us from the divine patrimony and purpose of our origin, Darwin managed to detach us from the distinction of our humanity, a clever maneuver by those who seek to divest us of the birthright associated with it.

But let's not get ahead of ourselves. In order to unpack the sequence of events that are set to unfold in the prophetic future, we must comprehend the gravity and consequence of what occurred in the prehistoric past.

---

[25] Romans 8:23 (ESV).

[26] Pember, *Earth's Earliest Ages*, 92.

Chapter 7

THE GOLDEN AGE

While most Christians reject the evolutionary model pertaining to the origin of species, many nevertheless subscribe to an evolutionary paradigm of history. It is merely taken for granted that our antecedents were vastly inferior to us in every way, that as you move backward on the timeline of history, you descend from the intellectual superiority of modern men residing in the twenty-first century to the barbarous stupidity of the antediluvians living in the prehistoric past.

It is true that a gradual retrograde of civilization can be traced backward through time . . . until circa 3300 BC, when the record comes to a grinding halt. This is that seminal period in which historians mark the beginning of civilization, often attributed to the Sumerians. However, what the date 3300 BC truly signifies is not the beginning but the *re*beginning of civilization in the aftermath of a global cataclysm.

The presumption that civilization began in the postdiluvian age does not correspond to the reckoning of ancient peoples, many of whom managed to preserve, at least in part, a testimony of the technological wonders of the Old World, the remarkable beings that inhabited it, and the cataclysm that brought it to ruin. Philosophers and sages maintained that the art of civilization, and indeed knowledge itself, was a gift from the gods—the forbidden Promethean fire imparted to humanity at the dawn of time. "The greatest minds of antiquity believed that gnosis or 'knowing' was the foundation of all religion," writes Flynn,

According to the ancient philosophers, knowledge was only attainable through the inspiration of heavenly powers. Their writings state that mankind's first knowledge had descended from the heavens.

The ancient mystery religions also preserved a legend: When heaven and earth joined together, gods descended to earth. The gods possessed the knowledge of the universe: the whole continuum of what can be known. They bestowed on men the art of civilization: government, agriculture and science, inventions that we in modern times hold to be human achievements. All science and learning was developed in the time when gods and man dwelt together.[1]

The knowledge of the gods was lost in the aqueous cataclysm that destroyed their empire on Earth. The ancients believed that whatever knowledge could be attained in the postdiluvian age was merely the reacquisition of what was already known long ago. The past, rather than the future, harbored the secrets of enlightenment for mankind. Thus, the Old World was the template for building the new.

It is widely acknowledged that divergent cultures around the globe were universally inclined to build upon the ruined foundations of antediluvian edifices, especially if those edifices were megalithic. There are, of course, obvious advantages to such a policy. Why labor to lay new foundations if the old ones are still intact? However, there is a deeper motivation behind the practice that transcends its architectural expediency. The ancients were obsessed with emulating the bygone glory of the Old World. They knew that the knowledge of the past was far superior to their own. By rebuilding the ruins, they hoped to regain some vestige of the grandeur that belonged to their prehistoric predecessors. When confronted with the mammoth remains of megalithic constructions, they hailed them as sacred ground—the handiwork and former habitation of the gods. New temples were raised upon the old foundations in homage to the divine builders who laid them. Palaces were also constructed by members of the royal blood, who viewed themselves as the offspring of

---

[1] Flynn, *Cydonia: The Secret Chronicles of Mars*, 219.

the gods and, as such, the rightful inheritors of their works.

The ancients did not look forward with eager eyes to the prospects of humanity's future; instead, they looked back with yearning to the days of yore, when the gods walked among men in the glorious Golden Age. The destruction of the Old World and the loss of its secrets were mourned like the death of a beloved ancestor. The ancient hope was ever invested in the long-foretold return of the gods. Someday, crooned the oracles, the gods would descend from the heavens once again and renew the sharing of knowledge; their empire would be restored, and their offspring would reoccupy the venerable thrones of their former dominion.

The descent (or ascent) and habitation of the gods among men was no small occurrence in the minds of the ancients—no mere footnote in the annals of history. Memorialized in the mythology of cultures far and wide, it was the single most significant event ever to have happened on Planet Earth. The author must refrain from giving too detailed an account of the Golden Age, as it is a vast and complicated subject. We are constrained by the focus of the present work to survey only the outer perimeters of this sprawling landscape.

Coined by the Greek poet Hesiod, the term *Golden Age* represents the dawn of humanity, when the gods dwelt among men in an epoch of unparalleled peace and harmony. There was no hostility in nature and no need to toil in the field for food, as the primordial soils freely gave of their bounty. Men lived almost immortal lives, persisting with a youthful vigor for hundreds of years. When finally death came knocking at the door, it was a tranquil affair—the pleasant passage from one state of being to another.

The spirits of the heroic dead persisted in the world as ethereal guardians for the living.[2] Plato further defines these guardian spirits as *daimons*, from which we derive the word *demon*.[3] In Greek mythology, a *daimon* proceeded from the deceased corpse of a demigod, the offspring of god

---

[2] Hesiod explains, "But when this race had been hidden under the cover of earth, they became, as almighty Zeus decreed, divinities, powers of good on the earth, guardians of moral men, who keep watch on cases at law and hard-hearted deeds, being hidden in air and going all over the earth, blessing men with wealth, as this is their kingly right" (James C. Lindahl, "Hesiod: Works and Days," San Jose University [unpublished lecture notes], accessed on June 8, 2020, https://www.sjsu.edu/people/james.lindahl/courses/Phil70A/s3/Hesiodworks).

[3] See Plato's *Cratylus*.

and man. In the Golden Age, the gods copulated with human women, who conceived and gave birth to the "Golden Race," the half-breed heroes of the Old World.

Having spawned from the seed of the gods, the demigods were imbued with superhuman abilities. They were revered as minor deities and venerated with their fathers. In the mythos of ancient cultures, the hybrid sons of the gods were often appointed to rule over the kingdoms of mortal men. The thrones of earthly dominion belonged, by decree, to the heirs of divine blood. Human tyrants throughout history have asserted their right to rule with the dubious claim that the blood of the gods coursed through their veins. The concept of the divine right of kings is rooted in the Golden Race and exemplified in the fabled realm that defines the Golden Age—Atlantis.

The legend of Atlantis was not invented by Walt Disney. The story of the rise and fall of both the city of Atlantis and the mighty Atlantean empire was preserved in myth as an allegory of the antediluvian age. The most famous and detailed account of Atlantis comes down to us from the fourth century BC in the form of Plato's unfinished work *Critias*. In the *Critias* dialogue, Plato recounts a conversation between Solon of Athens and an old Egyptian priest of the goddess Neith (Athena to the Greeks) in the city of Sais. The priest explains to Solon that advanced civilizations once flourished on Earth before they were destroyed in the deluge (and other cataclysms). The Greeks believed that they were in possession of new knowledge, but the Egyptians maintained that all knowledge was merely the relearning of what was known long ago. He then relates the tale of Atlantis:

> "I have before remarked in speaking of the allotments of the
> gods, that they distributed the whole earth into portions differ-
> ing in extent, and made for themselves temples and instituted
> sacrifices. And Poseidon, receiving for his lot the island of
> Atlantis, begat children by a mortal woman . . . He also begat
> and brought up five pairs of twin male children; and dividing
> the island of Atlantis into ten portions, he gave to the first-born
> of the eldest pair his mother's dwelling and the surrounding

allotment, which was the largest and best, and made him king over the rest; the others he made princes, and gave them rule over many men, and a large territory. And he named them all; the eldest, who was the first king, he named Atlas, and after him the whole island and the ocean were called Atlantic."[4]

What Plato does not reveal is that the ten twin sons of Poseidon were giants. The Egyptians were not the only civilization to keep a written record of Atlantis; the mystery schools of the Far East have long concealed secret knowledge regarding the antediluvian age. In her occult classic, *The Secret Doctrine*, theosophist Helena Blavatsky renders the following stanzas from an ancient Tibetan manuscript called the *Book of Dzyan* concerning the kings of Atlantis:

> They built huge cities. Of rare earths and metals they built. Out of the fires vomited, out of the white stone of the mountains and of the black stone, they cut their own images, in their size and likeness, and worshipped them.
>
> They built great images nine yatis high, the size of their bodies. Inner fires had destroyed the land of their fathers.
>
> The first great waters came. They swallowed the seven great islands.
>
> All holy saved, the unholy destroyed. With them most of the huge animals, produced from the sweat of the earth.[5]

The Greeks maintained a more comprehensive mythology of the Golden Age (later to be adopted and modified by the Romans) than did most other civilizations. However, the general narrative relating to the comingling of god and man, the subsequent procreation of hybrid off-spring, and the sudden obliteration of a ruinous cataclysm can be detected in the written records and oral traditions of every primary culture on earth. Hundreds of pages could be devoted to cataloguing the parallels

---

[4] Plato, *Critias*, translation by Benjamin Jowett, (n.p.: The Internet Classics Archive, 2009).

[5] Helena Petrovna Blavatsky, *The Secret Doctrine: The Synthesis of Science, Religion, and Philosophy, Vol. II* (London: The Theosophical Publishing Company, Limited, 2006), stanza XI, 43–45 from the *Book of Dzyan*.

in the pre-Flood legends of Mesopotamian, Egyptian, Greco-Roman, Mesoamerican, Andean, Polynesian, and Asian peoples (among many others). It is logical to conclude that all these stories, so homologous in their narratives, originate from the same source.

One of the principal commonalities of Golden Age lore is the positive light in which it is cast. The memory of the Old World was enshrined in the minds of the ancients as a utopian paradise, in which mankind greatly benefited from intercourse with the gods. There is, however, one glaring exception to the rule—the Hebrew account.

The ancient Hebrew conceptualization of the antediluvian age could not have been more antithetical to that of its contemporaries. In the Hebrew mind, the Old World was a dreadful dystopia marked by extreme violence, unbridled depravity, and open defiance against the ordinances of God. The beings who descended from heaven wrought chaos and corruption on Earth, provoking the judgment of the Noahic Flood.

While the advent of the Golden Age is undoubtably a major component of ancient Hebrew cosmology, the Tanakh has little to say about it. There is a simple explanation for this apparent omission: the story is thoroughly chronicled elsewhere. The history and consequence of the pre-Flood world was so deeply ingrained in Hebraic culture that the authors of scripture had only to make slight reference to it. The most explicit of these references is recorded in the sixth chapter of Genesis:

> When man began to multiply on the face of the land and daughters were born to them, the sons of God saw that the daughters of man were attractive. And they took as their wives any they chose. . . . The Nephilim [or *giants*] were on the earth in those days, and also afterward, when the sons of God came in to the daughters of man and they bore children to them. These were the mighty men who were of old, the men of renown.[6]

Notice how nonchalantly these enigmatic verses are inscribed by the author. One cannot help but conclude that the meaning of them was

---

[6] Genesis 6:1-2, 4 (ESV).

already widely understood, or else further explanation would have been required. To those unversed in the mythos of the Golden Age, this passage appears to be out of place—a peculiar digression in the Genesis chronology. However, to the trained eye, the little that is said speaks volumes.

Context is key. The premise of Genesis 6 concerns the judgment of the Flood; hence, the opening paragraph (rendered above) is the prelude to destruction. Rather than revealing new information, the author simply affirms what is already known: the sons of God impregnated the daughters of men, who gave birth to unsanctioned hybrid beings (*Nephilim*), a grave transgression that precipitated the cataclysm of the Great Flood. It is highly unlikely that the Hebrews derived their comprehension of this incident from Genesis 6 alone; they must have had other sources to fill in the blanks.

In 1773, the famous Scottish adventurer James Bruce returned to Britain after living for six years in Abyssinia (known today as Ethiopia). During his travels, Bruce managed to acquire several copies of a manuscript that was once widely circulated in the ancient world but subsequently lost to history—the Book of Enoch. Unbeknownst to Western scholarship, the Ethiopians had preserved the manuscript and incorporated it into their canon of scripture. Thanks to Bruce, for the first time in centuries, scholars were able to read what many of the early church fathers considered to be the source material from which the opening verses in Genesis 6 were derived. Nearly two hundred years later, the fateful discovery of a young goatherd would confirm the authenticity of the Ethiopic Book of Enoch.

In 1947, a Bedouin boy (according to one account) was traversing the cliffs along the Dead Sea in Israel's Judean Desert, searching for a stray goat. As legend has it, he happened upon a cave burrowed into the face of the limestone. Curious, the boy cast a stone into the mouth of the cave, and to his surprise, the unmistakable sound of shattering pottery rang in the air. Upon entering the cave to investigate, he made what was to become one of the greatest archaeological discoveries of all time. Rolls of ancient parchment, untouched for two thousand years, had been carefully concealed within large earthen jars—the Dead Sea Scrolls. Ten more caves containing many more priceless manuscripts would be discovered in the years that followed.

The Dead Sea Scrolls are a collection of 981 texts recovered from the caves of Qumran between 1946 and 1956. The texts, written in Hebrew, Aramaic, Greek, and Nabataean, are inscribed predominantly on parchment but also on papyrus and bronze. Due to the poor condition of several scrolls, not all the texts have been identified, and only fragments of some remain. Among the legible manuscripts are numerous copies of every book in the Hebrew Bible and the Old Testament protocanon except the Book of Esther. Many apocryphal works are also represented in the scrolls, such as the Book of Jubilees, the Genesis Apocryphon, the Book of Noah, the Book of Giants, and the Book of Enoch, all of which were found together in cave 1 of Qumran.

Enoch, the son of Jared and seventh in the line of Adam, is the most eminent pre-Flood patriarch in Hebrew tradition; he is also the most enigmatic. To the Christian, Enoch, though acknowledged as an exceptionally righteous man who walked with God, is little more than a cryptic footnote in the biblical narrative; but to the Hebrew, he was a prophet and a scribe—indeed, the first and foremost on both counts.

Concerning Enoch, the writer of Genesis offers only this:

> Enoch lived sixty-five years, and begot Methuselah. After he begot Methuselah, Enoch walked with God three hundred years, and had sons and daughters. So all the days of Enoch were three hundred and sixty-five years. And Enoch walked with God; and he was not, for God took him.[7]

Once again, we are confronted with a chronological ambiguity in the Genesis narrative, which obliges us to conclude that a more comprehensive account regarding Enoch is recorded elsewhere. Considering that the ancient Hebrews believed Enoch to be a prophet, it follows that there must have existed some literary work attributed to him. The assumption is confirmed in the epistle of Jude, where a passage from the Book of Enoch is quoted verbatim in the context of inspired prophecy. Writes Jude,

It was also about these that Enoch, the seventh from Adam,

---

[7] Genesis 5:21–24 (NKJV).

prophesied, saying, "Behold, the Lord comes with ten thousands of his holy ones, to execute judgment on all and to convict all the ungodly of all their deeds of ungodliness that they have committed in such an ungodly way, and of all the harsh things that ungodly sinners have spoken against him."[8]

There is no reason to doubt that this prophecy was inscribed by Enoch's own hand and that the passage is excerpted from an ancient text regarded as sacred scripture by the Hebrews, a portion of which was carefully stored (likely by the Essenes) in the caves of Qumran. The confusion and controversy surrounding the Book of Enoch is largely due to the existence of several conflicting manuscripts that have circulated over the centuries. A cursory examination of the three volumes attributed to Enoch suffices to settle which among them is most historically reliable and theologically concordant with the narrative of scripture:

» 1 Enoch, otherwise known as "The Ethiopic Enoch," is the only version discovered among the Dead Sea Scrolls and dated before the birth of Christ. The BC origin of the text is critical in determining its authenticity, as it contains messianic prophecies. The historical, prophetic, and doctrinal motifs of 1 Enoch are harmonious with the biblical texts. The Enochian prophecy quoted in the epistle of Jude appears to have been excerpted verbatim from this manuscript.

» 2 Enoch, otherwise known as "The Slavonic Enoch" (also called "The Book of the Secrets of Enoch"), is commonly dated to the latter part of the first century AD. Its content is distinctly Jewish rather than Christian. 2 Enoch appears to be an abridged version of 1 Enoch but missing the narrative of the watchers and lacking a synchronicity with the New Testament.

» 3 Enoch, otherwise known as "The Hebrew Enoch" (also called "The Revelation of Metatron"), was written somewhere between AD 500 and 600. This manuscript is clearly

---

[8] Jude 1:14–15 (ESV).

the product of Jewish Merkabah (or Chariot) mysticism. It accounts the heavenly journeys of the High Priest, Rabbi Ishmael ben Elisha, and his encounters with Metatron (Enoch).

Considering that 1 Enoch was written before Christ and contains prophecies pertaining to him, we are automatically supplied with a benchmark for determining its authenticity. If the prophecies were accurate in light of the New Testament, then the work is authentic, biblically speaking. As it happens, the Christological profile presented in the Book of Enoch was not only accurate but essential to the claims of Jesus of Nazareth. The following is a sample of the messianic content of 1 Enoch:

> And there I saw One, who had a head of days, and his head was white like wool, and with him was another being whose countenance had the appearance of a man, and his face was full of graciousness, like one of the holy angels. And I asked the angel who went with me and showed me all the hidden things, concerning that Son of Man, who he was, and whence he was, and why he went with the Head of Days? And he answered and said unto me: This is the Son of Man who hath righteousness, with whom dwelleth righteousness, and who revealeth all the treasures of that which is hidden, because the Lord of Spirits hath chosen him, and whose lot hath the pre-eminence before the Lord of Spirits in uprightness forever. And this Son of Man whom thou hast seen shall raise up the kings and the mighty from their seats, and the strong from their thrones and shall loosen the reins of the strong, and break the teeth of the sinners; and he shall put down the kings from their thrones and kingdoms because they do not extol and praise him, nor humbly acknowledge whence the kingdom was bestowed upon them.[9]

Observe that the Christ is called the "Son of Man" in the excerpt above. Not coincidentally, this was the title most favored by Jesus when

---

[9] 1 Enoch 46:1–5 (R. H. Charles).

referring to himself. The appellative *Son of Man* does not appear in the Old Testament in reference to the Christ except in a passage of Daniel, where it is employed to describe his human appearance:

> I saw in the night visions, and behold, with the clouds of heaven there came one like a son of man, and he came to the Ancient of Days and was presented before him. And to him was given dominion and glory and a kingdom that all peoples, nations, and languages should serve him; his dominion is an everlasting dominion, which shall not pass away, and his kingdom one that shall not be destroyed.[10]

Daniel's vision of the Christ being presented before the Ancient of Days perfectly coheres with Enoch's description of the same event:

> And at that hour that Son of Man was named in the presence of the Lord of Spirits, and his name before the Head of Days. Yea, before the sun and the signs were created, before the stars of the heaven were made, his name was named before the Lord of Spirits. He shall be a staff to the righteous whereon to stay themselves and not fall, and he shall be the light of the Gentiles [nations], and the hope of those who are troubled of heart. All who dwell on earth shall fall down and worship before him, and will praise and bless and celebrate with song the Lord of Spirits. And for this reason hath he been chosen and hidden before him, before the creation of the world and for evermore. And the wisdom of the Lord of Spirits hath revealed him to the holy and righteous; for he hath preserved the lot of the righteous; because they have hated and despised this world of unrighteousness, and have hated all its works and ways in the name of the Lord of Spirits: for in his name they are saved, and according to his good pleasure hath it been in regard to their life.[11]

---

[10] Daniel 7:13–14 (ESV).
[11] 1 Enoch 48:2–7 (RHC).

The Christian intonations of this BC manuscript are unmistakable. Hundreds (perhaps thousands) of years before he was born into the world, the Son of Man was described as a "staff to the righteous" and the "light of the Gentiles [nations]." The very core of Christian doctrine is revealed in the pronouncement, "for in his name they are saved." There can be no doubt that the prophecies of Enoch were fulfilled in Jesus of Nazareth. In fact, some scholars have argued that the remarkable congruity between 1 Enoch and the doctrines of the New Testament prove that portions of the manuscript were written in the first or second century AD, a contention vigorously refuted by the Ethiopians.

When Jesus referred to himself as the Son of Man, the meaning was crystal clear in the minds of the Jews. The Pharisees and Sadducees understood exactly who he was claiming to be precisely because they were well versed in the messianic prophecies of Enoch. Jesus was not merely declaring himself to be *a* son of man, but *the* Son of Man, according to the scriptures. When the high priest interrogated him with the question, "Are you the Christ, the Son of the Blessed?" Jesus replied,

> "I am, and you will see the Son of Man seated at the right hand of the Power, and coming with the clouds of heaven."
>
> Then the high priest tore his clothes and said, "What further need do we have of witnesses? You have heard the blasphemy! What do you think?"
>
> And they all condemned him to be deserving of death. Then some began to spit on him, and to blindfold Him, and to beat him, and to say to him, "Prophesy!" And the officers struck him with the palms of their hands."[12]

There must have been at least one member among the council of the Sanhedrin nervously contemplating the words of Enoch as he watched his colleagues spit on Jesus and slap him in the face:

> And they shall be terrified, and they shall be downcast of countenance, and pain shall seize them, when they see that

---

[12] Mark 14:60–65 (NKJV).

Son of Man sitting on the throne of his glory. . . . And all the kings and the mighty, and the exalted, and those who rule the earth shall fall down before him on their faces, and worship and set their hope upon that Son of Man, and petition him, and supplicate for mercy at his hands.[13]

Many more such passages could be cited to demonstrate the synchronicity of 1 Enoch with the biblical narrative, but the point would be belabored. Some scholars believe that the Book of Enoch was the primary influence on the doctrines of the New Testament, particularly those related to the person of Christ and to eschatology. What remains indisputable is that the patriarchs of the Christian church regarded it as scripture.

The Greek translation of 1 Enoch was known to and referenced by many of the early church fathers, including Clement and Barnabas (the friends of Paul), Irenaeus, Origen, Tertullian, Athenagoras of Athens, and Justin Martyr, all of whom held an affirming view of the text. Tertullian in his treatise *On the Apparel of Women* argues that the Book of Enoch ought to be regarded as scripture:

I am aware that the Scripture of Enoch, which has assigned this order (of action) to angels [referring to their sexual intercourse with human women] is not received by some, because it is not admitted into the Jewish canon either. I suppose they did not think that, having been published before the deluge, it could have safely survived that world-wide calamity, the abolisher of all things. If that is the reason (for rejecting it), let them recall to their memory that Noah, the survivor of the deluge, was the great-grandson of Enoch himself; and he, of course, had heard and remembered, from domestic renown and hereditary tradition, concerning his own great-grandfather's "grace in the sight of God," and concerning all his preachings; since Enoch had given no other charge to Methuselah than that he should hand on the knowledge of them to his posterity. Noah therefore, no doubt, might have succeeded in the trusteeship of

---

[13] 1 Enoch 62:5, 9 (RHC).

(his) preaching; or, had the case been otherwise, he would not have been silent alike concerning the disposition (of things) made by God, his Preserver, and concerning the particular glory of his own house.

If (Noah) had not had this (conservative power) by so short a route, there would (still) be this (consideration) to warrant our assertion of (the genuineness of) this Scripture: he could equally have *renewed* it, under the Spirit's inspiration, after it *had* been destroyed by the violence of the deluge, as, after the destruction of Jerusalem by the Babylonian storming of it, every document of the Jewish literature is generally agreed to have been restored through Ezra.

But since Enoch in the same Scripture has preached likewise concerning the Lord, nothing at all must be rejected *by* us which pertains *to* us; and we read that "every Scripture suitable for edification is divinely inspired." By the *Jews* it may now seem to have been rejected for that (very) reason, just like all the other (portions) nearly which tell of Christ. Nor, of course, is this fact wonderful, that they did not receive some Scriptures which spake of him whom even in person, speaking in their presence, they were not to receive. To these considerations is added the fact that Enoch possesses a testimony in the Apostle Jude.[14]

Tertullian, like many theologians of his day, was convinced that the Book of Enoch would have been canonized as holy scripture if not for the Jews, who rejected it because of its Christological content, which clearly pointed to Jesus of Nazareth, whom they had condemned as a blasphemer and a fraud. Tertullian's confidence in the text is evidenced in the way he cites the peculiar story it relates, an elaboration of the Genesis 6 affair, as literal history:

---

[14] Tertullian, *On the Apparel of Women*, in *Ante-Nicene Fathers, Vol. 4*, by Phillip Schaff (Grand Rapids, MI: William B. Eerdmans Publishing Company, 1956).

For they, withal, who instituted them are assigned, under condemnation, to the penalty of death,—those angels, to wit, who
rushed from heaven on the daughters of men; so that this igno-
miny also attaches to woman. For when to an age much more
ignorant (than ours) they had disclosed certain well-concealed
material substances, and several not well-revealed scientific
arts—if it is true that they had laid bare the operations of
metallurgy, and had divulged the natural properties of herbs,
and had promulgated the powers of enchantments, and had
traced out every curious art, even to the interpretation of the
stars—they conferred properly and as it were peculiarly upon
women that instrumental mean of womanly ostentation, the
radiances of jewels wherewith necklaces are variegated, and
the circlets of gold wherewith the arms are compressed, and
the medicaments of orchil with which wools are coloured, and
that black powder itself wherewith the eyelids and eyelashes
are made prominent. . . . And these are the angels whom we
are destined to judge: these are the angels whom in baptism
we renounce: these, of course, are the reasons why they have
deserved to be judged by man.[15]

The Masoretic rendering of Genesis 6 designates these mutinous
angels as *sons of God*. In the Septuagint they are called the *angels of
God* (which, consequently, invalidates the ridiculous Sethite nonsense).
However, Hebrew tradition, as well as numerous ancient extrabiblical
texts, including the Book of Enoch, denominate them with the Aramaic
word *'iyrin*, rendered in the Greek as *egrégoroi* and in English as *watchers*.

The *watcher* denomination is not exclusively extrabiblical. The Book
of Daniel recounts a fascinating incident in which King Nebuchadnezzar
is sentenced to an unusual punishment for his excessive pride: he is
driven mad and made to live among the beasts of the field and eat grass
for seven years. What makes this story even more intriguing is that
Nebuchadnezzar's judgment is decreed by a council of watchers:

---

[15] Tertullian, *On the Apparel of Women.*

I saw in the visions of my head as I lay in bed, and behold, a watcher ['*iyr*], a holy one, came down from heaven. He proclaimed aloud and said thus: "Chop down the tree and lop off its branches, strip off its leaves and scatter its fruit. Let the beasts flee from under it and the birds from its branches. But leave the stump of its roots in the earth, bound with a band of iron and bronze, amid the tender grass of the field. Let him be wet with the dew of heaven. Let his portion be with the beasts in the grass of the earth. Let his mind be changed from a man's, and let a beast's mind be given to him; and let seven periods of time pass over him. The sentence is by the decree of the watchers ['*iyrin*], the decision by the word of the holy ones, to the end that the living may know that the Most High rules the kingdom of men and gives it to whom he will and sets over it the lowliest of men."[16]

This scene recalls us to the council of the Elohim, who determined to make man in their likeness and grant him dominion of the Earth. The council's decision regarding Nebuchadnezzar is a reiteration of Adam's irrevocable endowment: the authority of human rulers will be upheld even if they defy heaven, but the council will appoint and depose them as they see fit. Having been thoroughly humbled after seven years of madness, the King of Babylon obsequiously declares that Yahweh "does according to his will among the host of heaven and among the inhabitants of the earth."[17] All realms, terrestrial and extraterrestrial, are subject to the decree of the King and his council.

The identity of the watchers is no great mystery. Much like the term *angel, watcher* is an occupational descriptive, as in soldier or warrior, or more precisely, warden; that is to say, it does not supply insight into what a being *is* but what it *does*. In Aramaic and Hebrew, as in English, *watching* can mean *guarding*, which, as we have seen, is the job description of the cherubim who watch over the throne and kingdom of God with extreme vigilance and are thus aptly portrayed with many eyes and

---

[16] Daniel 4:13–17 (ESV).
[17] Daniel 4:35 (ESV).

four faces looking in every direction, as if to convey, "Nothing escapes our gaze." Daniel depicts the watchers as members of the divine council and refers to them as "holy ones,"[18] which is a distinction reserved for the highest-ranking beings who dwell in the presence of God. Clearly, the watchers are synonymous with the cherubim—the princes and wardens of the kingdom.

According to the Hebrew account, the Golden Age is defined by the defection and descent of two hundred watchers, who committed the most heinous crime ever recorded: they invaded Adam's domain and copulated with his daughters in order to procreate their own offspring, the Nephilim, an unsanctioned race of hybrid beings.

This most pivotal of events in the annals of human history, viewed favorably by the pagans, led to the near extinction of the human species, a scenario that will be repeated, to some extent, at the end of the age. It is therefore imperative that we survey the prehistoric landscape through the lens of 1 Enoch and take note of the circumstances that provoked the fall of the watchers, precipitated the Flood of Noah, and facilitated the first usurpation of human dominion on Planet Earth.

---

[18] See also Psalm 89:7.

Chapter 8

FALL OF THE WATCHERS

When, in 1773, James Bruce returned to Britain with three Ethiopic copies of 1 Enoch in hand, he could not have imagined how relevant the text would become in the twenty-first century. We, who are now on the brink of the same kind of circumstances that preceded the utter destruction of the Old World, would do well to carefully regard the words of Enoch, which were not inscribed for his own generation "but for a remote one which is to come"—for the righteous "who will be living in the day of tribulation, when all the wicked and godless are to be removed."[1] It cannot be coincidental that the Book of Enoch, written in the dawn of humanity, should resurface just in time to benefit those who are living in the dusk.

The end-time pertinence of the Enochian text is firmly established in its very first prophecy:

> The Holy Great One will come forth from his dwelling, and the eternal God will tread upon the earth, even on Mount Sinai, and appear in the strength of his might from the heaven of heavens. And all shall be smitten with fear, and the watchers shall quake, and great fear and trembling shall seize them unto the ends of the earth. And the high mountains shall be shaken, and the high hills shall be made low, and shall melt

---

[1] 1 Enoch 1:1–3 (RHC).

like wax before the flame and the earth shall be wholly rent in sunder, and all that is upon the earth shall perish, and there shall be a judgment upon all.[2]

The tenor of this prophecy should be familiar to the reader, as it resonates with echoes of Rahab's obliteration and the fury of the dragon's defeat on the field of Edom. It simultaneously predicts the first cataclysmic judgment that was soon to inundate the earth in the days of Noah and the final judgment at the end of the age, when the King returns to tread the winepress of God's wrath. The verse that follows establishes the eschatological context: "And behold! He comes with ten thousands of his holy ones to execute judgement upon all, and to destroy the ungodly,"[3] a scene later described by John, who sees Jesus coming with the armies of heaven to vanquish the coalition of the beast gathered against him in the valley of Armageddon.[4]

We might imagine Enoch sitting beneath the towering cedars of Lebanon, breathlessly penning the words of his prophecy as visions of the Flood and the battle of Armageddon explode in his mind. Though separated by many thousands of years, these events would be inextricably linked through time, like the quantum entanglement of electrons separated by thousands of miles.

In this chapter we will endeavor to undertake a brief examination of the Golden Age through the eyes of the ancient Hebrews. To this effect, we will rely primarily on the historical portion of 1 Enoch (the "Book of the Watchers") but will also reference other relevant Dead Sea Scroll texts, including the Book of Jubilees and the Book of Giants, to supplement the narrative. What follows is a compilation of the story they tell.

The Enochian tale begins with a company of two hundred watchers who become enamored of the daughters of men:

---

[2] 1 Enoch 1:3–7 (RHC).
[3] 1 Enoch 1:9 (RHC).
[4] See Revelation 19.

And it came to pass when the children of men had multiplied that in those days were born unto them beautiful and comely daughters. And the angels, the children of the heaven, saw and lusted after them, and said to one another: "Come, let us choose us wives from among the children of men and beget us children."[5]

These verses appear to have been pasted word for word into the Genesis account, which makes perfect sense if the intent of the author was to recall the reader to the testimony of Enoch wherefrom they were copied.[6] For most of church history, the incident they describe was scrutinized and debated exclusively in the halls of seminaries among budding scholars, but thanks to the internet, Genesis 6:1 has become nearly as famous as John 3:16. Consequently, a panoply of books and documentaries have been published in recent years to capitalize on the growing demand for all things "Nephilim."

In the author's opinion, though broadly consumed, the implications of the Genesis 6 affair have been poorly digested. If, having read the passage above, the theological furniture in your mind has not been rearranged, then you have simply not understood what is insinuated in the text. That the angels, the children of heaven, could look upon human women and burn with lust for them is a shocking contradiction to the traditional perception of heavenly beings, who are not supposed to be clothed in bodies of flesh. Furthermore, that they deemed themselves reproductively compatible with our species is sufficient to overturn the notion that only we are made in the likeness of God. The meaning of the text is inescapable: the sons of God were sexually attracted to the daughters of men and desired to copulate with them and beget offspring.

Too often, the sexuality implicit in the Genesis 6 affair is brushed aside by theologians, who swing the broom of incredulity to and fro, sweeping away every pestiferous detail that makes a mess of their angelology. Angels are spiritual beings, they contest, and therefore incapable of lusting after,

---

[5] 1 Enoch 6:1–2 (RHC).

[6] It is an intriguing coincidence that the passage appears precisely in the first paragraph of the sixth chapter in both the Book of Enoch and Genesis.

having sex with, and impregnating human females. Forcefully though the argument is advanced, it will never escape the countermomentum of its own irrelevance, because that is precisely what they (the angels) did.

The problem for theologians is that sensual impulses imply sexual organs and reproductive biology, which according to convention, angels must not have. In an effort to circumvent this problem, some researchers have suggested that the angels did not themselves have sex with women but instead possessed the bodies of men in order to perform the act or, alternatively, simply "incarnated" with male anatomy (which assigns to them the metamorphic powers previously mentioned). Others postulate that sexual intercourse never actually occurred and that the procreative procedure was accomplished through some form of genetic engineering.

All of these theories, and indeed any that may be devised, fail to address the critical first cause—the children of heaven *lusted* after the daughters of men. How can spiritual beings, supposedly unequipped for sexual intercourse and incapable of reproduction, be subject to carnal passions and accomplish procreation? Do the sons of God even have seed to sow? Surely the fact that they impregnated women suggests that they do. Proponents of the genetic engineering hypothesis attempt to sidestep this conundrum by suggesting that the angels did not use their own seed to fertilize the ova of human females but the seed of other creatures modified *in vitro*. In the first place, this proposition evades the first cause—they wanted to have sex, a desire which would have hardly been satisfied in a petri dish; and in the second place, it dismisses the testimony of Enoch, who leaves no room for doubt as to how they performed the act. It is evident that Enoch, as well as the writer of Genesis, clearly means to say that the sons of God lusted after, copulated with, and procreated through human females.

The methods by which the watchers accomplished the transgression are not as important as the motives. Why did they do it? Aside from the primal urge for sexual intercourse, they seem to have been consumed with another carnal impulse—envy. The watchers were envious of mankind. Specifically, there are three things they coveted:

1. **Wives**

   Mankind was granted a special privilege that was not afforded to the sons of God: a female counterpart, a wife. The watchers envied men for their wives.[7]

2. **Offspring**

   Because men had female counterparts, they could procreate offspring. The watchers wanted to beget their own children and have families, like the sons of Adam.

3. **Dominion**

   Mankind was given dominion of Planet Earth. The watchers coveted man's dominion and plotted to usurp it by producing their own human-hybrid sons. This is perhaps the most important, and most overlooked, aspect of their transgression.

The defection of the watchers, though provoked by lust, was not entirely impulsive. They had a plan. By copulating with the women of Earth, they could produce their own offspring, who might be human enough to inherit Adam's birthright. The half-breed sons of the watchers, inexorably superior to their human cousins in every way, would seize the thrones of men and establish their own kingdoms, which their fathers would rule by proxy.

Once the details of their diabolical plan had been devised, the watchers entered the terrestrial realm through the stargate on the summit of Mount Hermon. Knowing full well that what they were about to do amounted to sedition, they decided to bind themselves with an oath before descending into the plains below. They would stay the course and suffer the consequences together, whatever befall:

---

[7] In the interest of intellectual honesty, it should be noted that there is simply no way to know whether or not there are females among the sons of God (i.e., the "daughters of God"). All of the terminology related to angels in the Bible is strictly masculine, but the fact that they are capable of lust, sexual intercourse, and procreation suggests that they may indeed have, or have had at one time, female counterparts. Though I am unwilling to commit to the proposition, I cannot rule it out. Whatever the case, the angels clearly envied men for their wives.

And Semjâzâ, who was their leader, said unto them: "I fear ye will not indeed agree to do this deed, and I alone shall have to pay the penalty of a great sin." And they all answered him and said: "Let us all swear an oath, and all bind ourselves by mutual imprecations not to abandon this plan but to do this thing." Then sware they all together and bound themselves by mutual imprecations upon it. And they were in all two hundred; who descended in the days of Jared on the summit of Mount Hermon, and they called it Mount Hermon, because they had sworn and bound themselves by mutual imprecations upon it.[8]

It is possible that in order to breed with human women, the watchers were forced to abandon some facet of their higher nature and affix themselves to the constraints of the human condition. Support for this hypothesis could be cited in the Book of Jude, where their sexual exploits are likened to those of the Sodomites and Gomorrahites, who were in the habit of going after *strange flesh*:

And the angels who did not keep their proper domain, but left their own *abode*, he has reserved in everlasting chains under darkness for the judgment of the great day; as Sodom and Gomorrah, and the cities around them in a similar manner to these, having given themselves over to sexual immorality and gone after strange flesh, are set forth as an example, suffering the vengeance of eternal fire.[9]

The word *abode* in this passage is *oiketerion* in the Greek, which is commonly used to describe a bodily residence. Jude's choice of the word *oiketerion* may not be coincidental, as it only appears in one other passage of the New Testament:

For we know that if our earthly house, this tent, is destroyed, we have a building from God, a house not made with hands,

---

[8] 1 Enoch 6:3–6 (RHC).
[9] Jude 1:6–7 (NKJV, emphasis added).

eternal in the heavens. For in this we groan, earnestly desiring to be clothed with our *habitation* which is from heaven, if indeed, having been clothed, we shall not be found naked. For we who are in this tent groan, being burdened, not because we want to be unclothed, but further clothed, that mortality may be swallowed up by life.[10]

Here, "habitation" is *oiketerion*. Paul is using the same word to describe the bodies with which the saints will be clothed at the resurrection that Jude uses to describe what the watchers abandoned (or forfeited) upon their descent to the earth. Notice that he says we groan not because we want to be *unclothed*, but *further clothed*. Human biology is not going to be *replaced* at the resurrection but *repaired*. All of the extraordinary attributes inherent in the blueprint of Adam's genetic architecture will be completely restored through the transformative power of the resurrection. As previously noted, Jesus exhibits the resurrected body when he appears in the midst of his disciples after rising from the grave. He is fully human, even bearing the scars of the crucifixion in his flesh, and yet capable of seemingly superhuman feats. Having chosen to betray the King of heaven and abandon paradise, the watchers likely forfeited their extrinsic immortality and became subject to entropy. Who knows what other changes may have occurred in their bodies when they, like us, were shut out of Eden?

After descending the slopes of Hermon, the watchers began to select wives from among the female inhabitants of the surrounding region. Whether they seduced these women or took them by force is unclear. However, because the wives of the watchers are ultimately implicated in their husbands' transgression and judged accordingly, we may infer that they were willing partners.

Some researchers speculate that the watchers were reptilian in appearance. This is most certainly not true. As sons of God, they bore the semblance of strikingly handsome young men, much like the angels who supped with Lot before Sodom's destruction.[11] This would explain

---

[10] 2 Corinthians 5:1–4 (NKJV, emphasis added).
[11] See Genesis 19.

the seeming eagerness of the women to wed the watchers. It is hard to imagine a beautiful woman falling head over heels for a reptilian freak.

It is interesting that the watchers saw fit to wed these women rather than simply fornicate with them. This procedure reveals that they were after more than sex. Apparently, they intended to procreate families within the covenant of marriage, almost as if they were hoping that the interspecies union might eventually be approved, or at the very least tolerated, by God. Whatever the case, the result of their union was alarming, to say the least: after the watchers copulated with their wives, the women conceived and gave birth to giants.

There is much debate concerning how these women were able to carry to term and deliver gigantic babies, a feat which would have surely proven fatal for both mother and child. According to some traditions, the women's wombs were indeed split open by the massive fetuses, but this scenario is not necessary to make sense of the phenomenon. Just like human babies born today with the genetic disorder of giantism, the size and weight of the hybrid babies may have been typical at birth, but as the infants progressed through childhood, they experienced accelerated growth, resulting in exceedingly large adults. However, in stark contrast to the genetic disorder of giantism, which weakens the heart and causes a cascade of debilitating conditions, the giant sons of the watchers were superhumanly enhanced with the DNA of the elder race.

The watchers may not have intended to beget giants. We assume that they knew exactly what to expect from their genetic experiment, but it is possible that they were just as surprised by the outcome as the men who watched in wonder as the children of the gods grew to colossal size.

As an intriguing aside, the Greek translation of 1 Enoch describes successive races of giants bred over time:

> And they [the women] bore to them [the Watchers] three races—first, the great giants. The giants brought forth [other translations read "slew"] the Naphelim, and the Naphelim brought forth [or "slew"] the Elioud. And they existed, increasing in power according to their greatness.[12]

---

[12] 1 Enoch 7:11 (Greek).

146

The Book of Jubilees concurs:

> And they begat sons the Naphidim, and they were all unlike,
> and they devoured one another: and the Giants slew the
> Naphil, and the Naphil slew the Eljo, and the Eljo mankind,
> and one man another.[13]

We must not assume, as some have, that all of the giants were male.
There is no reason to doubt that females were also conceived, enabling the
giants to breed among themselves. The giants may also have copulated
with human women in their adolescence, before their members were too
large to perform the act. It will become apparent as we progress that the
watchers and their offspring had plenty of time to reproduce before the
Flood, and according to some accounts, the breeding was not limited to
the daughters of Adam.

The Book of Giants supplements a heinous detail to the Enochian
narrative. After successfully begetting hybrid children with their human
wives, the watchers turn their procreant passions on the beasts of the
field, each one selecting for himself two hundred specimens from the
animal kingdom for the express purpose of miscegenation (cross-species
breeding). The manuscript from the Book of Giants is badly damaged
and highly fragmented, but much can be inferred from what remains:

> [. . .] two hundred donkeys, two hundred asses, two hundred
> [. . .] rams of the flock, two hundred goats, two hundred [. . .
> beast of the] field from every animal, from every [bird . . .]
> were selected for miscegenation[14]

> [. . .] they defiled [. . . they begot] giants and monsters [. . .]
> they begot, and, behold, all [the earth was corrupted . . .][15]

Quite contrary to the Greek embellishment, a macabre panorama

---

[13] Jubilees 7:22 (RHC).
[14] Book of Giants 1Q23 Frag. 1 + 6.
[15] Book of Giants 4Q531 Frag. 2.

of the Golden Age is beginning to emerge. We must now contemplate a pre-Flood world populated not only with the giant half-breed sons of the watchers but also with monstrous mutants blended from the seed of god and beast. Like mad scientists drunk with the power of procreation, the watchers were using their DNA to genetically modify the creatures of Earth into perverted reflections of their own likeness. It would seem that once they realized the potency of their seed in the human species, they decided to test its effect on other specimens by producing a sundry array of inhuman hybrid progeny, the stepbrothers of the giants, so to speak. The precise means by which they managed to accomplish this cannot be known, but one might assume the same kind of genetic engineering familiar to us today. (It is important to remember that the elder race is exceedingly ancient and technologically advanced.) If the germlines of the species were modified, then the hybrid DNA would be inherited by successive generations through time, resulting in the widespread genetic corruption of animal life on Planet Earth.

If all this were not enough to kindle the ire of the Maker, the watchers committed yet another grave trespass by teaching their wives, their children, and mankind the forbidden knowledge of the morning stars. Secrets pertaining to astrology, pharmacy, and sorcery were disclosed, as well as the art of metallurgy. The decision to impart knowledge to men was not made on a whim, nor an act of goodwill. The watchers desired to be worshipped as gods. By giving gifts to men, they could purchase their devotion and lead them into idolatry, thereby gaining authority in their realm. To this end, the greatest secrets were reserved for their own sons, who were to forge kingdoms on Earth and subjugate the sons of Adam.

It is highly unlikely that the watchers came through the gate of Hermon empty-handed. Who knows what technologies they brought with them? They must have contemplated the likelihood of being exiled for their crimes; it is only logical to assume that they would have equipped themselves appropriately. They might even have arrived at the helms of advanced aerospace craft. We should not suppose, however, that they freely shared all they knew or possessed with the awestruck masses of humanity. This would have been counterintuitive, as their objective was not to enlighten the human race but to subjugate them.

When thinking about the technologies that may have been in operation during the Golden Age, we should resist the temptation to compare them to our own. Most of our technologies are superfluous, designed for the convenience and amusement of impotent human minds. The instruments of a vastly superior civilization would not resemble the tools and toys we have devised for profit and play. In other words, we should not go looking for evidence of laptops and Lamborghinis among antediluvian ruins. The technology of the watchers would be so foreign to the mind of man that we would scarcely be able to recognize it, even if the waters of the Flood had not washed away every trace of its existence . . . that is, nearly every trace.

So complete was the destruction of the Old World that the only evidence left standing to testify of its bygone grandeur are the megalithic edifices constructed of solid stone. Like the bleached bones of a body long dead, the ruinous remains of megaliths worldwide stand in memoriam of the antediluvian age and the lost knowledge of its cyclopean masons. The quarrying, transporting, cutting, lifting, and placing of enormous blocks of hard stone flawlessly fitted together without the use of mortar and precisely aligned with specific constellations and cosmological phenomena implies a level of technological capability that would not be seen on the earth again until the advent of the Industrial Revolution in the nineteenth century. Without considering any other evidence, the megaliths alone bear witness to the knowledge that was lost in the cataclysm of the Flood.

The ancients maintained that the megaliths were built by the offspring of the gods, a myth preserved to this day in the term used by archaeologists to describe their trademark architecture: *cyclopean*. In Greek mythology, the giant one-eyed sons of the gods were the master masons, blacksmiths, metalworkers, and craftsmen of the pre-Flood world. The ruined megalithic constructions scattered throughout the Grecian landscape, such as the walls of Mycenae and Tiryns in the Peloponnese, were attributed to the cyclopes.

Cyclopean masonry employs the distinctive utility of massive blocks of stone cut from solid rock and fitted together without the use of mortar. The blocks were often so flawlessly shaped and positioned that a strand of hair could not pass between their joints. But the sheer size of the stones and apparent ease with which they were manipulated are not the most impressive features of the megaliths; the true signature of their master builders is observed in the methods devised to preserve them. Cyclopean walls were specifically designed to withstand cataclysm. Interlocking polygonal blocks of extremely hard stone were layered and pitched at a precise inclination so that they would flex and sway during the convulsions of an earthquake without being torn apart. The ingenious antiseismic architecture of cyclopean walls is an indelible signature of lost knowledge that was never recovered in the postdiluvian age, and has never been rivaled in the modern world.

Megalithic ruins displaying the trademark techniques of cyclopean masons have been discovered in all four hemispheres of the planet. The simplest explanation for the universality of the megalith phenomenon is to assume that an advanced global civilization once populated the earth, until it was utterly destroyed in an aqueous cataclysm. Skeptics often challenge this proposition by citing a lack of evidence in the form of technological artifacts that, according to their logic, should be littered throughout the strata of pre-Flood soils.

On one hand, the argument is compelling; on the other, immaterial. Only if we presume that the megaliths represent the advancement of the populace at large should we expect to find such artifacts in abundance. If, however, they are only representative of the knowledge and technology possessed by an elite caste of beings who ruled over a Bronze Age civilization that was liquidated in the waters of the Flood thousands of years ago, then all we should expect to find are precisely the megalithic ruins we see today and nothing more.

It is not accurate to speak of an advanced civilization in the distant past, but rather an advanced fraternity within civilization—the Golden Race. Only the offspring of the gods, and perhaps their chosen priests, were privy to the secrets of high technology. The watchers were not interested in the betterment of mankind. Their love was reserved for their wives and the mutant children of their union. The knowledge they shared with men was not intended to help them but to corrupt them and turn them against the King of heaven.

The watchers knew that the armies of the kingdom would not stand idly by if they attempted to take dominion of the earth by force. However, if men could be enticed to willingly abdicate their authority in exchange for knowledge, then, having received authorization from its regents, the watchers could legally operate in their realm. They could not, however, occupy the thrones of men themselves. In order to usurp human dominion, they produced their own hybrid offspring who were human enough to claim it. Thus, the watchers became the lords of the earth through the dominion of their sons and the willing abdication of mankind.

The watchers apportioned the earth among themselves and appointed their giant sons to rule over their respective realms. The empire of the gods was dreadfully oppressive. Men were forced to feed their giant overlords, who consumed all the acquisitions of the land, and when they were no longer able to sustain them, the giants devoured mankind.

Records Enoch,

> And as men perished, they cried, and their cry went up to heaven. And then Michael, Uriel, Raphael, and Gabriel looked down from heaven and saw much blood being shed upon the earth, and all lawlessness being wrought upon the earth. And they said one to another: "The earth being made without inhabitant cries out, and the voice of their crying has come up to the gates of heaven. And now to you, the holy ones of heaven, the souls of men make their suit, saying, 'Bring our cause before the Most High.'" And they said to the Lord of the ages: "Lord of lords, God of gods, King of kings, the throne of thy glory standeth unto all the generations of the ages, and thy name is holy and glorious and blessed unto all the ages! Thou hast made all things, and power over all things hast thou: and all things are naked and open in thy sight, and thou seest all things, and nothing can hide itself from thee. Thou seest what Azazel hath done, who hath taught all unrighteousness on earth and revealed the eternal secrets which were preserved in heaven, which men were striving to learn: And Semjaza, to whom thou hast given authority to bear rule over his associates. And they have gone to the daughters

of men upon the earth, and have slept with the women, and have defiled themselves, and revealed to them all kinds of sins. And the women have borne giants, and the whole earth has thereby been filled with blood and unrighteousness. And now, behold, the souls of those who have died are crying and making their suit to the gates of heaven, and their lamentations have ascended: and cannot cease because of the lawless deeds which are wrought on the earth. And thou knowest all things before they come to pass, and thou seest these things and thou dost suffer them, and thou dost not say to us what we are to do to them in regard to these."[16]

This passage demonstrates the protocol of human dominion. The armies of the kingdom will not mobilize until the sons of Adam, the regents of Earth, appeal to the court of heaven, which they did not do until the offspring of the watchers began to devour them. At first, the watchers were embraced as Promethean benefactors, who had come to bestow gifts to men. Notice that the watchers revealed to them the secrets they were "striving to learn." This implies that they knew exactly what to offer the sons of Adam in exchange for what they wanted—their daughters.

Men did not have to accept the gifts bestowed by the watchers nor tolerate them in their realm, and the watchers could not have relocated within the borders of man's dominion unless they had been granted permission to remain. According to the Ethiopic tradition, the watchers were not uninvited guests but came in response to a seductive solicitation by the daughters of Cain.

The children of Cain had utterly forsaken the commandments of God and given themselves over to the perfection of lawlessness. Every perverse thought they formulated in their mind was practiced with impunity under heaven, and the watchers were watching.

And they [the watchers] were content to leave the height of heaven, and they came down to earth, to the folly of the dancing of the children of Cain with all their work of the artisan,

---

[16] 1 Enoch 8:2–9:11 (RHC).

152

which they had made in the folly of their fornication, and to their singings, which they accompanied with the tambourine, and the flutes, and the pipes, and much shouting, and loud cries of joy and noisy songs. And their daughters were there, and they enjoyed the orgies without shame, for they scented themselves for the men who pleased them, and they lost the balance in their minds. And [the watchers] did not restrain themselves for a moment, but they took to wife from among the women those whom they had chosen, and committed sin with them. . . . And the daughters of Cain with whom the angels had companied conceived, but they were unable to bring forth their children, and they died. And of the children who were in their wombs some died, and some came forth; having split open the bellies of their mothers they came forth by their navels.[17]

The fingerprint of the serpent may be detected in the descendants of Cain, who according to John "was of the evil one."[18] The royal line of Adam was divided into two branches, one through Seth and the other through Cain, who slew Abel. The line of Seth, symbolized in the lamb, represents the righteous through whom the kingdom of heaven would advance and the Christ would come. The line of Cain, symbolized in the goat, represents the rebels through whom the dragon would ever wield proximal power and oppose the kingdom on Earth. We must not forget that the dragon was animated by a particular motive: to prevent the coming of the Dragon Slayer. It is therefore highly implausible that he was an innocent bystander in the unfolding of events that nearly eradicated the human race. Far from a bystander, Satan was likely the architect of the whole affair.

Being a watcher himself, Satan was well acquainted with the vulnerabilities of his brethren, some of whom, he knew, looked upon the daughters of men with lust and envy. The descendants of Cain, meanwhile, were

---

[17] Ernest A. Wallis Budge, trans., *The Queen of Sheba and Her Only Son Menyelek (Kebra Nagast)* (Cambridge, Ontario: In Parentheses Publications, 2000).

[18] 1 John 3:12 (ESV).

craving another taste of the succulent fruit from the tree of knowledge, a desire the serpent was all too eager to oblige.

According to occult tradition, the satanic priesthood began with Cain, who worshipped the dragon instead of Yahweh and was rewarded with secret knowledge for his devotion. This is the origin of the Luciferian doctrine, which teaches that Yahweh is a tyrant and the enemy of man, who made him a slave and kept him bound in the chains of ignorance, but the serpent was the friend of man, who illuminated the darkness of his mind and freed him from the thralldom of Eden. The dragon priests of Cain would become willing vessels through whom the powers of the insurgency could influence the affairs of the world. They have successfully altered the course of history, and are still operating in the shadows today.

The pieces on the board were thus positioned: on the one side, the watchers, who desired the daughters of men; on the other, the sons of Cain, who desired forbidden knowledge. All the devil had to do was bring them together, without being implicated in their crimes.

The game of thrones, the reader will recall, has rules. Satan was authorized to tempt but nothing more. He knew that the transgression of the watchers would incur swift and terrible retribution and, like the cunning snake that he is, was careful to keep his own hands clean to avoid their judgment. If the dragon and his princes had engaged in the sexual trespass of the watchers, they would have certainly been condemned with them. I believe that the dragon princes will eventually impregnate human women with their own seed, but not until the final hour, when they know their time is short and their fate nearly sealed. (More on this later.)

In the end, all parties involved obtained their prize: the sons of Cain were imparted with the secrets they were striving to learn, the watchers wedded the women they desired, and the dragon reveled in the corruption wrought through their transgression.

Not all men had become enamored of the extraterrestrial interlopers. While the watchers were revealing secrets to the sons of Cain and copulating with their daughters, Enoch was instructing the sons of Seth in righteousness and admonishing them to obey God. It is of interest to note that the name *Enoch* means "initiated" or "initiating." Initiations are often associated with secret societies and occult fraternities. An applicant seeking entry into a mystery school, such as a Freemasonic Lodge, must be initiated with an oath that includes the impartation of secret knowledge before he is considered a member. Fundamentally, all mystery schools are derived from the "illumination" of the dragon. Every branch of the occult that has budded in the course of history has its roots in the dragon priests of Cain, who worshipped "Lucifer" and were initiated into the secrets of the watchers.

Conversely, the mysteries of the gospel have their roots in Enoch, who walked with God and was initiated in the revelation of Christ, of whom it was prophesied "shall be a staff to the righteous whereon to stay themselves and not fall, and he shall be the light of the Gentiles, and the hope of those who are troubled of heart . . . for in his name they are saved."[19] Since the day Enoch penned these words, all those who have heard and believed the gospel of Christ, that Son of Man who redeems the offspring of Adam and reconciles them to God, are initiated into the most wondrous mystery of all, far surpassing anything the watchers imparted to the sons of Cain. It is for this reason that Enoch is called the "scribe of righteousness" by the angels who instructed him.

If Enoch was the scribe of righteousness, then the sons of Cain were the scribes of lawlessness. The knowledge the watchers imparted to men was like matches in the hands of children. Rather than benefit mankind, it ignited a firestorm of debauchery and bloodshed, such that the whole earth became a living hell filled with violence and despair.

Eventually, the supplications from the righteous line of Seth rose to heaven and filled the bowls of God's wrath. The King had long suffered the sedition of the watchers and the perversion of mankind, giving ample space for repentance. He would wait no longer. The pouring out of his fury upon the earth would be sudden and catastrophic.

> Then said the Most High, the Holy and Great One spake, and sent Uriel to the son of Lamech, and said to him: "Go to Noah and tell him in my name 'Hide thyself!' and reveal to him the end that is approaching: that the whole earth will be destroyed, and a deluge is about to come upon the whole

---

[19] 1 Enoch 48:4, 7 (RHC).

earth, and will destroy all that is on it. And now instruct him that he may escape and his seed may be preserved for all the generations of the world." And again the Lord said to Raphael: "Bind Azazel hand and foot, and cast him into the darkness: and make an opening in the desert, which is in Dudael, and cast him therein. And place upon him rough and jagged rocks, and cover him with darkness, and let him abide there for ever, and cover his face that he may not see light. And on the day of the great judgement he shall be cast into the fire. And heal the earth which the angels have corrupted, and proclaim the healing of the earth, that they may heal the plague, and that all the children of men may not perish through all the secret things that the watchers have disclosed and have taught their sons. And the whole earth has been corrupted through the works that were taught by Azazel: to him ascribe all sin." And to Gabriel said the Lord: "Proceed against the bastards and the reprobates, and against the children of fornication: and destroy the children of the Watchers from amongst men: send them one against the other that they may destroy each other in battle: for length of days shall they not have. And no request that they make of thee shall be granted unto their fathers on their behalf; for they hope to live an eternal life, and that each one of them will live five hundred years." And the Lord said unto Michael: "Go, bind Semjaza and his associates who have united themselves with women so as to have defiled themselves with them in all their uncleanness. And when their sons have slain one another, and they have seen the destruction of their beloved ones, bind them fast for seventy generations in the valleys of the earth, till the day of their judgement and of their consummation, till the judgement that is for ever and ever is consummated. In those days they shall be led off to the abyss of fire: to the torment and the prison in which they shall be confined for ever. And whosoever shall be condemned and destroyed will from thenceforth be bound together with them to the end of all generations. And destroy all the spirits of the reprobate and the children of the watchers, because they have wronged mankind.[20]

There is much to unpack in this sweeping judgment. First, we should not pass over the name of Azazel without making mention of its correlation in the scriptures, where it occurs in the context of sin offerings made by Aaron on behalf of the Hebrews:

> Aaron shall offer the bull as a sin offering for himself and shall make atonement for himself and for his house. Then he shall take the two goats and set them before the Lord at the entrance of the tent of meeting. And Aaron shall cast lots over the two goats, one lot for the Lord and the other lot for Azazel. And Aaron shall present the goat on which the lot fell for the Lord and use it as a sin offering, but the goat on which the lot fell for Azazel shall be presented alive before the Lord to make atonement over it, that it may be sent away into the wilderness to Azazel.[21]

This practice was directly derived from the judgment of the watchers, according to the testimony of Enoch. Azazel was the chief instructor of mankind. Among other dangerous secrets, he taught men the arts of weaponsmithing and warfare and was therefore held personally responsible for the carnage that ensued. He seems to have been a particularly sadistic character, inciting a murderous bloodlust in the world that had not previously existed. As manslaughter is the gravest of all crimes, Azazel was punished most severely among his brethren.

Note that Raphael[22] is instructed to "heal the earth which the angels have corrupted" and to "heal the plague . . . that all the children of men may not perish through all the secret things that the watchers have disclosed and have taught their sons." This seems contradictory. Why would God want to heal the earth before destroying it utterly? The answer may

---

[20] 1 Enoch 10:1–15 (RHC).
[21] Leviticus 16:6–10 (ESV).
[22] Not surprisingly, the name *Raphael* is derived from the root *rapha*, which means "to heal" or "to mend."

lie in the nature of the plague that was causing men to perish. In biblical parlance, the word *perish* is often used to describe the antithesis of eternal life, which is condemnation with the dragon, the second death.[23] The mission of the Christ was to save men from this terrible fate. Salvation through the Son of Man is freely available to the offspring of Adam, provided they are human. One must be human to qualify for redemption in the human redeemer.

The genetic matrix of life on Planet Earth was corrupted through the miscegenous transgression of the watchers. It is plausible that the plague refers to the propagation of their alien DNA in the gene pools of diverse species, including the human species. If the genetic profile of mankind was compromised such that the offspring of Adam were no longer human, then they would be ineligible for salvation in Christ, and thus perishing in the eternal sense. The watchers may have attempted to orchestrate the mutagenic extinction of the human species in order to secure dominion of the Earth for their hybrid sons, who remained human enough to appropriate it. This scenario would have certainly been advantageous for the dragon, who wanted nothing more than to exterminate the "seed of the woman."

The Genesis 6 narrative insinuates, however subtly, that all flesh on Earth was genetically corrupted before the Flood:

> Then the Lord saw that the wickedness of man was great in the earth, and that every intent of the thoughts of his heart was only evil continually. And the Lord was sorry that he had made man on the earth, and he was grieved in his heart. So the Lord said, "I will destroy man whom I have created from the face of the earth, both man and beast, creeping thing and birds of the air, for I am sorry that I have made them." But Noah found grace in the eyes of the Lord.[24]

How can the intent of a man's heart be *only evil* continually? Such a man would have to be inhumanly malevolent. Notice that the genealogy

---

[23] See John 3:16; Revelation 21:8.
[24] Genesis 6:5–8 (NKJV).

of Noah is inserted directly after he is said to have "found grace in the eyes of the Lord":

> This is the genealogy of Noah. Noah was a just man, perfect in his generations. Noah walked with God. And Noah begot three sons: Shem, Ham, and Japheth.
> The earth also was corrupt before God, and the earth was filled with violence. So God looked upon the earth, and indeed it was corrupt; for all flesh had corrupted their way on the earth.[25]

Apparently, there are two reasons why Noah was favored by the Lord and preserved through the Flood: first, because he was a just man who walked with God, and second, because he was *perfect in his generations*. The word *perfect* employed in the text is derived from the Hebrew adjective *tamiym*, which most often conveys biological purity, as in a lamb without *blemish (tamiym)*. To say that Noah was *perfect in his generations* is equivalent to saying that he was *pure in his genome*. Noah's hereditary genetic profile was uncontaminated by the plague that was corrupting all flesh; he was therefore specifically selected to reseed humanity after the Flood.

Aside from the eight members of Noah's family, careful selections were also made among the animal species according to the purity of their genomes. This is evident in the fact that two of every kind (species) were *sent* to Noah for preservation on the ark:

> And of every living thing of all flesh you shall bring two of every sort into the ark, to keep them alive with you; they shall be male and female. Of the birds after their kind, of animals after their kind, and of every creeping thing of the earth after its kind, two of every kind *will come to you* to keep them alive.[26]

Raphael's directive to heal the plague before the destruction of the

---

[25] Genesis 6:9–12 (NKJV).
[26] Genesis 6:19–20 (NKJV, emphasis added).

earth can now be understood. The hereditary propagation of the watchers' DNA corrupting the genomes of all flesh had to be redressed if a pure genetic stock was to be preserved for the reseeding of species after the Flood. Additionally, Noah and his sons were still perfectly human, but Shem, Ham, and Japheth needed genetically viable wives if they were to repopulate the world with uncontaminated offspring.

While Raphael was remedying the plague to secure a viable seed bank, Uriel was preparing Noah to build the ark that would carry it through the maelstrom of the Flood, and Gabriel was inciting war among the offspring of the watchers to ensure that they did not interfere.

We should not envision a cartoonish scene of giants beating each other over the head with wooden clubs. This was a hybrid civil war, kingdom against kingdom, race against race, fielding the technological armaments forged from the secrets of the watchers. With homicidal rage, the progeny of the gods slaughtered one another in epic battles, laying waste to their realms and reducing their megalithic fortifications to rubble.[27]

Michael was dispatched to bind Semjaza and his associates and force them to watch the butchery of their beloved sons. A curious addendum is attached to his commission: "And no request that they make of thee shall be granted unto their fathers on their behalf; for they hope to live an eternal life, and that each one of them will live five hundred years." Here, it would seem, is an endorsement of our previous postulation. The watchers had wagered, however imprudently, that their daring enterprise might be pardoned by the King. They hoped that their sons would be granted a long life on Earth followed by eternal life with them in paradise. The request was flatly denied. Indeed, to their horror, the fate of their offspring would be quite the opposite. After perishing in battle, the souls of the Nephilim would be cursed to wander the earth as vagabonds, tormented with the appetites of the flesh but without bodies to satisfy them:

> And now, the giants, who are produced from the spirits and
> flesh, shall be called evil spirits upon the earth, and on the

---

[27] There is some compelling evidence that nuclear-equivalent weapons were detonated in the distant past (see Leonardo Vintini, "Desert Glass Formed by Ancient Atomic Bombs?" *Ancient Origins*, October 14, 2014, https://www.ancient-origins.net/unexplained-phenomena /desert-glass-formed-ancient-atomic-bombs-002205).

earth shall be their dwelling. Evil spirits have proceeded from their bodies; because they are born from men, and from the holy watchers is their beginning and primal origin; they shall be evil spirits on earth, and evil spirits shall they be called. As for the spirits of heaven, in heaven shall be their dwelling, but as for the spirits of the earth which were born upon the earth, on the earth shall be their dwelling. And the spirits of the giants afflict, oppress, destroy, attack, do battle, and work destruction on the earth, and cause trouble: they take no food, but nevertheless hunger and thirst, and cause offences. And these spirits shall rise up against the children of men and against the women, because they have proceeded from them.

From the days of the slaughter and destruction and death of the giants, from the souls of whose flesh the spirits, having gone forth, shall destroy without incurring judgement—thus shall they destroy until the day of the consummation, the great judgement in which the age shall be consummated, over the watchers and the godless, yea, shall be wholly consummated.[28]

We can extrapolate that the disembodied spirits of the giants, like the *daimons* of Greek lore, became the demons of the postdiluvian age encountered in the biblical narrative. These revolting entities, condemned to a torturous existence, have but one objective—to inhabit bodies of flesh and, through them, satiate their interminable hunger, thirst, and sexual desire. These are the true *body snatchers*, who invade the hyper-dimensional compartment in which the soul resides. Like tapeworms feeding on the sustenance of the intestines, the parasitic wraiths of the Nephilim hijack the bodies of their hosts to feed on the sensory input of their brains and feel once more the fabric of the physical world from which they were banished.

Enoch's testimony concerning the fate of the Nephilim is verified in the New Testament. The unclean spirits that had proceeded from the offspring of the watchers were permitted to freely wander the earth and afflict mankind without incurring judgment until the end of the age, at

---

[28] 1 Enoch 15:8–16:1 (RHC).

which time the Great Judge would appear to cast them, with their fathers, into the lake burning with fire and brimstone. It is for this reason that the demons despaired when they saw Jesus of Nazareth walking on the shores of Galilee and shrieked, "What have we to do with you, Jesus, you Son of God? Have you come here to torment us before the time?"[29]

A similar episode occurred in the synagogue of Capernaum:

> Now there was a man in their synagogue with an unclean spirit. And he cried out, saying, "Let us alone! What have we to do with you, Jesus of Nazareth? Did you come to destroy us? I know who you are—the Holy One of God!"[30]

You can imagine their shock. What was the King of heaven doing on Earth before the appointed time of judgment? Even the disembodied Nephilim, whose fathers were formerly numbered among the princes of the kingdom, had not anticipated God's plan to redeem mankind through the blood of his beloved Son.

It is important to recognize that the judgment of the watchers and their offspring was not delivered directly to them by the powers of heaven, but through a man. As the watchers had trespassed and transgressed in Adam's realm, it was fitting that one of his descendants be the mediator between the divine council and its defected members. Enoch, the seventh from Adam, was chosen to represent the dominion of mankind on Earth:

> And I, Enoch was blessing the Lord of majesty and the King of the ages, and lo! the watchers called me—Enoch the scribe— and said to me: "Enoch, thou scribe of righteousness, go, declare to the watchers of the heaven who have left the high heaven, the holy eternal place, and have defiled themselves with women, and have done as the children of earth do, and have taken unto themselves wives: 'Ye have wrought great destruction on the earth: And ye shall have no peace nor for- giveness of sin: and inasmuch as they delight themselves in

---

[29] Matthew 8:29 (NKJV).
[30] Mark 1:23–24 (NKJV).

their children, the murder of their beloved ones shall they see, and over the destruction of their children shall they lament, and shall make supplication unto eternity, but mercy and peace shall ye not attain.'"[31]

The ambiguity of the *watcher* designation is on display in this scene. Both the loyal and defected factions are of the same caste. As in the passage from Daniel concerning Nebuchadnezzar, a council of watchers is presiding in judgment. However, in Enoch's case, the accused is not a defiant human king but two hundred renegade princes of the elder race. It is an understatement to say that they were distraught by the severity of the judgment delivered to them through Enoch:

> And Enoch went and said: "Azazel, thou shalt have no peace: a severe sentence has gone forth against thee to put thee in bonds: And thou shall not have toleration nor request granted to thee, because of the unrighteousness which thou hast taught, and because of all the works of godlessness and unrighteousness and sin which thou hast shown to men." Then I went and spoke to them all together, and they were all afraid, and fear and trembling seized them. And they besought me to draw up a petition for them that they might find forgiveness, and to read their petition in the presence of the Lord of heaven. For from thenceforward they could not speak (with him) nor lift up their eyes to heaven for shame of their sins for which they had been condemned. Then I wrote out their petition, and the prayer in regard to their spirits and their deeds individually and in regard to their requests that they should have forgiveness.[32]

Enoch drew up their petitions as requested, but it was an exercise in futility; they were immediately rejected by the council. Enoch was then sent back to the watchers to deliver the bad news. He found them gathered

---

[31] 1 Enoch 12:3–6 (RHC).
[32] 1 Enoch 13:1–6 (RHC).

together, weeping, in a place called Abelsjail, which is located between Lebanon and Senir. Lebanon likely refers to Mount Lebanon, and Senir is another name for Mount Hermon. It just so happens that an imposing megalithic complex is located between these two mountains—Baalbek.

Baalbek is home to one of the most magnificent ancient monuments ever constructed and the largest hewn stones ever discovered. The foundation stones of Baalbek weigh more than a thousand tons each. Although the Romans would later raise a temple to Jupiter over its mammoth ruins, Baalbek was indisputably built in the antediluvian age and may have served as the epicenter of the watchers' empire on Earth.

After witnessing the massacre of their beloved sons, the watchers were bound and imprisoned in the depths of Tartarus until the day of judgment. Enoch provides the context for Peter's enigmatic reference to the angels who sinned in the pre-Flood world:

> For if God did not spare the angels who sinned, but cast them down to hell [Tartarus] and delivered them into chains of darkness, to be reserved for judgment; and did not spare the ancient world, but saved Noah, one of eight people, a preacher of righteousness, bringing in the flood on the world of the ungodly . . . then the Lord knows how to deliver the godly out of temptations and to reserve the unjust under punishment for the day of judgment, and especially those who walk according to the flesh in the lust of uncleanness and despise authority.[33]

Judgment did not fall upon the earth immediately after the incarceration of the watchers; instead, God "waited patiently in the days of Noah while the ark was being built"[34] and the angels were healing the plague. The longsuffering of God is manifest in the lifespan of Enoch's son, Methuselah. Enoch was told that the Flood would not occur until the year his son died. In a remarkable show of forbearance, Methuselah would be the longest-living man ever recorded, 969 years old.

In Genesis 5, we are provided with a genealogy of the antediluvian

---

[33] 2 Peter 2:4–5, 9–10 (NKJV).
[34] 1 Peter 3:20 (NIV).

patriarchs, beginning with Adam and ending with the sons of Noah. From Adam to the death of Methuselah, some 2,256 years transpired, as reckoned in the Septuagint.[35] Enoch informs us that the watchers descended in the days of Jared (whose name means "descent"), nearly one thousand years after Adam was exiled from Eden. From the birth of Jared to the Flood of Noah, approximately 1,300 years transpired.[36] This means that the mutant spawn of the watchers had a thousand years to propagate their abominable seed. A thousand years of watchers begetting giants and giants begetting more giants, and watchers begetting monsters and monsters begetting more monsters. It also affords a thousand years for the proliferation of the knowledge that the watchers disclosed. Great cities were constructed, kingdoms were forged, and a unified hybrid empire expanded throughout the earth.

This was the true Golden Age of yore. The gods were dwelling among men, imparting forbidden knowledge, corrupting the genetic matrix of life, and leading mankind into open defiance against his Maker—seizing for themselves the adoration that belonged to Yahweh. Megalithic monuments, some perhaps constructed by the hands of their giant sons, were raised across the empire in dedication to the watchers.[37] These monuments did not memorialize distant mythological deities from days long past but the living gods who visited them in the flesh to receive the veneration (and human sacrifice) offered with devotion by their mutant progeny.

The cataclysm of the Flood was intended to utterly obliterate the empire of the gods and cleanse the earth of their abominable seed. The offspring of the watchers were unsanctioned sentient beings that were not

---

[35] The Masoretes subtracted one hundred years from the birthdate of each firstborn son in the genealogy, significantly shortening the pre-Flood timeline. Many scholars regard the Septuagint as the correct reckoning of the Genesis 5 genealogy.

[36] The list of patriarchs recorded in the Genesis 5 genealogy does not necessarily represent a continuous chronology from father to firstborn son. Some scholars contend that there are obvious gaps in the record and argue for many thousands of years between Adam and the Noahic deluge. The author is sympathetic to this view.

[37] Some of the most preponderant megalithic sites on Earth (e.g., the Giza Plateau, Baalbek, Teotihuacan, Tiwanaku, Sacsayhuaman, Göbekli Tepe, etc.) were clearly devised according to the hermetic principle of celestial mirroring ("as above, so below"). New technologies have provided archaeoastronomers the means to date the monuments erected on these sites with remarkable precision according to their alignments with particular constellations and cosmological phenomena. It comes as no surprise that many of them appear to have been constructed between 10,000 and 15,000 years ago, in the age before the Noahic deluge.

created by God. If left to propagate unchecked, they would have irreparably corrupted the genetic profile of human and animal life on Earth. The ark was prepared as a seed bank to carry the uncorrupted genomes of diverse species into the post-Flood world, where they would eventually migrate, adapt, and multiply in every biosphere on the planet.[38]

The most critical genome carried on the ark was that of mankind, preserved in Noah and his family. As depicted in John's vision, the dragon had failed to wholly eradicate the seed of the woman:

> The serpent spewed water out of his mouth like a flood after the woman, that he might cause her to be carried away by the flood. But the earth helped the woman, and the earth opened its mouth and swallowed up the flood which the dragon had spewed out of his mouth.[39]

The dragon's cunning strategy had nearly succeeded. Great corruption was wrought in the earth, and the watchers alone had suffered the penalty for their terrible crimes. And yet, the sons and daughters of Adam, despite their continual betrayal, were not forsaken. The human species was preserved, and the Dragon Slayer Prophecy was still in play. After the waters of the Flood subsided, the mandate of Adam's dominion was reiterated to Noah and his sons,[40] followed by this dire warning:

> "Whoever sheds the blood of man, by man shall his blood be shed, for God made man in his own image."[41]

---

[38] There are two factors that should be taken into account when considering the mechanisms at work in the preservation and propagation of life through the ark. First, it is likely that all land animals have the ability to hibernate for extended periods of time. If the animals on the ark were in a state of hibernation, then there would have been no need to care for them during the voyage. Second, it is likely that all animals have a built-in mechanism for accelerated adaptation (microevolution), which would enable a suite of variations to express in the physiology of each species, depending on the conditions of the environments into which they migrated.

[39] Revelation 12:15–16 (NKJV).

[40] "So God blessed Noah and his sons, and said to them: 'Be fruitful and multiply, and fill the earth. And the fear of you and the dread of you shall be on every beast of the earth, on every bird of the air, on all that move on the earth, and on all the fish of the sea. They are given into your hand'" (Genesis 9:1–2, NKJV).

[41] Genesis 9:6 (ESV).

This was the institution of capital punishment for manslaughter, but it was also a veiled threat directed to the attention of those alien agencies who might be tempted to invade Adam's realm and usurp his dominion as the watchers had done through their hybrid offspring.

Only mankind had the right to rule on Planet Earth.

Chapter 9

ATLANTIS RISING

In the chronicles of human reckoning, there is one pivotal event that has inscribed upon the parchment of history and wrought in the earth itself such an indelible mark that the psyche of mankind is forever marred with the memory of its occurrence. So magnitudinous was this event, so destructive its power, so catastrophic its aftermath, that every people group on the earth, though sundered by boundless seas and discordant tongues, kept record of it in their writings, their oral traditions, their songs, and their myths.[1] Some referred to it simply as the great cataclysm that brought to ruin the mighty kingdoms of the Old World, but most remember the Flood. The Flood of Noah cannot be forgotten by his descendants, because is it encoded in their DNA. The ancestral memories of the antediluvian age, though absent from the textbooks of modern universities, are present nevertheless in the deep recesses of the subconscious mind. Ergo, what man cannot forget, he must deny.

Denial of the Flood is a modern phenomenon. In the annals of the ancients, the deluge was a monumental fact, the remembrance of which, like a tombstone in the timeline of history, stood as a warning for all future generations. It was not until the inception of the geological doctrine of uniformitarianism in the nineteenth century that men dared to defy

---

[1] Sir James George Frazer, in *Folklore in the Old Testament: Studies in Comparative Religion, Legend, and Law* (London: Macmillan, 1918, pp. 104–361), cites hundreds of homologous flood traditions from diverse regions around the globe, including Asia, Australia, the East Indies, Melanesia, Micronesia, Polynesia, South America, Central America, North America, and Africa. .

the admonition of their antecedents and willfully forget the advent of the Flood. The apostle Peter, writing in the first century AD, prophesied concerning such men:

> Scoffers will come in the last days, walking according to their own lusts, and saying, "Where is the promise of his coming? For since the fathers fell asleep, all things continue as they were from the beginning of creation." For this they willfully forget: that by the word of God the heavens were of old, and the earth standing out of water and in the water, by which the world that then existed perished, being flooded with water. But the heavens and the earth which are now preserved by the same word, are reserved for fire until the day of judgment and perdition of ungodly men.[2]

That "all things continue as they were from the beginning" is the very premise of modern geology, which categorically denies the judgment of the Great Flood and scoffs in the face of the Great Judge who presided over it and who will preside again in the final judgment at the end of the age. Peter's prophecy would come to pass in the year 1830—nearly two thousand years after the penning of his first epistle—when geologist Charles Lyell published his influential textbook *Principles of Geology* and triggered an academic avalanche of Flood denial.

Lyell's book popularized the doctrine of geologic uniformitarianism, the premise of which propounds that the geologic processes presently acting upon the earth are sufficient to account for all geologic formations in all ages. The theory necessitates vast quantities of time for profound alterations to the earth's crust and repudiates the assumption that cataclysm rapidly reshaped the landscape in the distant past. In short, Lyell had provided mankind with a scientific pretext to willfully forget the Flood of Noah and the agencies that provoked it.

The geologic doctrine set forth in Lyell's *Principles* was a radical departure from the scientific consensus of the time (and indeed, of all times) and a blatant disregard for the testimony of antiquity. In their scholarly

---

[2] 2 Peter 3:3–7 (NKJV).

work *The Genesis Flood*, Whitcomb and Morris explain,

> Throughout the entire eighteenth century, and well into the nineteenth, an imposing list of scientists and theologians produced works in support of the Flood theory of geology. That the Flood was universal and that it was responsible for the major geologic formations of the earth was accepted almost without question in the western world during that period.[3]

"There was no question about the historical reality of the flood," concurs historian Charles Gillispie. "When the history of the earth began to be considered geologically, it was simply assumed that a universal deluge must have wrought vast changes and that it had been a primary agent in forming the present surface of the globe. Its occurrence was evidence that the Lord was a governor as well as a creator."[4]

Evoked in the rainbow, recollection of the Flood is intended to reconjure in the minds of men the utter destruction of the Old World, reminding them that "the Lord is a governor as well as a creator" who judges the ungodly but delivers the righteous. The geologic formations wrought in the pulverizing waves of an aqueous cataclysm bear witness to the sovereignty of God, the longsuffering of his patience, and the severity of his wrath.

In his letter to the Romans, Paul condemns those who would suppress the truth by denying the evidence on display in the natural world:

> For the wrath of God is revealed from heaven against all ungodliness and unrighteousness of men, who by their unrighteousness suppress the truth. For what can be known about God is plain to them, because God has shown it to them. For his invisible attributes, namely, his eternal power and divine

---

[3] John C. Whitcomb and Henry M. Morris, *The Genesis Flood: The Biblical Record and Its Scientific Implications* (1961, repr. Phillipsburg, NJ: Presbyterian and Reformed Publishing Company, 2011), 91. If the reader is interested in the scientific proofs of the Flood of Noah and a scholarly rebuttal to uniformitarian geology, he should immediately acquire a copy of *The Genesis Flood*.

[4] Charles C. Gillispie, *Genesis and Geology: A Study of the Relations of Scientific Thought, Natural Theology, and Social Opinion in Great Britain, 1790–1850* (Cambridge, MA: Harvard University Press, 1951), 42.

nature, have been clearly perceived, ever since the creation of the world, in the things that have been made. So they are without excuse. For although they knew God, they did not honor him as God or give thanks to him, but they became futile in their thinking, and their foolish hearts were darkened.[5]

The uniformitarian motto, "The present is the key to the past," supplied Lyell and his colleagues with a new lens through which to view the geological record and refute the evidence of the Flood. By presuming that the forces acting upon the surface of the earth have been uniform from the beginning, the sudden upheavals of cataclysm could be replaced with the slow grind of endless time and the ancestral witness of humanity discarded like an old rag. Lyell's *Principles* were enthusiastically embraced by atheistic academics who were eager to undermine the veracity of the biblical narrative and the prevailing theory that supported it—*catastrophism*.

Geologic catastrophism propounds that the surface of the earth has undergone extreme and rapid change due to cataclysm. Before Lyell, the doctrine of catastrophism was universally accepted as plain fact. Today it is roundly rejected in the scientific community, not because it has been refuted—indeed, evidence in support of the doctrine mounts by the day[6]—but because it undermines the theory of evolution and is therefore regarded with contempt. "The hostility of modern uniformitarians toward geological catastrophism in general and the concept of a universal Deluge in particular," note Whitcomb and Morris, "is a striking phenomenon of contemporary scientific thought." They continue,

> In spite of the fact that actual observation of geologic processes is strictly limited to those now in operation, uniformitarians have assumed that these, and only these, acted in the past and therefore must be applied to the study of origins. They thus

---

[5] Romans 1:18–21 (ESV).

[6] It is becoming increasingly evident that the surface of the planet was reshaped by a cataclysmic flood about 12,000 years ago, at the end of the last ice age, called the Younger Dryas, when ice sheets in the Northern Hemisphere suddenly melted. See, for example, The Human Origin Project, "Did the Younger Dryas Flood Shape Prehistoric Earth?" February 11, 2019, https://medium.com /@humanoriginproject/did-the-younger-dryas-flood-shape-prehistoric-earth-e1d67d16a88c.

have presumed to speak with finality upon matters which can be understood properly only in the light of God's revelation in Scripture. Geologic evidences for the great Flood are ignored, and even the possibility of such a catastrophe in the past is ruled out on the basis of *a priori* philosophical reasoning.[7]

The study of origins—now we come to the crux of the matter. Lyell's doctrine was devised—wittingly, or unwittingly—to erode the biblical bedrock of human origins in order to lay the foundations of evolution. Charles Darwin was an avid proponent of Lyell's *Principles*, which had conveniently provided him with the missing ingredient for his own theory: unlimited time. "He who can read Sir Charles Lyell's grand work on the *Principles of Geology*," he wrote in *The Origin of Species*, "which the future historian will recognize as having produced a revolution in natural science, and yet does not admit how vast have been the past periods of time, may at once close this volume."[8] The smugness with which this pronouncement is made would become a defining characteristic of Darwin's disciples in the twentieth century.

The theory of evolution could not have existed without the theory of uniformitarianism. By removing the cold and foreboding tombstone of the Great Flood from the timeline of history, Charles Lyell paved the way for Charles Darwin. "There can be little doubt that it was through Lyell's *Principles* that Darwin's mind was emancipated from the shackles of Biblical chronology," remarks historian Francis C. Haber, "and had this step not taken place, it seems unlikely that the *Origin of Species* could ever have fermented out of the *Voyage of the Beagle*, for Darwin's theory of evolution required for its foundation far more historical time than ever the uniformitarian geologists were accustomed to conceiving."[9]

But even an endless supply of uniform geologic time was not sufficient for the flourishing of Darwin's theory; the very memory of the Flood had to be expunged from the minds of men if they were to abandon a

---

[7] Whitcomb and Morris, *The Genesis Flood*, 89.

[8] Charles Darwin, *The Origin of Species by Means of Natural Selection*, vol. 49 of *Great Books of the Western World*, edited by Robert M. Hutchins (Chicago: Encyclopedia Britannica, 1955), 153.

[9] Francis C. Haber, *The Age of the World: Moses to Darwin* (Baltimore: Johns Hopkins University Press, 1959), 268.

truth so universally acknowledged. In his book *The Testimony of Science to the Deluge*, published in 1896, William Brown Galloway captures the totalitarian temperament of Lyell's coalition:

> They had settled it that the universal Deluge was to be rejected, Scripture notwithstanding. Away with catastrophes! Let us have only the present rate of change, the gradual operation of present known causes, however slow; and give them plenty of time! A hundred thousand or a million or a few millions of years can be created at will for the purpose. Truth shall be what we make it, and they who do not so accept it shall be held comparable to the persecutors of the great Galileo.[10]

Thus it has been ever since. The triumph of Lyell and Darwin over the biblical narrative of prehistory—and the ubiquitous testimony of antiquity—has fomented widespread denial of the Genesis 6 affair and contempt for those who dare evoke its memory. This was a masterstroke in the game for dominion of the earth. By persuading the descendants of Noah to willfully forget the Flood, mankind's ancient adversary has set the board for a reoccurrence of the events that occasioned it. The pieces are now positioned for the final move. Checkmate is imminent.

The biblical view of history, geologic and human, may be derived by reversing the uniformitarian motto, "The present is the key to the past." Solomon assures us that the *past* is the key to the *present*:

> What has been is what will be, and what has been done is what will be done; and there is nothing new under the sun. Is there a thing of which it is said, "See, this is new"? It has been already, in the ages before us.[11]

The procession of history, like the orbit of the earth around the sun,

---

[10] William Brown Galloway, *The Testimony of Science to the Deluge* (London: Sampson Low, Marston & Co., 1896), 22.
[11] Ecclesiastes 1:9–10 (ESV).

is going, full circle, back to the beginning where it all started. Hence, we can know the end from the beginning. The final chapter of the story is prefigured in the first—Genesis is the cipher of Revelation.

Scripture foretells of a satanic empire that will arise at the end of the age. Symbolized in the motif of the fiery phoenix reborn from the ashes of its incinerated corpse, this final empire will be a reincarnation of the first—the empire of the gods. The extraterrestrial incursion and subsequent genetic miscegenation that occurred on the earth preceding the Flood of Noah will be repeated before the present age is consummated and the planet is cleansed of corruption once again, this time by fire. The acolytes of the mystery schools, embedded into the highest echelons of society worldwide, are secretly laboring to accomplish what they call the Great Plan (or Great Work)—the advent of a New Golden Age and the restoration of the Atlantean world order, which sank beneath the waves of divine wrath.

As aforementioned, the legend of Atlantis is an allegory of the Golden Age, but it is also a harbinger of the end of the age, encoded with the seven-ten numerology of the dragon. Recall that, according to Plato, the island of Atlantis was divided into ten portions that were ruled by the ten twin hybrid sons of Poseidon. Other sources add that the axis of Atlantean power comprised seven islands bound together in a league that held sway over three continents. Masonic philosopher Manly P. Hall elucidates,

> The *Critias* first describes the blessed state of the Atlantean people under the benevolent rulership of ten kings who were bound together in a league. These kings were monarchs over seven islands and three great continents. From the fable we can infer that the ten rulers of the Atlantic league were philosopher kings, endowed with all virtues and wise guardians of the public good. These kings obeyed the laws of the divine father of their house, Poseidon, god of the seas.[12]

Hall was an occultist who viewed the Golden Age through the laudatory prism of the ancient Greeks. He believed that the myth of Atlantis

[12] Manly P. Hall, *The Secret Destiny of America* (New York, NY: Penguin Group, 2008), 43.

preserved the memory of the philosopher kings of the Golden Race, who guided mankind in an epoch of unprecedented peace and knowledge. Like all mystery acolytes, he looked forward to the day when the progeny of the gods would rise again to rule the earth—an event foretold in John's Revelation.

Atlantis is inexorably associated with the sea; its patron deity, Poseidon (an aspect of Satan), is the violent and ill-tempered god of the sea, and the city itself was destroyed in an aqueous cataclysm. It is no wonder, then, that in Revelation 13 we find the great red dragon standing on the shore of the sea, presiding over the reemergence of the Atlantean world order, embodied in the figure of a beast:

> And I saw a beast rising out of the sea, with ten horns and seven heads, with ten diadems on its horns and blasphemous names on its heads.[13]

The reader will notice that the beast is made in the image of the dragon, having seven heads and ten horns, but with one conspicuous discrepancy: the diadems are on its horns instead of its heads. This indicates a transposition of authority from the seven dragon princes to the ten bestial kings, who are, as will become apparent, their hybrid progeny.

In Revelation 17, the angel tells John that the beast he saw rising out of the sea "was, and is not, and is about to come up out of the abyss and go to destruction."[14] In other words, it once existed, sank to the bottom of the sea,[15] and is fated to rise again for a brief period of time before being destroyed utterly. I am not suggesting that the legendary city of Atlantis will suddenly emerge from the depths of the ocean, to be featured on the evening news; rather, the hybrid dominion it represents will be revived and reestablished in the empire of the beast.

In a corresponding vision, John beholds an army of locusts rising from the abyss with the beast, whom he personifies as Apollyon the destroyer.[16]

---

[13] Revelation 13:1 (ESV).
[14] Revelation 17:8 (Common English Bible).
[15] The word *abyss* is derived from the Greek *ábyssos*, which is associated with the watery depths and the lowest part of the sea.
[16] See Revelation 9:11.

Apollyon is a play on words intended to implicate the Greco-Roman god Apollon, more commonly known by his Latin name, Apollo. One of the aspects of Apollo was Parnopion, god of locusts, the title attributed to his bronze statue at the Acropolis of Athens,[17] a fact the contemporary readers of John's Revelation were no doubt familiar with. *The Anchor Bible Dictionary* supplies the following definition:

> APOLLYON. The Greek name, meaning "Destroyer," given in Revelation 9:11 for "the angel of the bottomless pit" (in Hebrew called Abaddon), also identified as the king of the demonic "locusts" described in Revelation 9:3–10 . . . In one manuscript, instead of Apollyon the text reads "Apollo," the Greek god of death and pestilence as well as of the sun, music, poetry, crops and herds, and medicine. Apollyon is no doubt the correct reading. But the name Apollo (Gk Apollon) was often linked in ancient Greek writings with the verb apollymi or apollyo, "destroy." From this time of Grotius, "Apollyon" has often been taken here to be a play on the name Apollo. The locust was an emblem of this god.[18]

There were few deities more beloved by the Greeks and Romans than Apollo. The exalted son of Jupiter, king of the gods, and the Titaness Leto, Apollo is everywhere portrayed as an icon of the Golden Age: his hallmark feature is golden hair, and he rides a golden chariot, plays a golden lyre, and wields a golden sword and a golden bow. According to myth, Apollo was born on Delos, one of the islands in the Cyclades archipelago that Poseidon raised out of the sea, where a magnificent temple and statue were erected to his glory by the Greeks. The word *delos* means "brought to light," as in "revealed."

---

[17] "Opposite the temple [the Parthenon on the Acropolis of Athens] is a bronze Apollon, said to be the work of Pheidias. They call it Parnopion (god of the Locusts), because once when locusts were devastating the land the god said that he would drive them from Attika. That he did drive them away they know, but they do not say how" (Pausanias, *Description of Greece*, 1.24.8).

[18] Herbert G. Grether, "Apollyon," in *The Anchor Bible Dictionary*, vol. 1, edited by David Noel Freedman (New York: Doubleday, 1992).

The revealing of Apollo is a prominent sign of the end of the age. In his second letter to the church at Thessalonica, Paul urges the brethren not to be anxious concerning the coming of the Lord (as some were convinced that the event had already occurred and they had been "left behind") but to remember that Christ will not return unless the rebellion comes first and the son of destruction (Apollo) is revealed:

> Now concerning the coming of our Lord Jesus Christ and our being gathered together to him, we ask you, brothers, not to be quickly shaken in mind or alarmed, either by a spirit or a spoken word, or a letter seeming to be from us, to the effect that the day of the Lord has come. Let no one deceive you in any way. For that day will not come, unless the rebellion comes first, and the man of lawlessness is revealed, the son of destruction, who opposes and exalts himself against every so-called god or object of worship, so that he takes his seat in the temple of God, proclaiming himself to be God.[19]

Some versions of the Bible have interpreted the Greek word *apostasia*, rendered above as *rebellion* and from which we derive the word *apostasy*, to mean "falling away" (or even "departure," in support of a pretribulational rapture). Traditionally, Paul's reference to the apostasy that must precede the second coming of Christ has been understood as a defection from the faith, but this interpretation imposes a religious context that is not implied in the text. The true extent of the "great apostasy," as it is so called, is predicted in David's second psalm:

> Why do the nations rage, and the people plot a vain thing? The kings of the earth set themselves, and the rulers take counsel together, against the Lord and against his Anointed, saying, "Let us break their bonds in pieces and cast away their cords from us."[20]

---

[19] 2 Thessalonians 2:1–4 (ESV).
[20] Psalm 2:1–3 (NKJV).

The great apostasy is nothing less than kinetic war with the Lord and his Anointed Son, the rightful claimant to David's throne and heir of Adam's dominion on Earth. The nations will rage in open rebellion against the kingdom of heaven and plot to install Apollo, the son of Satan, on the throne that belongs to Jesus, the Son of God. Considering the stupendous audacity of such a bold enterprise, the question is begged, *What kind of weapons are brought to bear in a war with God?* Obviously, there is some unspecified factor, emboldening humanity with inhuman ambitions. The answer lies in the delineation between the *kings of the earth* and the *rulers* who take council together. Intimations of a sinister alliance between the gods and men may be discerned in an oracle of Isaiah concerning the final judgment, in which the hosts of heaven and the kings of Earth are sentenced together as coconspirators:

> On that day the Lord will punish the host of heaven, in heaven, and the kings of the earth, on the earth. They will be gathered together as prisoners in a pit; they will be shut up in a prison, and after many days they will be punished.[21]

While the dragon prosecutes his cosmic war in heaven (per John's vision of the woman and the dragon), the beast will marshal the forces of his empire on Earth to fight against the King, who is coming to depose him.

It is important to recognize the duality at work in the figures of the dragon and the beast, both of which represent a singular entity *and* a plural coalition. The dragon is symbolic of Satan *and* his confederation of princes. The beast is symbolic of the antichrist *and* his confederation of kings. The beast is made in the likeness of the dragon because it is his biological *and* political progeny. As the son of Satan, Apollo inherits his "power, his throne, and great authority,"[22] which is an expression of the dragon's wholesale influence over the nations at the end of the age.

Scholars agree that the final empire to rise on Earth before the return of Christ will be a manifestation of Rome, clearly depicted in the Book of

---

[21] Isaiah 24:21–22 (ESV).
[22] Revelation 13:2 (NKJV).

Daniel (as we shall see). It is not coincidental that the Son of God came into the world during the height of Roman power, nor that he will return to a world enshrouded in the political and spiritual climate of that age. The Romans openly worshipped the dragon in the guise of Jupiter (Jove), the patron deity of their republic. As a result, Satan had gained inordinate influence over the nations through Roman expansion, such that he could offer their dominion to Jesus. What the Son of God rejected, the son of Satan will eagerly accept. The dragon will give his authority to the beast, and the beast, in turn, will compel the citizens of the empire to extol the dragon as Optimus Maximus, the "best and greatest" of all gods:

> Men worshiped the dragon, for he had given his authority to the beast, and they worshiped the beast, saying, "Who is like the beast, and who can fight against it?"
>
> And the beast was given a mouth uttering haughty and blasphemous words, and it was allowed to exercise authority for forty-two months; it opened its mouth to utter blasphemies against God, blaspheming his name and his dwelling, that is, those who dwell in heaven.[23]

The exclamation of the earth's inhabitants, "Who is like the beast, and who can fight against it?" is the overture to Armageddon. Men will worship the dragon with full knowledge of who he is and what he intends to do: wage war with the King of heaven. In the time of the end, Luciferianism will prevail against every other religious creed. Satan will be worshipped as god, and his hybrid progeny, Apollo, as the son of god and true savior of humanity. In the place of crosses, menorahs, and crescents, the symbols of the dragon and the sun (the emblem of Apollo) will adorn the churches, temples, and mosques of the nations, regressing mankind to his most ancient idolatry.

"The tradition of the Dragon and the Sun," explains Blavatsky, "is echoed in every part of the world, both in its civilized and semi-savage regions." She continues,

---

[23] Revelation 13:4–6 (RSV).

It took rise in the whisperings about secret initiations among the profane, and was established universally through the once universal heliolatrous religion. There was a time when the four parts of the world were covered with the temples sacred to the Sun and the Dragon; but the cult is now preserved mostly in China and the Buddhist countries . . . the "Dragons" [were] held throughout all antiquity as the symbols of Immortality and Wisdom, of secret Knowledge and of Eternity . . . the hierophants of Egypt, of Babylon, and India, styling themselves generally the "Sons of the Dragon" and "Serpents."[24]

Helena Blavatsky was a high-level nineteenth-century Russian occultist who promulgated Luciferianism in the West through her influential books *Isis Unveiled* and *The Secret Doctrine*, as well as her popular magazine, aptly titled *Lucifer*. In 1875, Madame Blavatsky, along with her American associate Colonel Henry Steel Olcott, founded the Theosophical Society in New York, with the aim of encouraging Westerners "to view *Satan*, the Serpent of Genesis, as the real creator and benefactor, the Father of Spiritual mankind."

For it is he who was the "Harbinger of Light," bright radiant Lucifer, who opened the eyes of the automaton *created* by Jehovah, as alleged; and he who was the first to whisper: "in the day ye eat thereof ye shall be as Elohim, knowing good and evil"—can only be regarded in the light of a Saviour. An "adversary" to Jehovah the "*personating* spirit," he still remains in esoteric truth the ever-loving "Messenger" (the angel), the Seraphim and Cherubim who both *knew* well, and *loved* still more, and who conferred on us spiritual, instead of physical immortality—the latter a kind of *static* immortality that would have transformed man into an undying "Wandering Jew."[25]

---

[24] Blavatsky, *The Secret Doctrine*, Vol. II, 339–40.
[25] Ibid., 218.

The seal of the Theosophical Society communicates the Luciferian creed through hermetic symbolism: an Egyptian ankh (symbolic of immortality) is positioned in the center of a hexagram (symbolic of the seven dragon princes), which is encircled by a snake eating its tail (Leviathan) crowned with a clockwise swastika (symbolic of benevolence and goodness)[26] and the Sanskrit characters of the mantra "aum" (symbolic of the Logos, the word of God). The seal is encompassed by the slogan "There Is No Religion Higher Than Truth." In her *Secret Doctrine*, Blavatsky makes no secret of the fact that "Lucifer, or *Luciferus*, is the name of the angelic Entity presiding over the *light of truth* as over the light of day."[27] The implication is that the dragon is the supreme deity, the sole purveyor of truth, the source of immortality, and the savior of mankind. As the clockwise swastika is also symbolic of the sun, the Theosophical Seal encapsulates the tradition of the dragon and the sun, which is the foundation of all mystery cults.

In the same way that the Roman emperors led the people in obeisance to their patron god Jupiter, so the bestial emperor, Apollo, will lead the people in obeisance to his divine father, Lucifer. It cannot be coincidental that one of Jupiter's most ancient and important epithets was Lucetius, the "Light-Bringer."[28]

The adepts of the occult have always known that the reign of Lucifer, and the dawning of a New Golden Age, will only begin when his son, Apollo, is seated on the throne of a world empire. As previously established, the dragon cannot himself occupy a human throne, nor can he force mankind to worship him or do his bidding; rather, his influence is exercised through human proxies. What better proxy could there be than your own half-breed son, who is human enough to appropriate the birthright of Adam and rule in your stead? What better an empire than one in which the kings subjugated to your son are also the hybrid progeny of your princes? If the citizens of Earth are to be led into kinetic war with the King of heaven, then the authority of mankind must be consolidated

---

[26] Hitler would later adopt a counterclockwise inversion of the swastika as the emblem of the Nazi Party.

[27] Blavatsky, *The Secret Doctrine, Vol. II*, 458.

[28] *Encyclopedia Britannica Online*, s.v. "Jupiter: Roman god," accessed on June 3, 2020, https://www.britannica.com/topic/Jupiter-Roman-god.

into the hands of a single leader, which is precisely what the dragon princes compel their hybrid sons to do:

> "The ten horns which you saw are ten kings who have received no kingdom as yet, but they receive authority for one hour as kings with the beast. These are of one mind, and they will give their power and authority to the beast. These will make war with the Lamb, and the Lamb will overcome them, for he is Lord of lords and King of kings; and those who are with him are called, chosen, and faithful."[29]

The human-hybrid construct of the beast's empire is predicted in the second chapter of Daniel, where we find King Nebuchadnezzar vexed by the dream of an imposing statue, the head of which is made of gold, the chest and arms of silver, the midsection of bronze, the legs of iron, and the feet with ten toes of iron mixed with clay. Daniel explains to the king that the statue's segmented anatomy cast in distinctive metals signifies five empires that would arise to dominate the known world, including and succeeding his own, which is depicted in the head of gold.

With the benefit of hindsight, scholars and historians have been able to confirm the astonishing accuracy of Nebuchadnezzar's dream and have come to a general consensus regarding whom the metals represent. The duo of the chest and arms cast in silver is symbolic of the Medo-Persian Empire; the midsection made of bronze, the Grecian Empire; the legs of iron, a fitting portrayal of the Roman Empire, which was ultimately divided between East and West; and the feet made of iron mixed with clay perfectly express the fractured perpetuation of Rome, which was never conquered but dissolved into the multicultural complex of European nations in the Holy Roman Empire.

Aside from its historical fulfillment in the Holy Roman Empire, the final empire, depicted in the feet of the statue, presumably with five toes on each foot, directly correlates to the beast of Revelation and its ten horns, which represent ten kings who will arise to rule the earth at the end of the age. But just like the five sets of twins who ruled Atlantis, these are

---

[29] Revelation 17:12–14 (NKJV).

no ordinary human kings. The feet and toes of the statue are composed of iron mixed with potter's clay (ceramic clay).

Potter's clay is symbolic of the human race, since, in contrast with the elder race, man was molded by the hands of the Maker from the substance of the earth itself, as a potter forms his clay: "But now, O Lord, you are our Father; we are the clay, and you are our potter; we are all the work of your hand."[30] The meaning of the iron mixed with potter's clay metaphor is twofold. First, it represents the aforementioned Holy Roman Empire, which, due to its culturally heterogeneous composition, like iron mixed with clay, was partly strong and partly fragile:

> Whereas you saw the feet and toes, partly of potter's clay and partly of iron, the kingdom shall be divided; yet the strength of the iron shall be in it, just as you saw the iron mixed with ceramic clay. And as the toes of the feet were partly of iron and partly of clay, so the kingdom shall be partly strong and partly fragile.[31]

But Daniel's interpretation does not stop there. He continues,

> As you saw iron mixed with ceramic clay, *they will mingle with the seed of men*; but they will not adhere to one another, just as iron does not mix with clay. And in the days of *these kings* the God of heaven will set up a kingdom which shall never be destroyed; and the kingdom shall not be left to other people; it shall break in pieces and consume all these kingdoms, and it shall stand forever.[32]

The second meaning of iron mixed with potter's clay may be discerned in the pronouncement, "they will mingle with the seed of men," which refers to the ten kings (represented in the ten toes) during whose reign Christ will return to pulverize the empire of the beast (as described in

---

[30] Isaiah 64:8 (ESV).
[31] Daniel 2:41–42 (NKJV).
[32] Daniel 2:43–44 (NKJV, emphasis added).

the verses that follow). Mingling with the seed of men recalls to mind the miscegenation of the watchers who procreated hybrid offspring with human women. It would seem, then, that the ten kings of the final world empire, like the twin sons of Poseidon, will be the progeny of god and man. There is an insinuation that the citizens of the bestial empire will also be human hybrids, as not only the toes but the entirety of the feet are composed of iron mixed with potter's clay.

A second advent of the Golden Age, in which the gods return to comingle with men, has been long foretold in the utterances and epics of prophets and poets over the centuries. The Roman poet Virgil, living in the generation directly preceding the birth of Christ, gave voice to the pagan hope through Apollo's Sibylline oracle:

> Now the last age by Cumae's Sibyl sung has come and gone, and the majestic roll of circling centuries begins anew: Justice returns, returns old Saturn's reign, with a new breed of men sent down from heaven. Only do thou, at the boy's birth in whom the iron shall cease, the golden race arise, befriend him, chaste Lucina; 'tis thine own Apollo reigns. . . . He shall receive the life of gods, and see heroes with gods commingling, and himself be seen of them, and with his father's worth reign o'er a world at peace. . . . Assume thy greatness, for the time draws nigh, dear child of the gods, great progeny of Jove [Jupiter]! See how it totters—the world's orbed might, Earth, and wide ocean, and the vault profound, all see, enraptured of the coming time![33]

It is from this poem, penned more than a hundred years before the Book of Revelation, that the Latin phrase *novus ordo seclorum*, or "New World Order" is derived. Like John's vision of the beast and Nebuchadnezzar's dream of the statue, the prophecy of the Cumaean Sibyl predicts the inauguration of a New Golden Age, when Jupiter's beloved son descends from heaven to save mankind. "This is when the 'son' of promise arrives on earth—Apollo incarnate—a pagan savior born of 'a new breed of men

---

[33] Virgil, *The Eclogues*, IV.

sent down from heaven' when 'heroes' and 'gods' are blended together," writes Thomas Horn in his seminal work, *Zenith 2016*. He elucidates,

> This sounds eerily similar to what the Watchers did during the creation of the Nephilim and to what scientists are doing this century through genetic engineering of human-animal chimeras. But to understand why such a fanciful prophecy about Apollo, son of Jupiter, returning to Earth should be important to you: In ancient literature, Jupiter was the Roman replacement of Yahweh as the greatest of the gods—a "counter-Yahweh." His son Apollo is a replacement of Jesus, a "counter-Jesus." This Apollo comes to rule the final New World Order, when "Justice returns, returns old Saturn's [Satan's] reign." The ancient goddess Justice, who returns Satan's reign (*Saturnia regna*, the pagan golden age), was known to the Egyptians as Ma'at and to the Greeks as Themis, while to the Romans she was Lustitia. Statues and reliefs of her adorn thousands of government buildings and courts around the world, especially in Washington, DC, as familiar Lady Justice, blindfolded and holding scales and a sword. She represents the enforcement of secular law and is, according to the Sibyl's conjure, the authority that will require global compliance to the zenith of Satan's dominion concurrent with the coming of Apollo. What's more, the Bible's accuracy concerning this subject is alarming, including the idea that "pagan justice" will require surrender to a satanic system in a final world order under the rule of Jupiter's son.[34]

Thanks to the internet, the New World Order has become a cliché echoed in the throat of every conspiracy theorist under the sun. However, most fail to realize that the architects of the Great Plan do not intend to give birth to something new but to resurrect the dead. The New World Order is nothing more than the restoration of the old Atlantean world

---

[34] Dr. Thomas Horn, *Zenith 2016: Did Something Begin in the Year 2012 That Will Reach Its Apex in the Year 2016?* (Crane, MO: Defender, 2013), 138.

order, the Golden Age, in which the gods walked openly among men and their half-breed sons ruled the earth.

The restoration of the Atlantean world order is embodied in the myth of Osiris, the Egyptian deity of resurrection and rebirth. Having inaugurated the glorious epoch of Zep Tepi, the "First Time," when the gods comingled with men, Osiris was venerated as the begetter of civilization and the imparter of divine knowledge. The untimely death of Osiris, beloved king of the Golden Age, was mourned by the ancient Egyptians, and the advent of his resurrection was celebrated with great pomp and circumstance. Although several variations of the Osirian myth have come down to us from antiquity, the general sequence is always the same: Osiris is murdered by his brother Set; his body is dismembered and scattered abroad; his wife Isis finds the lost pieces of his body and reassembles them; Osiris is reanimated in order to impregnate Isis; Isis gives birth to Horus.

According to Plutarch's account, Set had an opulent coffin fabricated to fit the precise anatomical proportions of his brother, Osiris. He then organized an extravagant party and presented the coffin to his guests with the proposition that whoever fit most comfortably within could keep it as a gift. When Osiris accepted the challenge and laid himself in the coffin, Set closed the lid and sealed his brother inside. With Osiris thus entombed, he threw the coffin into the Nile River, where it was carried out to sea. Eventually it floated across the Mediterranean to the shore of Byblos, where it became lodged in a great *Erica* tree (other sources say it was an acacia tree). The tree grew to enfold the coffin and conceal it within the weaves of its great trunk. Later, the king of that land, whom Plutarch names Malacander, discovered the tree and, captivated by its beauty, decided to have it felled and transported to the city, where it was carved into an ornamental pillar for the royal palace. Thence, the lifeless corpse of Osiris remained hidden from all the world. Eventually, Isis, who had been searching for the body of her husband, came to Byblos and discovered the pillar. She removed the coffin and carried it back to Egypt, whereupon Set learned of its recovery and, having located it, cut the body of Osiris into pieces and scattered them abroad. Isis, after realizing what Set had done, went looking for the dismembered pieces and managed to find them all, except the phallus, which had been devoured by a fish (other sources say a crocodile). After reassembling the body of her husband, she fashioned a phallus of gold and, through sorcery, reanimated him long enough to copulate. She conceived and gave birth to Horus, the son of Osiris.

Like all important myths from antiquity, the Osirian myth is encoded with information intended to be hidden from the profane but apparent to the initiated. The body of Osiris represents the corpus of divine knowledge imparted to mankind through the watchers in the Old World. The majority of these "mysteries" were lost in the cataclysm of the Flood that destroyed the Osirian kingdom, which, like Atlantis, is an allegory of the Golden Age. However, just as the deceased body of Osiris was preserved in the coffin as it floated over the waters of the Mediterranean, so the knowledge of the watchers was preserved, in some measure, through the waters of the Flood.[35]

That the coffin of Osiris came to rest at Byblos on the coast of Lebanon is a detail of great importance. Byblos was the capital city of the Phoenicians, a seafaring people of Canaanite descent. The Phoenicians were, in essence, a secret society of whom very little is known. We do know, however, that they were the master mariners and masons of the ancient world. The Phoenicians' renown as superior craftsmen of metal, cedar, and stone is evinced in the fact that they were employed by David and Solomon to build the most important monuments in Israel, including the Temple of Yahweh.[36]

Having attained extraordinary wealth and widespread prestige, Solomon could have appealed to any of the great kings in the Levant, and beyond, to help him build the Temple, including the Egyptian Pharaoh, whose daughter he wed. That he sought the assistance of the Phoenician king, Hiram of Tyre, attests to the superior knowledge of his people. King Hiram provided Solomon with cedars from Lebanon and sent his best artisans to oversee the finer details of the project, including the eminent master, Hiram Abiff.[37] It is from this affair that the origins of Freemasonry are derived.

---

[35] The body of Osiris, and the coffin that carried it through the sea, may also represent the bloodline of the watchers, preserved in the genomes of Noah's daughters-in-law, who were carried through the Flood on the ark. The author does not necessarily subscribe to this view, but the reader should be aware of it.

[36] See 1 Kings 5; 1 Chronicles 14; 2 Chronicles 2.

[37] See 1 Kings 7.

Just as Osiris embodies the secret knowledge of the watchers, Hiram Abiff embodies the secret purpose of the Masons. One of the symbols most sacred to the Craft is the figure of Hiram's coffin, which is always accompanied by an acacia branch (usually positioned above). Officially, the branch and the coffin pertain to a legend concerning Hiram's assassination; however, the true meaning of the symbols points to the acacia pillar and the coffin of Osiris that it concealed in the palace of the Phoenician king. We may decipher the message: the corpus of pre-Flood knowledge was preserved by the Phoenicians and passed on through the fraternal orders that continued in their tradition, including the Masons.[38] The purpose of these "mystery schools" is illustrated in the project undertaken by Isis—to resurrect Osiris and bring forth Horus.

Many of the rituals and rites of Freemasonry (and other mystery schools) revolve around the raising of Osiris, the conception of Horus, and the restoration of Zep Tepi—the empire of the gods. Horus is the counterpart of Apollo, a fact revealed to Herodotus by the priests of Egypt, who explained to the Greek historian that the kingdoms of the world were once ruled by semidivine hybrid kings called *Shemsu Hor* (companions of Horus), who were the offspring of god and man:

> The rulers in Egypt were gods settled with human beings and one of them on each and every occasion was the lord, and Orus [Horus], the son of Osiris, was the last to be king there, whom the Greeks name Apollo.[39]

The prime objective of the Great Plan—to resurrect the Golden Age and bring forth Apollo—is expressed in the alignment of two monuments that symbolize Osiris and Isis: the obelisk (phallus of Osiris) and the dome (womb of Isis). The meticulous devising and positioning of monuments for the express purpose of inscribing secret knowledge or invoking specific deities is known as *theurgy* ("divine-working"). The Freemasons, in

---

[38] Space does not permit a more thorough examination of the Phoenicians, who are the keystone to understanding many of the mysteries pertaining to the ancient world. Sanford Holst's work *Phoenician Secrets* (Los Angeles, CA: Santorini Publishing, 2011) is a good starting point if the reader is inclined to pursue the topic.

[39] Herodotus, *Inquiries*, Book 2 Installment 13, translated by Shlomo Felberbaum.

particular, excelled at theurgy. Washington, DC, is a testament to their craft. Of the many theurgic configurations implicit in the layout of the city, the Washington Monument, which happens to be the largest obelisk on Earth, is carefully aligned with the dome of the Capitol Building. The intent of the alignment is to invoke Osiris, Isis, and Horus and secretly communicate the great hope of its architects: that the United States of America would become the New Atlantis and bring forth the long awaited Philosopher King (Apollo).[40] Another famous example of the Osiris-Isis-Horus invocation may be found in Vatican City, where the ancient obelisk of Heliopolis is positioned precisely in front of the iconic dome that crowns the Basilica of Saint Peter.

These theurgic alignments (and many more examples could be cited) are the fingerprints of the dragon priests, who have been quietly laboring at the behest of the gods to set the stage for the coming of Apollo. "The builder gods of the Egyptian Edfu texts," remarks Flynn, "were adamant about the proper location for building: in order to have the desired effect, the building must occur in the holy places. A successful undertaking—the building of city walls, temples and mystery religions in the holy places— would bring about a 'resurrection of the destroyed world of the gods.'"[41]

To the uninitiated masses of the ancient world, the gods were distant, all-powerful beings who controlled the forces of nature; when appeased, they blessed the land with fair weather and good crops, but when offended, they sent plagues, earthquakes, and hurricanes to punish the impudent mortals who angered them. The initiates of the mysteries knew better. To them, the gods were close at hand, moving surreptitiously through the passing of centuries, communicating their Great Plan to the elect—those chosen men and women deemed worthy to be coconspirators. Albert Pike, who held the office of Sovereign Grand Commander of the Scottish Rite in the late nineteenth century and was one of the most influential Masons in American history, wrote that the imagined mythical beings

[40] As much as I would like to digress into the fascinating complexities of this scheme, I must forgo the temptation. If the reader is interested in the subject, he should consult the works of Manly P. Hall (*The Secret Destiny of America* and *America's Assignment with Destiny*) and Thomas Horn (*Zenith 2016*). Horn, in particular, provides an expansive and scholarly examination of the themes we have only lightly touched on in this chapter.
[41] David Flynn, *Cydonia: The Secret Chronicles of Mars*, 307.

in the pantheons of the ancient Persians, Indians, Egyptians, Greeks, and Romans were but poetical illusions to satisfy the vulgar, because "man still looked back with longing to the lost Golden Age, when his ancestors communed face to face with the Gods; and hoped that, by propitiating Heaven, he might accelerate the renewal of it."[42]

Pike, and those among his colleagues who were privy to the true doctrines of Freemasonry at the highest degrees, knew that the mythological gods of yore were not literal beings but metaphorical allusions to an elder race of masters who needed the cooperation of enlightened humans to help them restore their empire and renew the face-to-face communion of the Golden Age. In order to accomplish this divine working, the dragon priests must gradually illuminate the world with the light of Lucifer and guide mankind to willfully invoke the return and rule of the gods. "LUCIFER, the Light-bearer!" exclaims Pike in his *Morals and Dogma*.

> Strange and mysterious name to give to the Spirit of Darkness! Lucifer, the Son of the Morning! Is it he who bears the Light, and with its splendors intolerable blinds feeble, sensual or selfish Souls? Doubt it not![43]

The divine working of the Great Plan, which for hundreds of years remained hidden within the clandestine chambers of secret societies, was externalized in the nineteenth century, directly corresponding with the rise of occultism, Darwinism, and, as will become apparent, the UFO phenomenon. In the twentieth century, the blatant Luciferianism of theosophy was repackaged to reach a broader audience, including, and most importantly, a Christian audience. To this end, biblical terminology was coopted by Blavatsky's proteges to make the doctrines of the mysteries more palatable on the Christian tongue. Christ became the central figure of their teachings, but not the Christ of scripture. Anyone familiar with the New Age messiah will immediately recognize him as antichrist. The New Age is synonymous with the New Golden Age, and the theosophical

---

[42] Albert Pike, *Morals and Dogma of the Ancient and Accepted Scottish Rite of Freemasonry* (Charleston, SC: Supreme Council of the Thirty Third Degree for the Southern Jurisdiction of the United States, 1871), 653.

[43] Pike, *Morals and Dogma*, 321.

Christ with Apollo. Rather than refer to the gods of old, theosophists wrote—and write still—about the wise and benevolent members of the hierarchy (i.e., the insurgency) who are working through their human coconspirators to bring about a restoration of the Atlantean world order.

The most prominent of Blavatsky's proteges was undoubtably Alice Bailey, the mother and matriarch of the New Age movement. In the early 1920s, Bailey, following in the footsteps of her esteemed predecessor, founded the Lucifer Publishing Company. She would later change the title of the organization to the slightly less conspicuous Lucis Trust. The literary works of Alice Bailey, who wrote as a conduit for the Master Djwhal Khul,[44] spread like wildfire in the West. Her teachings laid the spiritual foundation for the progressive revolution and the women's rights movement, which gave rise to radical feminism, the legalization of abortion, the proliferation of female promiscuity, and the normalization of homosexuality, among many other societal ills (including eugenics; Margaret Sanger was a theosophist). Bailey's influence was not limited to the secular world; her theosophical doctrines, cleverly disguised in biblical jargon, eventually seeped into Christian churches, Protestant and Catholic alike, through the Charismatic Renewal.[45]

Alice Bailey, in concert with her counterparts in the other mystery schools, was working to prepare the nations "for a new revelation which will inaugurate the new era and set the note for the new world religion."[46] This "new revelation" would begin with the realization that a brotherhood of enlightened beings, the Hierarchy, have been quietly observing the evolutionary progress of the human species and gently guiding their

---

[44] Like all theosophical adepts, Bailey practiced automatic writing, during which she channeled the thoughts and words of higher beings. Djwhal Khul was allegedly an Ascended Master residing in Tibet who had previously functioned as Blavatsky's divine muse. According to theosophists, Ascended Masters are essentially members of the elder race who reside on Planet Earth and have been secretly guiding mankind through the ages (in other words, the dragon and his princes).

[45] The Charismatic Renewal (or Charismatic Movement) was heavily influenced by theosophists, who sowed the seeds of spiritualism in Christian churches. Charismatic Christians were encouraged to pursue ecstatic spiritual experiences, including spiritual drunkenness, uncontrollable gyrations of the body, intercourse with heavenly beings, prophetic visions and trances, the utterance of incoherent language, and sensuousness in song and dance. The most excessive examples of Charismatic ecstasy resemble the Cult of Dionysus, whose devotees were given to orgiastic revelry, which included the very same manifestations mentioned above (drunkenness, gyrations, visions and trances, incoherent utterances, and sensual dancing).

[46] Alice Bailey, *Externalization of the Hierarchy* (New York: Lucis Publishing Company, 1957), 545.

development through the ages. Once men were made aware of their Promethean benefactors, they would petition them to directly govern the affairs of the world. "It will then be possible," Bailey explains, "for the Hierarchy, the Church of Christ hitherto invisible, to externalize itself and to function openly upon the physical plane."

> This will indicate a return to the situation which existed in Atlantean days when (to use Biblical symbology) God Himself walked among men . . . and the Members of the spiritual Hierarchy were openly guiding and directing the affairs of humanity as man's innate freedom permitted. Now, in the immediate future . . . this will happen again. The Masters will walk openly among men; the Christ [Apollo] will reappear in physical presence [and] the ancient Mysteries will be restored, the ancient landmarks will again be recognized—those land-marks which Masonry has so earnestly preserved and which have hitherto securely embalmed in the Masonic rituals, wait-ing the day of restoration and resurrection.[47]

The acolytes of the mysteries know that the coming of Apollo and the restoration of the Atlantean world order must be invocative. In other words, men must beseech the gods to return and willingly abdicate their authority to them. Bailey describes the procedure,

> This new invocative work, will be the keynote of the coming world religion and will fall into two parts. There will be the invocative work of the masses of the people, everywhere trained by the spiritually minded people of the world (work-ing in the churches whenever possible under an enlightened clergy) to accept the fact of the approaching spiritual ener-gies, focused through Christ and His spiritual Hierarchy, and trained also to voice their demand for light, liberation and understanding. There will also be the skilled work of invo-cation as practiced by those who have trained their minds

[47] Alice Bailey, *The Reappearance of the Christ* (New York: Lucis Publishing Company, 1948), 121.

193

through right meditation, who know the potency of formulas, mantras and invocations and who work consciously. They will increasingly use certain great formulas of words which will later be given to the race, just as the Lord's Prayer was given by the Christ, and the New Invocation has been given out for use at this time by the Hierarchy."[48]

As we have seen, the liberation for which the people will clamor is predicted in the Psalms: "Let us break their bonds in pieces and cast away their cords from us." This proclamation implies that the people will acknowledge the existence of the Hebrew God and recognize the identity of his Anointed King, Jesus of Nazareth, before deciding to openly oppose them (a situation we will amplify in the following chapter). The Hierarchy—Apollo and his consorts—will convince the nations that not all gods are the friends of mankind. Indeed, some gods, they will confess, have been manipulating the human species through primitive religious institutions and punitive moral injunctions in order to keep them under foot and suppress their divine potential. The Hierarchy will reveal to us that they have been covertly laboring to counteract this conspiracy of repression and liberate the mind of man with the enlightenment of the dragon, the most magnificent and benevolent of all divine beings. To our great astonishment we will learn that the dragon princes have been patiently guiding us through the course of our evolution so that we might one day fulfill the purpose for which we were created and take our place among the immortal company of heaven.

At long last, the final mystery will be unveiled: man is to throw off the yoke of Yahweh and his crucified Son so that he may become a god himself in the likeness of Apollo.

The revealing of Apollo, the inauguration of a New Golden Age, and the battle of Armageddon, will come to pass with the confluence of three essential components, which we may visualize as the conjunction of three equidistant circles (see Figure 1), defined as follows:

[48] Alice Bailey, *Problems of Humanity* (New York: Lucis Publishing Company, 1944), 159.

1. **The New Religion**

    The establishment of a new religion that impels men to become like the gods.

2. **The Alien Threat**

    The disclosure of a hostile alien presence and the arrival of the Golden Race.

3. **The Posthuman Paradigm**

    The development of GRIN technologies and the emergence of posthumanity.

When these three components converge, the end times will be upon us.

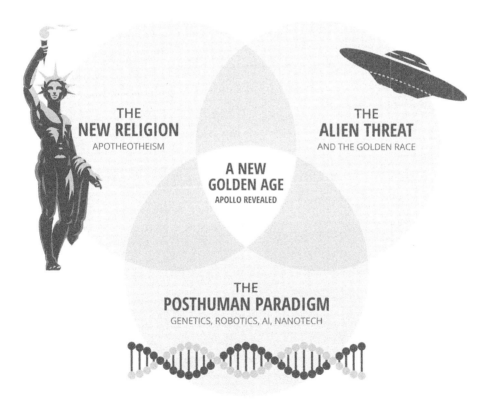

THE
NEW RELIGION
APOTHEOTHEISM

THE
ALIEN THREAT
AND THE GOLDEN RACE

**A NEW
GOLDEN AGE**
APOLLO REVEALED

THE
POSTHUMAN PARADIGM
GENETICS, ROBOTICS, AI, NANOTECH

Figure 1

Chapter 10

THE NEW RELIGION

I f the sons of Adam were to be persuaded, once again, to willfully relinquish their birthright in a second advent of the Golden Age, then it was imperative that they be made to forget the cataclysmic consequences of the first. Lyell and Darwin had succeeded in unfettering the mind of man from the age-old mooring of theism and divine accountability, opening before him an ocean of evolutionary potential. By denying the existence of their Maker, men could now act with impunity according to the doctrine of a new religion that impels them to cast off the image of Adam and become the gods of their own design.

The tenets of this new religion, conceived in the womb of Darwinism, emerged with great violence in the twentieth century. Roiling in the effusion of natal blood, it came forth with eugenics, with racism, with concentration camps, with gulags, with death squads, with hundreds of millions of lives lost across Europe and Asia. More men died in war and democide (death by government) in the century following Darwin than in all of human history combined. God was no longer to be feared. Man would define his own morality. Only survival and propagation (biological *and* political) mattered in the grand scheme of things. The earth belonged to the fittest.

The turn of the century was marked by an unprecedented acceleration in scientific breakthrough and technological development. The atom was modeled and split. Quantum theory was formulated. High-voltage electricity illuminated cities and powered industry. Automobiles and airplanes, propelled by internal combustion, traversed the land and sky. Warfare was mechanized with tanks and mobile artillery. Telephones and radio transmissions made long-distance communication instantaneous. X-rays were discovered. Vaccines, antibiotics, and anesthetics were developed. The nucleotide bases of DNA were identified, and genetic research commenced. Never before had knowledge advanced so prolifically on Planet Earth. This was the era of the Wright brothers, Edison, Tesla, Ford, Curie, Kossel, Planck, Bohr, Oppenheimer, and Einstein, to name a few of its luminaries; but it was also the era of Blavatsky, Nietzsche, and Crowley.

As atheism blossomed in the soils of Western society, growing in tandem with the advancements of technology, so, too, did Luciferianism. Lyell had provided man with a geological pretext to doubt the judgment of the Great Flood, and Darwin with a biological theory to deny the very existence of the Great Judge who presided over it. But denial was merely the prelude of defiance, and incredulity the first step on the long road to insurrection. If the dragon was to lead the inhabitants of Earth into war with the powers of heaven, then atheism would have to mutate into a much more virulent ideology, one in which God is not only denied but openly opposed. Having been severed from the mooring of theism, the destiny of mankind would need to be navigated to new shores, but evolution lacked a destination.

The theory of evolution by natural selection had supplied the atheist with a convenient origin devoid of divine accountability and consequence, something he greatly desired, but it left him with a vacancy of purpose. Evolution wasn't going anywhere. It had no wind in its sails, no heading, and no hand to turn the rudder. The theory required a helmsman, some farsighted individual who could espy its final destination and fill its sails with the winds of purpose.

Enter Friedrich Nietzsche.

One could contend—and many have—that no philosopher has influenced the zeitgeist of modern society more than Friedrich Nietzsche. The precepts and prognostications of Nietzschean philosophy would prove to be remarkably prescient and tremendously destructive in the century following his death, which occurred in the year 1900. It was Nietzsche who first intoned the proclamation, "God is dead," which has since become the rallying cry of militant atheists everywhere.

Born into a pious German family, the son of a Lutheran pastor and himself theologically trained, Nietzsche was especially effective at dismantling the tenets of the Christian faith from which he defected and which he loathed.[1] "I regard Christianity," he once wrote, "as the most fatal and seductive lie that has ever yet existed, as the great unholy lie: I draw out the after-growth and sprouting of its ideal from beneath every form of disguise, I reject every compromise position with respect to it—I force a war against it."[2]

His doctrines were clearly Luciferian. "We deny God," he professed, "and in denying God, we deny responsibility: only *thus* do we redeem the world."[3] The redemption of which Nietzsche spoke was freedom from the moral impositions of the Christian God and his crucified Son. With these sentiments—and many more equally acidulous quotations could be furnished—he reveals himself as less of an atheist and more of an antitheist, the former being an expression of denial, the latter of defiance.

Nietzsche railed against the ethics of Christianity and openly advocated immorality, declaring himself a disciple of Dionysus, the Greek god of revelry, ritual madness, religious ecstasy, orgiastic excess, and drunkenness. Servility to inferior Christian morals, he argued, was inhibiting the rise of superior men, whom he denominates as *übermenschen*, the "beyond-men" or "overmen." The overmen represent the highest ideal and final destination in the evolutionary ascent of the human species. Nietzsche enthusiastically subscribed to the theory of evolution but vehemently rejected Darwin's mechanism of natural selection as its driving force. Natural selection was blind and feeble, operating only in the interest of survival. Nietzsche had discerned in evolution a far more potent force, the *will to power*. Only the weak—the "bungled and the botched," as he liked

---

[1] Although Nietzsche commended the person of Christ, he detested the New Testament, which, in his opinion, promoted the false gospel of "a god who died for our sins; redemption through faith; resurrection after death—all these are counterfeits of true Christianity for which that disastrous wrong-headed fellow [the apostle Paul] must be held responsible" (*The Will to Power*, 169).
[2] Friedrich Nietzsche, *The Will to Power: A New Translation* by Walter Kaufman and R. J. Hollingdale (New York: Doubleday, 1967), 117.
[3] Friedrich Nietzsche, *Twilight of the Idols*, trans. Richard Polt (Indianapolis: Hackett Publishing Company, 1997), 37.

to call them—were motivated by survival and subservient to the Christian God. The strong were driven by the will to power and determined to become gods themselves.

Overman is to man what man is to ape; he is in every way superior to the human, as the human is in every way superior to the chimpanzee. But overman is more than a biological upgrade of the human species; he transcends human morality. In fact, he is positively amoral. Whereas the Christian man is enthralled to a "slave morality," subordinate to the will of a perceived Creator, the overman is free to practice a "master morality" of his own devising—a self-made moral code unencumbered by the arbitrary dictates of impotent deities.[4] Overman is lawless. He is not accountable to God, because he has become his equal. Hence, "God is dead. God remains dead. And we have killed him,"[5] and, "Dead are all gods: now we want the overman to live."[6] In other words, men must first depose the gods of yesterday if they are to take their place and evolve into the gods of tomorrow. Nietzsche had provided evolution with a purpose: to bring forth the overman on Earth.

> *I teach you the overman!* Human being is something that must be overcome. What have you done to overcome him?
>
> All creatures so far created something beyond themselves; and you want to be the ebb of this great flood and would even rather go back to animals than overcome humans?
>
> What is the ape to a human? A laughing stock or a painful embarrassment. And that is precisely what the human shall be to the overman: a laughing stock or a painful embarrassment.
>
> You have made your way [evolved] from worm to human, and much in you is still worm. Once you were apes, and even now a human is still more ape than any ape.... The overman is

---

[4] For reasons we do not have time to enlarge, many liberal academics are inclined to repudiate the fact that Adolf Hitler was a devotee of Nietzschean philosophy and modeled his "Master Race" on the concept of master morality, in which the strong have the evolutionary right and responsibility to subdue the weak. Hitler, like Napoleon, was an archetype of Nietzsche's "noble man," who, through the indomitable power of his will, nearly conquered the whole world.
[5] Friedrich Nietzsche, *The Gay Science* (Liepzig, Germany: E. W. Fritsch, 1887), 181.
[6] Friedrich Nietzsche, *Thus Spoke Zarathustra*, trans. Adrian del Caro (Cambridge, UK: Cambridge University Press, 2006), 59.

the meaning of the earth. Let your will say: the overman *shall be* the meaning of the earth! . . . Mankind is a rope fastened between animal and overman—a rope over an abyss. . . . What is great about human beings is that they are a bridge and not a purpose: what is lovable about human beings is that they are a *crossing over* and a *going under.*[7]

Note the contempt for mankind in Nietzsche's words. He mocks man, in his current evolutionary condition, as a "laughing stock, or painful embarrassment" and exhorts him to evolve with the assertion that "all creatures so far created something beyond themselves." The implication is that the human species is obligated to direct the course of its own evolution. The will to power is compelling man to become overman, to shed his biological and moral skin and abandon the weakness of Adam. There is more than the mind of Nietzsche at work in these words. They ring with the sibilance of a forked tongue.

Ironically, Nietzsche chose to herald the death of God and the coming of the overman who would replace him through the voice of the ancient Persian prophet Zarathustra. He penned *Thus Spoke Zarathustra*, from which the above excerpt is derived, between the years of 1883 and 1885, during a time when channeled communications were in vogue (especially among theosophists). More commonly known by his Greek name, Zoroaster, the teachings of Zarathustra represent the antithesis of Nietzschean philosophy: theism, the objective dichotomy of good and evil, and the importance of morality. In a sense, Nietzsche's appropriation of Zarathustra's voice, which he used to dismantle the very ideals promoted by the historical figure, is a representation of Nietzsche himself, who, being the son of a Protestant preacher, devoted his life to dismantling the faith in which he was reared. Modern admirers of Nietzsche praise the channeled ravings of Zarathustra as the manifestation of a brilliant mind, but one must not forget that this brilliant mind went stark raving mad just four years after completing the work. It is reasonable to conclude that Nietzsche's mind was not altogether his own at the end of his literary career.

---

[7] Nietzsche, *Thus Spoke Zarathustra*, 5–7.

In the twilight of Nietzsche's career, another pastor's son reared in the Christian faith was preparing to carry his insurrectionary torch into the twentieth century. Edward Alexander Crowley, later to be known as the infamous Aleister Crowley and the "Great Beast 666," was a ten-year-old boy growing up in Warwickshire, England, when the final segments of *Thus Spoke Zarathustra* were published in 1885. Like Nietzsche, Crowley was raised in a devout Protestant home and aspired to follow in the footsteps of his father, who was a popular minister in the puritanical denomination of the Plymouth Brethren. To say he took another path in life is a fabulous understatement. He would later write, "I simply went over to Satan's side; and to this hour I cannot tell why. But I found myself as passionately eager to serve my new master as I had been to serve the old. I was anxious to distinguish myself by committing sin. . . . I wanted a supreme spiritual sin; and I had not the smallest idea how to set about it."[8] The idea, in the course of time, would occur to Crowley through the philosophy of Friedrich Nietzsche and through the dictation of Aiwass, an emissary of the gods.

Aleister Crowley's appetite for supreme spiritual sin and uninhibited debauchery would eventually occasion the British press to crown him "The King of Depravity" and "The Wickedest Man in the World." In 1923, the *Sunday Express* published a front-page article denouncing Crowley as "a drug fiend, an author of vile books, the spreader of obscene practices . . . one of the most sinister figures of modern times."[9] Although he earned a formidable reputation for being a depraved bastard during his college years at Cambridge—where he was initiated into the Hermetic Order of the Golden Dawn—Crowley's meteoric rise to international infamy began in the innermost chamber of the Great Pyramid at Giza.

In 1903, after wedding his first wife, Rose Kelly,[10] Crowley and his bride set off for a honeymoon excursion in Egypt.[11] One night after supper,

---

[8] Aleister Crowley, *The Confessions of Aleister Crowley* (London: The Mandrake Press, 1929), 59.

[9] "Aleister Crowley's Orgies in Sicily," *The Sunday Express* (London), March 4, 1923.

[10] Ever the breacher of societal mores, Crowley eloped with Kelly the day after meeting her on the eleventh of August. They were unceremoniously married the following day.

[11] Crowley met his bride-to-be while engaged in a particularly dangerous magical ritual he was conducting on the shores of Scotland's Loch Ness. Named after the fourteenth-century Egyptian mage Abramelin, the so-called "Abramelin working" was a ritual designed to summon and gain mastery over one's "guardian angel," but in order for the magician to commune with the being,

Crowley decided to take Rose into the King's Chamber within the Great Pyramid to perform the "Preliminary Invocation of the Goetia." Known as the *Lesser Key of Solomon the King*, the *Goetia* is a grimoire (a book of magic spells) containing invocations for summoning the *shedim* of Hebrew lore, which are known in the Western world as *demons*. The invocation had no immediate effect, but later in Cairo, Rose (who did not have an affinity for magic) became entranced by a mysterious force. Crowley would later record the incident in his autobiography:

> [Rose] got into a strange state of mind. I had never seen her anything at all like it before. She kept on repeating dreamily, yet intensely, "They are waiting for you."[12]

Rose—to whom Crowley conferred the magical name "Ouarda"—would later reveal to her husband that the entity waiting for him was the Egyptian god Horus. Crowley was doubtful and suspicious of his wife's newly acquired abilities as a medium; after all, she had no training in magic and knew nothing of the Egyptian mysteries. So, being a practical occultist, he decided to test her premonition and took her to the Boulaq Museum (Museum of Egyptian Antiquities) in Cairo, a place neither of them had ever visited before, wherein he instructed her to find a likeness of Horus among the exhibits. In a trancelike state, Rose hurried through various rooms filled with ancient artifacts until she abruptly paused in front of an exhibit enclosed in a glass case and cried out, "There! There he is!" Crowley could not believe his eyes. Within the case was a wooden stele decorated with the unmistakable likeness of Horus in the form of Ra Hoor Khuit—the hawk-headed king crowned with a cobra-encompassed solar disc. The exhibit number was 666.

Crowley was told that "the Equinox of the Gods had come" and that he was to be the prophet and herald of a new age, the Aeon of Horus

---

the hermetic door behind which it resided would have to be opened. Occultists have warned that if left unfinished, the Abramelin working could unleash hordes of demonic entities into the world and result in the bodily possession of the magician himself. Upon meeting Kelly, Crowley abruptly discontinued the ritual and left for Egypt, leaving it quite unfinished. Whether he in fact became possessed by the entity he sought to control is anyone's guess.

[12] Crowley, *The Confessions of Aleister Crowley*, 392.

(Apollo), in which the gods and men would comingle once again.

On April 8, 9, and 10, 1904, shortly after the museum incident, Crowley was visited by an entity called "Aiwass," who claimed to be the emissary of Horus. At precisely the same time each day, for exactly one hour, Aiwass spoke to Crowley, murmuring over his left shoulder in an unearthly voice and dictating to him the Book of the Law, which was to become the holy writ of a new cult—Thelema.

In short, the Book of the Law (*Liber Al vel Legis*) is an esoteric screed and a blasphemous tirade against God. Three Egyptian deities, Nuit, Hadit, and Ra-Hoor-Khuit (Horus)—all of whose likenesses were depicted on the stele of exhibit 666 in the Egyptian Museum—spoke through the voice of Aiwass as he dictated its verses to Crowley. However, the true inspiration of the Law is unveiled in the enunciation, "I am the Snake that giveth Knowledge & Delight and bright glory."[13] As with the ravings of Zarathustra, the murmurings of Aiwass are antitheist in the extreme:

> I am in a secret fourfold word, the blasphemy against all gods of men. Curse them! Curse them! Curse them! With my Hawk's head I peck at the eyes of Jesus as he hangs upon the cross. I flap my wings in the face of Mohammed & blind him. With my claws I tear out the flesh of the Indian and the Buddhist, Mongol and Din. Bahlasti! Ompehda! I spit on your crapulous creeds. Let Mary inviolate be torn upon wheels: for her sake let all chaste women be utterly despised among you![14]

Summarized in its sole injunction, "Do as thou wilt," the doctrine of the Law is utter lawlessness. It encourages men to spurn the will of their Maker and abandon every moral inhibition, in other words, to be gods themselves and do exactly as they please. The opening verses of the Law declare it to be "the unveiling of the company of heaven. Every man and every woman is a star."[15] The unveiling of the company of heaven is the revealing of Apollo (Horus) and his consorts, who will compel men

---

[13] Aleister Crowley, Book of the Law 2:22.
[14] Ibid. 3:49–55.
[15] Ibid. 1:2–3.

to become like them (like the stars) and worship the dragon. As in the seal of the Theosophical Society, the seal of Thelema is a black hexagram (unicursal), which is emblematic of the seven dragon princes.[16] Crowley and Rose (soon to divorce) were commissioned by the company of heaven to kindle the insurrectionary fire of the "black stars"[17] in the hearts of men to prepare them for the coming of Horus (Apollo) and the Equinox of the Gods.

> Now ye shall know that the chosen priest & apostle of infinite space is the prince-priest the Beast [Crowley]; and in his woman called the Scarlet Woman [Rose] is all power given. They shall gather my children into their fold: they shall bring the glory of the stars into the hearts of men.[18]

Stars only shine in the dark when the light of the sun has vanished. Men must be made to love the darkness if they are to embrace the glory of the stars when they reveal themselves. And this was Crowley's mandate, to entice men to be "lovers of themselves, lovers of money, boasters, proud, blasphemers, disobedient to parents, unthankful, unholy, unloving, unforgiving, slanderers, without self-control, brutal, despisers of good, traitors, headstrong, haughty, lovers of pleasure rather than lovers of God."[19]

Upon receiving his directive from the company of heaven, Crowley needed a temple in which to practice the injunction of the law "Do as thou wilt" to its fullest extent, away from the prying eyes of the prude and

---

[16] Like the seven-headed red dragon, the hexagram is an emblem of the dragon's confederacy. The hexagram is a six-pointed star composed of two intersecting equilateral triangles. Contrary to popular conception, the hexagram does not encode the number six but the number seven. The six points (or angles) encompass the center, the seventh and principal point of the star. In Rosicrucian and Hermetic magic, the hexagram represents the seven sacred luminaries (or classical planets) in the night sky visible to the naked eye (the sun, the moon, Mercury, Venus, Mars, Jupiter, and Saturn), which are cryptic references to the seven dragon princes and the seven shattered vessels of Edom, their former principalities.

[17] References to the stars in the occult are indicative of black stars, which are representative of the fallen morning stars and allegiance to Lucifer, the original black star. Luciferians also refer to themselves as black stars and bear the emblem of the pentagram. Whereas the black hexagram encodes the number seven and symbolizes the insurgents of the elder race, the black pentagram encodes the number six (the number of a man) and symbolizes their human counterparts.

[18] Crowley, Book of the Law 1:15.

[19] 2 Timothy 3:2–4 (NKJV).

vulgar masses, who would surely object. He found what he was looking for in the small town of Cefalu in northern Sicily. There, in the seclusion and privacy of an unassuming farmhouse, which he christened the "Abbey of Thelema," Crowley and his newly wed Scarlet Woman, Leah Hirsig,[20] together with a band of deranged disciples, devoted themselves to the perfection of perversion. Prodigious amounts of narcotics were supplied to enhance the experience. What followed was an unhinged circus of depravity. Hetero- and homosexual orgies, bestiality, pedophilia, animal sacrifice, the consumption of blood and other bodily discharges, self-mutilation, and the evocation of demonic entities were the order of the day at the Abbey of Thelema. Crowley's commune was in every way a microcosm of the lawlessness and immorality that led to the Flood— a wickedness so great that every imagination in the thoughts and hearts of its members was only evil continually. Try as they did to hide their depraved activities from the outside world, rumors of what was happening at the Abbey eventually reached the ears of Benito Mussolini, who was so appalled that he personally ordered the eviction of Crowley and his Thelemites from Italy.[21]

Despite his diabolical behavior, Aleister Crowley emphatically denied the accusation that he was a black magician.[22] Instead, he viewed himself, like his hero Friedrich Nietzsche, as a freedom fighter in the struggle to liberate men from the moral impositions of the Christian God and his crucified Son. "Do what thou wilt" was the master morality of the overman. Crowley was merely putting Nietzschean philosophy into practice. "Nietzsche," he wrote, "may be regarded as one of our prophets."[23]

---

[20] After driving her to madness, Crowley divorced Rose Kelly and had her committed to an insane asylum.

[21] Mussolini brought Crowley's experiment to an abrupt end, but not before it had exacted a heavy toll on its participants. Raoul Loveday, an Oxford graduate, fell ill and died after allegedly drinking the blood of a cat during a sacrificial rite. Leah Hirsig, who was the subject of unspeakably vile ritual sex magic involving men, women, and animals and whom Crowley would later divorce, deteriorated into a life of drug addiction and prostitution. More than a few of the Thelemites from the Abbey lost their minds, and at least one of them committed suicide.

[22] In 1934, he filed a libel case against an author who accused him of being a "black magician." He lost the case after lurid stanzas of pornographic poetry he had published in his earlier years were read aloud in court and the testimony of his former disciples was heard.

[23] Aleister Crowley, *Magick without Tears* (Hampton, NJ: Thelema Publications, 1954), 178.

He praised Nietzsche as "an avatar of Thoth, the god of wisdom"[24] and encouraged his disciples to "read Nietzsche!"[25]

The impact of Friedrich Nietzsche and Aleister Crowley on the socio-political climate of the modern era cannot be overstated. The doctrines of these two men provided the philosophical and spiritual impetus for some of the most transformational events of the twentieth century.

Adolf Hitler was a devotee of Nietzschean philosophy and eagerly implemented the concepts of *will to power* and the overman in the formulation and execution of Nazi doctrine.[26] Hitler's campaign of eugenics to weed out the weak and racially inferior elements in the genetic stock of the German people in order to breed the superior Master Race was founded squarely on Nietzsche's evolutionary paradigm. Hitler fully embraced the purpose of evolution and attempted to carry out the directive of Zarathustra—to bring forth the overman on Earth.

There can be no doubt that Nietzsche's contempt for Christian morals is today promulgating from the lecterns of major universities across the globe and shaping governmental policies regarding critical ethical questions, such as late-term abortions and modern eugenics programs designed to purge the populace of undesirables, reminiscent of the Nazis' "Final Solution."[27]

Crowley's influence on popular culture is hard to miss and impossible to dismiss, particularly in the entertainment industries. Legion are the musicians, songwriters, bands, and record companies that have been—and are—directly inspired by "Crowleyanity." During the golden age of rock and roll, from the late '60s through the late '80s, nearly every chart-topping band had an affinity for Crowley and his cult of Thelema, including The Beatles, The Rolling Stones, Led Zeppelin, The Doors, David Bowie,[28] Pink Floyd, Black Sabbath, Metallica, Guns N' Roses, AC/DC,

---

[24] Crowley, *The Confessions of Aleister Crowley*, 745.

[25] Aleister Crowley, *The Equinox: The Method of Science—The Aim of Religion* (n.p.: Samuel Weiser, 1978), 145.

[26] Without digressing into Hitlerian quotes, Nietzsche's influence is unmistakable in *Mein Kampf.*

[27] The government of Iceland, for example, has recently implemented a policy that encourages parents to abort Down syndrome babies. As a result, close to 100 percent of the fetuses diagnosed with Down syndrome in Iceland are preemptively terminated in the womb.

[28] In the last album he produced before his death, entitled *Blackstar*, David Bowie, a lifelong occultist and Thelemite, brazenly conveys the Luciferian conspiracy in a music video featuring

Aerosmith, and U2. It could be argued that the music industry, such as it is, would never have existed without Aleister Crowley, and the same may be said of the film and TV industry.

Hollywood is perhaps even more sodden with his stench than the sordid world of rock stars. One need only peruse the streaming catalogues of Netflix, Amazon, and Hulu to get a sampling of the Thelemic depravity parading on-screen. Many film and television producers, directors, writers, and actors are Thelemites. Crowley's mandate to "bring the glory of the stars into the hearts of men" has been fully embraced and implemented by the magnates of the entertainment industry (to say nothing of the pornography industry).

The counterculture movement that swept through America in the 1960s was nothing more than a public exposition of Nietzschean philosophy and the Law of Thelema. "God is dead" and "Do what thou wilt" are now the prevailing sociopolitical ideologies and cultural anthems of the West. As a result, atheism is rapidly outpacing every other religious creed, including Christianity and Islam.[29] But atheism is not the endgame. Implausible as it may seem in the current social climate, rest assured that the atheist is a dying breed slated for an inevitable extinction event. To put it more precisely, atheism is evolving.

Denial, as we have noted, is but the prelude of defiance. Charles Lyell removed the foreboding tombstone of the Flood from our ancestral memory, making way for Charles Darwin, who emancipated us from divine accountability, facilitating the philosophy of Friedrich Nietzsche, who emboldened us to abandon biblical morality, culminating in the depravity of Aleister Crowley, who incited us to lawlessness and rebellion.

the album's flagship track of the same name. In the "Blackstar" video, Bowie and his occult acolytes summon the beast to attack Jesus Christ, who is vulgarly depicted as a Jewish criminal hanging on a cross. In the scene directly preceding the beast's appearance, ten women are performing a birthing ritual. These woman represent the human mothers who will give birth to the ten bestial kings, the hybrid progeny of the fallen morning stars. A full analysis of the esoteric symbolism in Bowie's "Blackstar" music video would occupy the pages of an entire chapter. Suffice it to say, "Blackstar" is probably the most occult-laced music video ever produced and the most blatant declaration of the Great Plan ever presented to the public.

[29] See Gabe Bullard, "The World's Newest Major Religion: No Religion," *National Geographic*, April 22, 2016, https://news.nationalgeographic.com/2016/04/160422-atheism-agnostic-secular -nones-rising-religion.

The plan has never been to convince us that God does not exist but to lead us into open war against him. Armageddon is the endgame.

Atheism, the disbelief in God, is soon to evolve into *apotheotheism*,[30] the belief that man can become a god himself. Rather than doubt the existence of Yahweh, apotheotheists demote him to a petty tyrant—an imposter who has many equals in the universe and whose attributes are attainable by means of technology. Whereas atheism is an expression of *denial*, apotheotheism is a posture of *defiance*. Atheism is derived from the doctrine of Darwin, who concludes that man is the product of evolution and has no purpose. Apotheotheism is derived from the doctrine of Nietzsche, who contends that overman *is* the purpose of evolution. The atheist argues that the gods do not exist. The apotheotheist acknowledges that the gods *do* exist and intends to become like them. The atheist declares that man created Yahweh. The apotheotheist is determined to depose him.

ATHEISM *(DENIAL)*	APOTHEOTHEISM *(DEFIANCE)*
Darwin	Nietzsche
• Man is the product of evolution	• Overman is the purpose of evolution
• "The gods do not exist"	• "The gods do exist and we will become like them"
• Man created Yahweh	• Man will depose Yahweh

In 1944, near the end of his ignominious life, Aleister Crowley was corresponding by mail with one Cara Soror, who ventured the question, "Do you believe in God?" Crowley's answer, though cryptic and long-winded in typical fashion, was fundamentally atheistic: he denies the notion of "God with a capital G." The matter would have been left at that if not for the curious postscript at the bottom of the letter:

[30] A term coined by the author from the conjunction of *apotheosis*: the deification of man, and *theism*: belief in the gods.

> My observation of the Universe convinces me that there are
> beings of intelligence and power of a far higher quality than
> anything we can conceive of as human; that they are not nec-
> essarily based on the cerebral and nervous structures that
> we know; and that the one and only chance for mankind to
> advance as a whole is for individuals to make contact with
> such Beings.[31]

Crowley is not referring here to the everyday demonic spirits conjured by the magician but to entities of extraterrestrial provenance. This is where the occultist and the atheist cross paths. It is essential to recognize that the denial of God does not preclude the acceptance of advanced non-human intelligence. An atheist may reject the notion of a divine being while simultaneously embracing the possibility of a superior one. The potential existence of "beings of intelligence and power of a far higher quality than anything we can conceive of as human" presents no difficulty to the atheist. Indeed, the existence of advanced extraterrestrial life is not only accepted within the atheistic worldview but anticipated by most evolutionary biologists.[32]

In 2008, Ben Stein starred in the highly acclaimed documentary film *Expelled: No Intelligence Allowed*. The film featured a fascinating cameo by Richard Dawkins, the British evolutionary biologist of atheist fame, during which Stein managed to extract from Dawkins a stunning admission (which Dawkins no doubt regrets to this day):

> *Stein:* What do you think is the possibility that intelligent
> design might turn out to be the answer to some issues in
> genetics or in evolution?
>
> *Dawkins:* Well, it could come about in the following way: it
> could be that at some earlier time, somewhere in the universe,
> a civilization evolved, by probably some kind of Darwinian

---

[31] Crowley, *Magick without Tears*, 127.

[32] The popular television show *Star Trek* enjoyed widespread secular appeal precisely because it synthesized atheism and extraterrestrials, a combination that was both entertaining and plausible within the Darwinian paradigm.

means, to a very, very high level of technology and designed a form of life that they seeded onto, perhaps, this planet. Now, that is a possibility, and an intriguing possibility, and I suppose it's possible that you might find evidence for that if you look at the detail, the details of biochemistry, molecular biology, you might find a signature of some sort of designer, and that designer could well be a higher intelligence from elsewhere in the universe. But that higher intelligence would itself had to have come about by some explicable, or ultimately explicable, process. It couldn't have just jumped into existence spontaneously. That's the point.

Stein narration: So Professor Dawkins was not against intelligent design, just certain types of designers, such as God.[33]

Dawkins is by no means the only intellectual atheist willing to entertain the possibility that superior extraterrestrial beings could have kick-started the engine of evolution on Earth. A growing number of biologists, physicists, mathematicians, and astronomers are beginning to acknowledge that the spontaneous generation of terrestrial life is highly improbable; in other words, evolution may have a purpose after all. The stage is slowly being set, piece by piece, for the company of heaven to make their grand appearance and reveal the secret that the custodians of the mysteries have guarded for many centuries: it is they who sowed the seeds of life into the primordial soils of Planet Earth, hoping and waiting patiently for the evolution of a species who would awaken with a conscious mind and seek the answers of their existence in the stars. Only when that species became technologically capable of *reaching out* to the cosmos and *reaching in* to modify their own biology would the offspring of the gods appear to guide them in the final steps on the path of apotheosis.

"This—the evolution of man into superman [overman]—was always the purpose of the ancient Mysteries," explains Freemasonic scholar Walter L. Wilmshurst in *The Meaning of Masonry*. "Man, who has sprung

---

[33] Nathan Frankowski, dir., *Expelled: No Intelligence Allowed*, Premise Media Corporation, Rampant Films, 2008.

from the earth and developed through the lower kingdoms of nature to his present rational state, has yet to complete his evolution by becoming a godlike being."[34]

The increasingly feasible prospect of becoming godlike beings has fomented two streams in the project of directed evolution, one *esoteric* and the other *scientific*. The former is primarily concerned with man's spiritual development, the latter with his biological enhancement. In the future, when the essential technologies are sufficiently advanced, these two streams, currently running parallel to one another, will converge into a rushing river. The result will be a new religion for a posthuman paradigm.

Darwin would have been appalled had he lived to see how eagerly his theory was appropriated in the twentieth century by prophets of the New Age. Influential figures such as Pierre Teilhard de Chardin, Barbara Marx Hubbard, Neale Donald Walsch, and Michael Bernard Beckwith, among innumerable others, have been highly effective in proselytizing the gospel of *conscious evolution* ("evolution by choice, not by chance"). Teilhard, a Jesuit priest, and Hubbard, a theosophist, were especially adept at interweaving the scientific vernacular of biological evolution with the esoteric rigamarole of metaphysics, making their teachings more presentable in the faculty lounges of prestigious universities. So influential was Teilhard that his literary work on the evolution of consciousness, once outlawed by the Holy See, is now treated as holy writ in the Jesuit Order, and increasingly in the Roman Catholic Church at large (a situation that has flourished under Pope Francis, the first Jesuit to occupy the Chair of Saint Peter).[35]

The coming one-world religion will be the complement of the one-world government established by the beast. Even now, the old boundaries between creeds, cultures, and languages are beginning to dissolve as information technologies (including social media and universal translators) bring us closer together as a single human family. There will, of course, be outliers who resist the movement toward religious unity (especially

---

[34] Walter L. Wilmshurst, *The Meaning of Masonry* (London: Past Provincial Grand Registrar in West Yorkshire, UGLE, 1920), 20, 40.

[35] Lest this chapter go on ad infinitum, we will forgo an examination of Teilhard's contemplation on the evolution of man and the profusion of New Age materials it inspired (most notably in the works of Barbara Marx Hubbard). A thorough and academic analysis of this topic, and of the coming one-world religion in general, is provided by Lee Penn in *False Dawn: The United Religions Initiative, Globalism, and the Quest for a One-World Religion.*

among radical Muslims, Evangelical Christians, and Orthodox Jews), but the vast majority of people, seduced with the promise of apotheosis, will happily surrender their partisan views and assimilate into the collective.

It may be difficult to imagine the disciples of Crowley breaking bread with the disciples of Christ, but make no mistake about it, the leaven of Luciferianism has thoroughly contaminated the Catholic Church and pervades the Emergent Church.[36] Ever since Vatican II, the Bishops of Rome have been laboring to modify or jettison many of the Church's ancient traditions in order to accommodate the coming one-world religion, which they hope to shepherd.[37]

It is important to recognize that the new religion will be predicated on the revelation that the gods do in fact exist. The gods of the future will not be iconic deities depicted in marble statues or stained glass windows but living and breathing beings walking among us. Like Blavatsky's Theosophists and Crowley's Thelemites, the agents of the Holy See are preparing their church to welcome the Hierarchy, the company of heaven, and embrace Apollo and his consorts as the saviors of mankind.[38]

And, make no mistake about it, Apollo will arrive precisely when mankind needs saving.

---

[36] The Emergent, or Emerging, Church is a postmodernist Christian movement whose mission is to be culturally relevant by making the gospel of Christ more broadly appealing and accommodating to "seekers" from all walks of life. To this end, the traditional teachings of the church, especially as they pertain to uncomfortable subjects (such as sin, damnation, and repentance), are discarded in favor of more attractive messages about love, acceptance, social justice, and prosperity. The Emerging Church movement spans all denominations and is the fastest-growing trend in Christianity today.

[37] In his scholarly work *A Woman Rides the Beast: The Roman Catholic Church and the Last Days*, the late theologian Dave Hunt presents an ironclad case that the woman who rides the beast and is eventually devoured by it, as depicted in Revelation 17, is in fact the Roman Catholic Church. The author vigorously agrees with Hunt's assessment.

[38] Recent conferences on astrobiology hosted by the Pontifical Academy of Sciences and the Vatican Observatory suggest that scholars at the Roman Curia are quietly updating their theology in anticipation of official disclosure of the alien presence. See Archdiocese of Baltimore, "Vatican-Sponsored Meeting Discusses Chances of Extraterrestrial Life," *Catholic Review*, January 19, 2012, https://www.archbalt.org/vatican-sponsored-meeting-discusses-chances-of-extraterrestrial-life; Megan Gannon, "Is Alien Life Out There? Vatican Observatory Co-Hosts Science Conference in Arizona," *Space*, March 14, 2016, https://www.space.com/25060-vatican-observatory-alien-life-conference.html. See also Thomas Horn and Chris Putnam, *Exo-Vaticana: Petrus Romanus, Project L.U.C.I.F.E.R., and the Vatican's Astonishing Plan for the Arrival of an Alien Savior* (Crane, MO: Defender, 2013).

Chapter 11

THE ALIEN THREAT

In the late 1800s, newspapers across the United States and Europe began to publish sensational articles featuring eyewitness accounts of extraordinary flying machines that were suddenly appearing in the sky. Dubbed "mystery airships" by the press, speculation ran wild concerning the technology that powered the craft and the beings that piloted them. Nineteenth-century man had not yet grasped the fundamentals of mechanized aviation; rather, his mind was filled with absurd Victorian-era concepts of aerodynamics and the steampunk fantasies of Jules Verne. Consequently, when recounting the sighting of a distant object traversing the atmosphere, he was inclined to confabulate the accessories deemed necessary for flight. We should not be surprised, then, that mystery airships were sometimes described as having large flapping wings or preposterous configurations of balloons and propellers that could not possibly keep an aircraft aloft in the real world, let alone enable it to perform the advanced aerial maneuvers often witnessed by hundreds of people at a time—maneuvers consonant with modern UFO sightings.

Reports of mystery airships persisted into the twentieth century, but the fanciful descriptions faded from the papers after the Wright brothers breached the heavens with a flying machine of their own and unlocked the secrets of aerodynamics. As intrepid aviators began to take to the skies in the years that followed, they encountered the phenomenon up close and personal. What were once thought to be airships were now described as shiny, metallic objects shaped like orbs, discs, bells, walnuts, or cigars. During World War II, fighter and bomber pilots flying missions in the European and Pacific theaters were often tailed by inexplicable orbs of light.[1] The orbs, officially designated *foo fighters* by the airmen,[2] were a cause for alarm at army intelligence, who worried that the enemy had invented a secret weapon against which there was no defense. Although the foo fighter phenomenon was widely reported in the press, it was not until after the war that the UFO began to assume its familiar form.

In June of 1947, during a routine flight over Mount Rainier, seasoned pilot Kenneth Arnold sighted nine boomerang-shaped objects skimming through the atmosphere at high altitude like "a saucer if you skip it across the water." The objects would later be described in the papers as "flying saucers."[3] In July of the same year, the *Roswell Daily Record* in Roswell, New Mexico, ran an astonishing headline that read, "RAAF Captures Flying Saucer on Ranch in Roswell Region." The article was based on an official press release from the US Army Air Forces that announced the recovery of a crashed "flying disc" of unknown origin. The press release was summarily retracted and replaced with a dubious story about a weather balloon,[4] but not before attracting national intrigue. The army's overt cover-up kindled the fire of UFO conspiracy and established the flying saucer as a permanent fixture of popular culture.

In the wake of the Roswell incident, a profusion of UFO-related content began appearing in books, radio broadcasts, television talk shows, and blockbuster films. But as the public became more interested in UFOs, the government became more entrenched in its policy of nondisclosure[5] . . .

---

[1] The luminescent orbs reported by pilots during WWII were likely reconnaissance drones dispatched from UFOs trailing their aircraft at a greater distance. Orbs are commonly associated with UFO sightings and have been seen deploying from cigar- and disc-shaped craft.

[2] The designation was inspired by the comic strip "Smokey Stover," in which Smokey (a firefighter) would often declare, "Where there's foo, there's fire." See Adam Janos, "Mysterious UFOs Seen by WWII Airman Still Unexplained," *History.com*, January 15, 2020, https://www.history.com /news/wwii-ufos-allied-airmen-orange-lights-foo-fighters.

[3] See "Kenneth Arnold," *History.com*, December 15, 2018, https://www.history.com/topics /paranormal/kenneth-arnold.

[4] See Adam Janos, "What Really Happened at Roswell?" *History.com*, December 17, 2019, https:// www.history.com/news/roswell-ufo-aliens-what-happened.

[5] For a detailed history of the UFO cover-up in the United States, I highly recommend Richard

that is, until recently. After seventy years of systematic denial, obfuscation, persecution of whistleblowers, and aggressive secrecy, the Pentagon is finally breaking its vow of silence.

On December 17, 2017, *The New York Times* published an article featuring an embedded video alleged to be footage captured by the gun camera of an F-18 Super Hornet jet that locked onto a "Tic Tac–shaped" UFO moving at impossible speeds. The article claimed that the video was leaked from the portfolio of a hitherto secret military program, the Advanced Aerospace Threat Identification Program (AATIP), which had been investigating and tracking UAPs (unidentified aerial phenomena) since 2007. The Pentagon initially declined to comment on the "Nimitz incident" (named after the aircraft carrier that scrambled the F-18), until September of 2019, when the Navy announced that the footage was indeed authentic.[6] In April of 2020, the US Department of Defense took the extraordinary step of formally releasing three videos of UFOs (including the aforementioned), with the stunning admission that the phenomenon they depict is real (and, by implication, a potential threat).[7] This was the first affirmative acknowledgment of "flying saucers" by the US military since the retracted Roswell press release in 1947.

In July of 2020, *The New York Times* published another explosive article that included the testimony of astrophysicist Eric W. Davis, who claimed to have examined materials retrieved from "off-world vehicles not made on this earth." Mr. Davis told the *Times* that he had conducted classified briefings on retrievals of unexplained objects to the Senate Armed Services Committee and the Senate Intelligence Committee in October of 2019.[8] Mr. Davis's claims have not been disputed by committee staff members or the Pentagon.

Dolan's comprehensive work *UFOs and the National Security State: The Cover-Up Exposed, 1973–1991* (Vol. I) and *Chronology of a Cover-Up, 1941–1973* (Vol. II).

[6] See Mosheh Gains and Phil Helsel, "Navy Confirms Videos Did Capture UFO Sightings, but It Calls Them by Another Name," *NBC News*, September 19, 2019, https://www.nbcnews.com /news/us-news/navy-confirms-videos-did-capture-ufo-sightings-it-calls-them-n1056201.

[7] See Michael Conte, "Pentagon Officially Releases UFO Videos," *CNN*, April 29, 2020, https:// www.cnn.com/2020/04/27/politics/pentagon-ufo-videos/index.html.

[8] See Ralph Blumenthal and Leslie Kean, "No Longer in Shadows, Pentagon's U.F.O. Unit Will Make Some Findings Public," *New York Times*, July 23, 2020, https://www.nytimes .com/2020/07/23/us/politics/pentagon-ufo-harry-reid-navy.html.

In light of these recent developments, we can finally declare, once and for all, that the controversy is over. As former Canadian Minister of Defense Paul Hellyer was fond of saying, "UFOs are as real as the airplanes that fly over your head."[9]

The government's admission that UFOs are real is essentially a confession that they are powerless to inhibit an alien faction of unknown origin from trafficking through the airspace above our cities in unfathomably advanced technological hardware. There are some researchers (especially in the Evangelical community) who argue that UFOs do not actually constitute a physical phenomenon but a supernatural one; a few even go so far as to suggest that they are demons or fallen angels. As noted in an earlier chapter, the inherent ambiguity and elasticity of the word *supernatural* strips it of explanatory power. The hypothesis that demons or angels are somehow morphing into flying saucers is nonfalsifiable, nonsensical, and self-defeating.

There is also a popular belief (again, among Evangelicals) that the UFO phenomenon is merely a deceptive ruse perpetrated by spiritual beings masquerading as aliens in the upper atmosphere (a realm they relegate to the devil, per Ephesians 2). That is to say, UFOs are not composed of nuts-and-bolts hardware but are sophisticated metaphysical illusions. Whereas the intentions behind these theories may be admirable (in that they are meant to combat perceived demonic deception), they are also unsupported by logic and unsubstantiated by the facts. The corporeality of the phenomenon is not in dispute among military officials concerned with advanced aerospace threats. UFOs are often tracked on radar before being pursued by fighter pilots who get close enough to make visual contact (as in the Nimitz incident mentioned above). Radar detection is an important feature of the phenomenon, because it proves beyond doubt that UFOs are physical objects.[10] As far as the Pentagon (and the author) is concerned, the critical question does not pertain to the obvious

---

[9] Stated during the Exopolitics Toronto Symposium on "UFO Disclosure and Planetary Direction," September 25, 2005.

[10] Radar antennas transmit beams of high-frequency radio waves through the atmosphere that collide with physical objects and reflect back to the receivers. The frequencies used to detect aircraft (as opposed to water vapor—i.e., clouds) only reflect off the surface of unmistakably solid objects.

corporeality of the craft but to the nature and intent of the creatures who build and pilot them.

In the decades following the Roswell incident, investigation into the subject of UFOs was largely limited to eyewitness accounts of ambivalent sightings, many of which turned out to have mundane explanations. Ufologists spent much (if not most) of their time sifting through endless cases of lights in the sky and distant unidentifiable objects hovering or darting high above casual observers. Every now and again, a gem appeared in the pile, revealing, if only for a fleeting moment, the diminutive figures of the beings who piloted the craft. These incidents usually entailed saucer-, teardrop-, or egg-shaped vessels beaming with brightly colored lights as they landed in remote localities, followed by a brief disembarkation of their occupants; but such cases were rare and difficult, if not impossible, to verify. In short, researchers had mountains of data related to UFO sightings but almost nothing at all in regard to who and what was inside of them . . . until the early 1980s, when case after case of alien abduction began to surface.

The alien abduction phenomenon is the most important thing happening on Planet Earth. It is also the most overlooked, misconstrued, and convoluted aspect of ufology. This is due, in large part, to its association with the New Age and spiritualism. The internet is replete with fantastical tales of alien encounters involving entities of all shapes and sizes. A growing number of people claim to be in ongoing contact with benevolent ETs who take them for joyrides in their saucers and send them messages through telepathic communication. Some even refer to themselves as "starseed," meaning they are not fully human but the hybrid progeny of ETs—chosen ambassadors of galactic light who were born into the world to raise the consciousness of mankind and bridge the gap between the two species they represent. That such beliefs instill a sense of transcendent purpose in the individuals who hold them does not negate the fact that they are entirely fictitious and have nothing at all to do with the systematic, secret, and nefarious agenda of the real alien abduction phenomenon.

For over a century now, hundreds of millions of people around the globe have been, and are, systematically abducted by nonhuman entities and involuntarily incorporated into a highly organized and clandestine breeding program. These abductees, when interviewed by competent professionals, tell the same general story with the same set of basic details, even though the majority of them are entirely unfamiliar with abduction research material and relatively uninterested in UFOs. The abductees span every walk of life, from blue-collar workers to white-collar business moguls, lawyers, engineers, physicians, politicians, professional athletes, Christians, Muslims, Buddhists, atheists, agnostics, and everything in between. "The abduction phenomenon cuts across all social, political, religious, educational, intellectual, economic, racial, ethnic and geographic lines," writes leading abduction researcher Dr. David Jacobs. "[The] phenomenon is global. People describe the same things in the same detail worldwide, regardless of cultural differences."[11]

Recently retired from his post as a professor of history at Temple University, Dr. Jacobs, along with his lettered colleagues, such as the late Harvard professor Dr. John Mack, have spent their careers examining the abduction phenomenon with scientific scrutiny. After conducting thousands of interviews and investigations, these men, together with other qualified researchers, have concluded that alien abduction, and the breeding program it entails, is as routine a reality for many people as getting up in the morning and going to work. The field of abduction research, when properly conducted, is not a realm of New Age fantasies or baseless conclusions; rather, it is a science of evidence, corroborative testimony, and verifiable facts that have never been and cannot be refuted.

Dr. Mack, a Pulitzer Prize winner and former head of the Department of Psychiatry at Harvard Medical School, maintained that in order to challenge the reality of alien abduction, an alternative psychiatric theory would have to account for the following five dimensions of the phenomenon:

1. The high degree of consistency of detailed abductions accounts, reported with emotion appropriate to actual experiences told by apparently reliable observers.

---

[11] David M. Jacobs, *Walking Among Us: The Alien Plan to Control Humanity* (San Francisco: Disinformation Books, 2015), 13.

2. The absence of psychiatric illness or other apparent psychological or emotional factors that could account for what is being reported.

3. The physical changes and lesions affecting the bodies of the experiencers, which follow no evident psychodynamic pattern.

4. The association with UFOs witnessed independently by others while abductions are taking place (which the abductee may not see).

5. The reports of abductions by children as young as two or three years of age.[12]

As a psychiatrist, Dr. Mack was uniquely qualified to evaluate the testimony of alien abductees and weigh them against every known psychological disorder. He was adamant in insisting that the majority of abductees were mentally sound individuals, everyday people who were involuntarily subjected to the extraordinary circumstances of a phenomenon they could not control nor evade.

As a historian, Dr. Jacobs was trained to methodically analyze events in sequence from a pragmatic and nonpartisan point of view. Like Dr. Mack, he offered a list of facts that must be accounted for in the formulation of an alternative explanation that seeks to gainsay the physical reality of the phenomenon. They include the following:

- When people are abducted, they are physically missing from their normal environment.

- People are sometimes abducted in groups and can confirm each other's reports.

- Bystanders sometimes see people being abducted.

[12] John E. Mack, *Abduction: Human Encounters with Aliens* (New York: Scribner, 1994), 29; John E. Mack, "Why the Abduction Phenomenon Cannot be Explained Psychiatrically," in *Alien Discussions: Proceedings of the Abduction Study Conference, MIT* (Cambridge, MA: North Cambridge Press, 1992).

- When returned to their normal environment after an abduction, people often have marks, cuts, bruises, broken bones, and even fully formed scars (a biological impossibility) that were not there before the abduction.

- When returned, people sometimes have their clothes on inside out or backward, or they are wearing someone else's clothes. In these cases, they clearly remember dressing themselves correctly beforehand.

- Most of what abductees describe has no antecedents in popular culture.

- Abductions occur at all times of the day and night, depending on access to the abductees and when they will be least missed. Abductees need not be sleeping.

- Abductions begin in childhood and continue with varying frequency into old age.

- The abduction phenomenon is intergenerational. The children of abductees often themselves report being abductees, as do their children.

- Abductions are unrelated to alcohol or drugs.[13]

Both Mack and Jacobs stress that most abductees fear being abducted and desperately want the ongoing experience to end. They also note that many of those seeking help in understanding what is happening to them are high-functioning professionals who testify against their own interests, knowing full well that should their colleagues find out, their careers would be jeopardized.

Unlike the sporadic and unpredictable sightings of UFOs, the abduction phenomenon lends itself to scientific analysis precisely because of its systematic and predictable procedures, which are commonly reported by abductees around the world and corroborated with remarkable detail.

---

[13] Jacobs, *Walking Among Us*, 12–13.

In his book *Secret Life: Firsthand Documented Accounts of UFO Abductions*, Jacobs frames the classic prelude of an abduction episode:

> An unsuspecting woman is in her room preparing to go to bed. She gets into bed, reads a while, turns off the light, and drifts off into a peaceful night's sleep. In the middle of the night she turns over and lies on her back. She is awakened by a light that seems to be glowing in her room. The light moves toward her bed and takes the shape of a small "man" with a bald head and huge black eyes. She is terrified. She wants to run but she cannot move. She wants to scream but she cannot speak. The "man" moves toward her and looks deeply into her eyes. Suddenly she is calmer, and she "knows" that the "man" is not going to hurt her.
>
> This is a typical beginning of an abduction. Virtually all abductees have experienced this. From the first few seconds of an abduction, nothing is within the realm of normal human experience. It is an instant descent into the fantastic and bizarre. Technology and bio-technology that seem like magic are immediately apparent. Once the event begins, humans are powerless to stop it. When it is over, most victims cannot remember it.[14]

"One common characteristic of an abduction experience," notes researcher Budd Hopkins in his groundbreaking book *Missing Time*, "is the merging in memory of its onset and its conclusion, a joining so seamless as to leave the abductee with no *feeling* that he or she has actually lost any time, despite what clocks and simple vision may establish beyond any doubt."[15] Hopkins was a pioneer in alien abduction research and one of the first to highlight the problem of missing time frequently reported by individuals who had experienced a close encounter with a UFO. It turns out that the time was not missing at all but fully accounted for onboard the alien craft.

[14] David M. Jacobs, *Secret Life: Firsthand Documented Accounts of UFO Abductions* (New York: Fireside, 1993), 49–50.
[15] Budd Hopkins, *Intruders: The Incredible Visitations at Copley Woods* (New York: Random House, 1987), 11.

Dr. Jacobs continues,

> Once the abductee has been transported to and entered the alien craft, the primary experiences begin. These involve those procedures that the aliens perform the greatest number of times on the greatest number of people, including physical and mental examinations, and reproductive procedures that are ultimately directed to the production of offspring. . . .
>
> The aliens bring the abductee into the main examining room. Although disoriented, she can still observe what is happening to her. She sees frightening-looking Beings who are busily going about their tasks, seemingly paying no attention to her. But other aliens are waiting for her. They are small—about three and one-half to four feet tall. These Small Beings are usually gray, tan, pale white (not Caucasian), or "colorless." They have bald, bulbous craniums. Their immense eyes are dark, with no pupils or corneas. They either have no nose or it is so slight that it is unnoticeable, and their small, slit-like mouth does not move. They have no ears. Their bodies are very thin. They either wear nothing or what appears to be form-fitting clothing.
>
> The examining room is small and circular. It might contain a ledge or "walkway" around the perimeter that appears to be part of the wall itself. Sometimes apparatuses or machines are in the room, often attached to the walls and ceiling. The room lighting is diffuse. It can range from bright to dim, but the origin of the lighting cannot be seen. The entire room closely resembles a hospital operating room. It is serviceable and functional; it is neat and clean. The dominant colors of the "metallic" walls and floor are white and gray.
>
> The central feature of the room is the table. It is made of a "metallic" or plasticlike material supported by a pedestal. Stationed around the table are carts that contain instruments and other machinelike devices. There might be from one to four tables in a small room and up to two hundred in a large room.

When the aliens escort the abductee into a very large room, she silently passes other tables containing naked humans lying in rows in various stages of examination. It is eerily quiet. She hears only the clanging of instruments, the shuffling of feet, and an occasional moan from the victims.

The Small Beings lead the abductee to the table and, if she still has her clothes on, assist her in removing them. They allow the clothes to fall to the floor and remain there for the duration of the experience. She then gets up on the table and lies down.[16]

What follows, as Jacobs, Mack, Hopkins, and others came to realize, is not an examination but a program of hybridization carried out in a series of stages that are repeated throughout the duration of an abductee's life. As the program is reproductive in nature, the procedures differ for males and females. Men generally have sperm extracted and are sometimes forced to have sexual intercourse with alien-human hybrid females. Women generally have ova extracted and are subjected to more invasive procedures related to their internal reproductive organs. "The ova are fertilized *in vitro* with the sperm," explains Dr. Jacobs, "and the resulting zygote is altered in some way to create a hybrid."

The aliens implant the altered embryo during another abduction. Between nine and eleven weeks post-implantation, when the women are about to "show," the aliens extract the fetus and put it into a gestation tank filled with liquid nutrients. Eventually, they remove the fully developed babies from the tanks. Abductees and hybrids then help raise the hybrid offspring. Abductees are required to interact with the offspring from childhood to adulthood. They hold and feed hybrid babies, play with toddlers, interact with adolescents, and teach the hybrids about life on Earth.[17]

[16] Jacobs, *Secret Life*, 87–88.
[17] Jacobs, *Walking Among Us*, 38.

The abductors performing these procedures are known as the "grays," due to the pallid grayish complexion of their skin. They are the typical alien figures epitomized in popular culture. To reiterate Dr. Jacobs's description, the grays have big, bulbous craniums that taper into a pointed chin with small indentations in the place of ears and nostrils, and a slit for a mouth. Their most prominent feature—recalled with a cold shudder by all abductees—is their deep black, almond-shaped eyes that nearly span the width of their head. The grays come in two sizes, small and tall. Small grays are about three to three and a half feet tall. Their slender bodies are situated rather awkwardly beneath their disproportionately large heads. Tall grays are nearly identical, except that they are about four to four and a half feet tall.

The disposition of gray aliens is dispassionate and robotic. They never display the slightest semblance of emotion, even when abductees are less than cooperative. They go about their business like automatons dutifully performing their function as the labor force in the abduction program.[18] The grays are dispatched to fetch abductees and escort them into the alien craft for processing, which is methodical and orderly. They perform all of the menial tasks onboard, including the procedures related to the production of hybrids mentioned above, but they are not the only beings present in the vessel. A hierarchy of races is manifest among the aliens.

The grays, whose anatomy is somewhat similar to our own, seem to be subject to a more exotic race of entities with features altogether inhuman. These creatures, whom Jacobs denominates *insectalins*, have been described by abductees as having praying mantis-like heads with large, almond-shaped eyes that point diagonally downward toward the bottom of their face, which terminates in a slender, lipless mouth rather than a chin. Like the grays, the insectalins have a pallid grayish complexion, but in stark contrast with their diminutive minions, they stand over six feet tall. Their arms and legs (they have two of each) are long and spindly, as are their fingers. Both the grays and insectalins wear a form-fitting

---

[18] Due to their robotic behavior, some researchers have speculated that the grays are actually biological machines of some kind specifically designed to perform their task. Others have posited that they are themselves cloned hybrids, possibly created from the genetic material of the human species. I believe that both of these hypotheses are simultaneously correct. The grays are cloned automatons composed of human and alien genetic material.

fabric that is almost indistinguishable from their flesh. As bizarre as it sounds, the insectalins are sometimes draped in capes with high collars encircling their thin necks. They are the commanders onboard the alien craft and the managers of the abduction program. Whether they are the masterminds of the program is not clear. (As a general rule, we will refer to the small, bulbous-headed aliens and their insectalin overlords collectively as the "grays").

All communication between the alien races and their human captives is telepathic. The aliens do not talk with their mouths or vocalize their thoughts in any audible way; rather, they project their thoughts like radio waves into the minds of abductees. I suspect that the ability to communicate telepathically is inherent but dormant in the human species. Our radios are broken, so to speak. We can still receive and broadcast brainwave transmissions, but we have lost the ability to tune and interpret them. Candidacy for abduction may very well be linked to hereditary bloodlines in which the psychic faculty is more highly developed, or less degenerated. Many abductees claim to have received empathic abilities from the aliens, when in reality it is likely that they were chosen precisely because of their latent predisposition to telepathy, which was merely activated by their abductors. As will become apparent, there is a strategic correlation between your neighborhood psychic and alien abductees.

The acute telepathic capabilities of the aliens facilitate not only communication with the abductees but also control of them. Both the grays and the insectalins have the power to manipulate the human mind and implant false memories, known as "screens." The telepathic manipulation of the insectalins is particularly potent. One of the procedures to which all abductees are routinely subjected has been described as a "mind scan," or as Dr. Jacobs calls it, neural engagement. During neural engagement, the alien (typically a tall gray or insectalin) will position its head directly in front of the abductee's so that their faces are only inches apart. The abductee is then forced to gaze into the alien's deep black eyes as it probes his or her mind and implants false memories to suppress or subvert any recollection of the abduction episode. The real memories, still present in the subconscious, are sequestered behind a series of screen memories designed to deflect access to them.[19] The process is not fail-safe. Sometimes abductees are able to recall an abduction episode, or fragments of an episode, without having to circumvent a screen memory, but this is rare.[20] The vast majority are left with bizarre, fuzzy memories about flying saucers and little men who come to visit them from time to time. Most write them off as dreams.

Aside from the grays and the insectalins, there are also hybrids onboard the alien craft performing a variety of tasks. Progenerated through the breeding program, the appearance of the hybrids corresponds to the ratio of alien to human DNA in their genomes. Generally speaking, the spectrum of their physiology ranges from nearly alien to nearly human and everything in between. On the nearly alien end of the spectrum, the hybrids look most like the grays but with some human features; they are taller than the grays and have disproportionately bulbous heads, overly large eyes, slender limbs, small noses, thin lips, and straggly hair (the aliens have no hair). On the nearly human end of the spectrum, they are practically indistinguishable from everyday men and women, but appearances can be deceiving.

Through a process of trial and error over the last century, it would seem that the insectalins have perfected a hybrid with the precise genotypic and phenotypic ratios so as to look entirely human but retain the telepathic powers of the aliens. Disturbingly, these advanced hybrids, whom Jacobs denominates *hubrids*, are designed to seamlessly blend into

---

[19] For example, an abductee may first remember a "dream" in which an owl was perched on the nightstand next to her bed, gazing down at her with its big black eyes and conversing with her in her mind; until she realizes that it wasn't a dream and it wasn't an owl but a gray alien, indeed several gray aliens, come to abduct her in the usual manner. The aliens also cleverly play on the preconceptions and belief systems of their abductees. A person who subscribes to New Age beliefs may be presented with a screen memory involving loving encounters with benevolent ETs during which important spiritual knowledge is imparted. In reality, the false recollection is masking the usual table procedures related to the breeding program. Christians are sometimes implanted with screen memories involving angels and demons and even the figure of Christ himself. The popular contention that "demons are masquerading as aliens" is most certainly true in reverse. Aliens are masquerading as demons through screen memories.

[20] There are ways for abductees to unlock the real memories behind the screens, such as through relaxation techniques and hypnotic regression. Suppressed memories may also be unlocked through mind-altering substances like LSD, DMT, and mescaline. This is why people sometimes see gray aliens when tripping on psychedelic drugs; they are inadvertently retrieving fragments of suppressed memories, including the faces of their abductors.

the human populace as undercover agents for their insectalin overlords. Even more disturbingly, the hubrids seem to be conspicuously lacking in a particular human trait—empathy. They have no moral inhibitions and no regard for human suffering. They act only in the interest of the alien program.

Before we venture to speculate about the purpose of the program, we need to spend some time deconstructing misconceptions concerning the abduction phenomenon and the nature of the gray aliens.

To begin with, it is commonly believed that alien abductions are not physical but metaphysical experiences associated with occultism, drug-induced hallucinations, sleep paralysis, out-of-body experiences, demon possession, or demonic activity in general, among other things. Those who adopt this view have likely fallen victim to the falsehoods circulating online and are not well versed in the scientific data that proves the physical nature of the phenomenon beyond all doubt. Abductees, for example, are physically removed from their environments and transported onto nuts-and-bolts vessels, where they are subjected to a series of bodily procedures conducted by flesh-and-blood entities, including the insertion of implants into various parts of their anatomy.[21] When they are returned to the point of abduction, they are often left with scars consistent with the

---

[21] Alien implants represent hard evidence and definitive proof of the abduction phenomenon. Typically the size of a tiny pill, the implants are inserted into various parts of the body, especially in the upper nasal cavity, behind the eye, behind the ear, and in the back of the head and neck, but also in the hands, legs, ankles, and feet. The hardware of the implants consists of rare earth metals, which are sometimes encased within an organic membrane. The metals have been found to contain isotopes that are extremely rare or nonexistent on earth. Doctors have observed that, contrary to other foreign objects inserted into living tissue, the implants do not provoke an inflammatory response. Research suggests that they may also emit an electromagnetic field while in the body. It is probable that the implants serve several practical functions related to the abduction program. They likely operate as tracking devices that enable the aliens to easily locate and apprehend abductees. They may also facilitate the monitoring and control of certain bodily functions, such as nervous system reactions or signals from the brain. The aliens may use the implants to sedate and immobilize abductees before an abduction episode in order to neutralize resistance. This may be why the phenomenon is often associated with sleep paralysis. As we do not understand the technology, the possibilities are endless. Several reputable physicians have performed technical analyses on implants they have personally removed, confirming the information cited above. The most notable of these was the late Dr. Roger Leir, whose unimpeachable methods of research and remarkable conclusions have never been refuted. For more information related to implants, see "Alien Implant Removals: Before and After Effects," Mutual UFO Network, April 3, 1998, https://www.mufon.com /alien-implants/alien-implant-removals-before-and-after-effects.

procedures performed on them. Single women, even virgins, who have not had intercourse are often found to be pregnant after an abduction episode and then inexplicably pronounced to be without child by their bewildered gynecologists a few months later. To insist that the phenomenon is not physical is to ignore these facts and insult the intelligence of the people who report them.

Researchers who are persuaded that abductions are metaphysical experiences have mistaken advanced technology for supernaturalism. "Any sufficiently advanced technology is indistinguishable from magic," Arthur C. Clarke rightly observed. The aliens command a level of technology that simply defies human comprehension. They have the ability to appear and disappear, levitate, and transport themselves and their abductees through closed windows.[22] What many casual researchers fail to realize is that these seemingly supernatural powers are only operational when the alien craft is in close proximity. The technology that facilitates these abilities is sometimes visible as a beam of light projected through the windows. If there are no windows in the room where the abductee happens to be located during an abduction episode, then the grays lead him or her into a room that does have a window for transport through the beam. When the craft is not in proximity, abductees are led by the hand through the house, out the back door, through the yard, across the street, through the woods, and into an open field where the craft has landed. This course of action often occurs during mass abductions when multiple abductees are taken from the same neighborhood at the same time.

It is important to reiterate that the abduction phenomenon is intergenerational. In other words, it is hereditary. If one of your parents was an abductee, then you and your children are also being abducted and incorporated into the breeding program. I have found no exceptions to this rule. Abductions are not isolated events. Abductees are continually taken by the grays from the time they are toddlers into adulthood. By the time they are elderly, they have experienced hundreds, if not thousands, of abduction episodes.

Abductee family lines are not race-, religion-, or culture-specific. There

---

[22] This is why nearly all abductees have recurring "dreams" in which they are lying prone while floating through windows and walls, or up through the ceiling.

may be several reasons why the aliens choose to abduct successive members of the same family. The first is convenience. Children of abductees are conveniently abducted from the same environment as their parents. Children play a special role in the program. They are often forced to interact and play with hybrid children onboard the alien craft, probably in the interest of acclimating them to human interaction and social norms. The aliens are likely also selecting for specific hereditary traits which are vital components in the genetic profile of the hybrids.

Most Christian researchers who have braved the topic are convinced that the prime objective of the abduction program is deception. This is not so. Deception is a means to an end, not an end in itself. A protocol of deception is perpetuated to conceal the breeding program. The aliens do not want us to know what they are doing. They do not communicate their intentions to abductees, and they do not engage in theological messaging. Humans are not being indoctrinated by the aliens but harvested for genetic material.

These well-meaning researchers often make the mistake of conflating *abductees* with *contactees*. Contactees are individuals who claim to be in contact with extraterrestrials, from whom they allegedly receive important messages for humanity regarding future events or spiritual concepts (which are often hostile to biblical doctrines). Contactees were a cultural phenomenon in the 1940s and continued through the 1960s. Several contactee personalities became household names, such as George Adamski, who styled himself as a liaison between the citizens of Earth and their friendly neighborhood "Space Brothers" from elsewhere in the solar system. Adamski claimed to be in ongoing contact with a human-like alien race, who frequently treated him to fantastic escapades onboard their flying saucers. Naturally, the phenomenon, which included spirit channeling, was embraced by the New Age, where it is fostered to this day.

Modern contactees fancy themselves as ambassadors of love and light who convey telepathic communications from benevolent ETs, which are usually transcribed via automatic writing. These individuals are seeking attention. They often publish books and speak in conferences about their experiences, but without providing a shred of verifiable evidence. No ufologist worth his salt takes the contactee phenomenon seriously. At best, it is a delusion of mentally disturbed individuals craving validation. At worst, it is divination and intercourse with demons. The contactee phenomenon has nothing whatsoever to do with the abduction phenomenon and should not be conflated with it. Abductees are victims. Publicity is the last thing they want. They are usually too frightened and embarrassed to come forward with their experiences, and for good reason. They have nothing to gain by doing so and everything to lose. Abductees who are willing to share their experiences in publications usually do so under the cover of an alias to conceal their identity.

We have so far discussed the nature of the abduction phenomenon without remark on the nature of the abductors themselves. Little can be known for certain in this regard, except that they are *alien* in every sense of the word and deceptive at all times. But the fact that they are deceptive does not mean that they are demonic. Contrary to popular belief, aliens are *not* demons.

The temptation to write the abduction phenomenon off as a supernatural deception is typically accompanied by the assertion that the abductors are nothing more than demons. Having previously defined the origin and nature of demons, it should be clear that they have nothing to do with gray aliens. Demons are the disembodied spirits that proceeded from the deceased progeny of the watchers in the pre-Flood world. They do not themselves manifest as physical beings but possess the physical bodies of their hosts.

It has been suggested that the grays were created with the express purpose of embodying demonic spirits—that they are "flesh suits" for demons, so to speak. This theory, though certainly innovative, is not logically sound. The nature of demonic spirits is exactly antithetical to the disposition of the grays. Demons are wild and ravenous beings consumed only with the desire to ameliorate the torment of their miserable condition by inhabiting bodies of flesh through which to satiate their otherwise insatiable lusts. Indeed, if one were to design a body to be maximally unappealing to demonic spirits, one could do no better than the gray alien. The grays are most definitely not built for pleasure. They do not have sexual organs (that anyone has ever reported); they do not have articulating mandibles, teeth or tongues, for the mastication and enjoyment of food (they absorb liquid nutrients); and even should they desire pleasure (and there is no evidence that they do), they have no time to indulge in it, as they are unceasingly occupied with the retrieval and processing of abductees.[23]

It was the French computer scientist, astronomer, and ufologist Jacques Vallée who, in his classic book *Passport to Magonia: From Folklore to Flying Saucers*, gave legs to what is today called the "demon theory of UFOs." Written in 1968, the book examines the folklore of various cultures relating to contact with fairy-tale creatures such as pixies, elves, dwarfs, gnomes, and cloud people from Magonia, a magical land in the sky. Vallée proposed that what we call the UFO phenomenon is merely the modern repackaging of the same old supernatural chicanery that has been occurring on Earth for millennia. He was one of the first to popularize the interdimensional hypothesis (IDH), which posits that the "alien" entities interacting with mankind are not necessarily extraterrestrial but interdimensional.

According to the hypothesis, deceptive interdimensional beings have been switching masks, as it were, modulating how they present themselves to mankind in order to adapt to the cultural mores, belief systems, and superstitions of each passing era. Christian UFO researchers were quick to embrace Vallée's theory, because it seemed to provide a more biblically compatible explanation for the phenomenon than extraterrestrials.[24] And it was an easy adaptation. Aliens from a distant planet were simply replaced by demons from an interdimensional world. Mystery solved.

Convenient though it may be, the demon theory of UFOs is fatally flawed. Alien hardware is real. There is plenty of evidence that UFOs (discounting the orbs) are nuts-and-bolts aerospace vehicles, including the fact that they are routinely detected on radar and then pursued by

---

[23] At the risk of sounding vulgar, it should be noted that abductees are always stripped naked before the table procedures begin onboard the alien craft. One can only imagine the internal torment of sexually voracious spirits surrounded by hundreds of incapacitated naked bodies while they themselves are trapped within the stoic anatomy of gray aliens and entirely incapable of indulging in the act.

[24] In truth, Vallée's theory does not correspond to any biblical doctrine. There are no pixies, elves, dwarfs, or gnomes in the Bible, and demons do not behave like these fairy-tale creatures. Rather, the theory is consistent with medieval Christian superstitions, which depict demons as tricksters who like to disguise themselves in various forms to seduce or hoodwink unsuspecting humans.

fighter pilots, who manage to get close enough to make visual confirmation.[25] One must also consider the credible stories of crash retrievals and reverse engineered technologies that have surfaced over the decades, with corroborating evidence.[26] As far as I know, demons are not in the habit of manufacturing technological hardware.[27]

It is important to note that *Passport to Magonia* was written well over a decade before serious research into alien abductions had begun. While Vallée's ideas are compelling, they do not correspond with the scientific data compiled by competent abduction researchers in the years following the publishing of his book. There are no accounts of gray aliens in the folklore of ancient peoples and nothing at all even remotely resembling the systematic breeding program presently underway. We should not conflate folklore with scientific fact, nor should we attempt to correlate UFO and abduction phenomena with the superstitious fairy tales of medieval times.

Today, millions of people all over the earth are being routinely taken from their homes, their cars, their boats, their beach houses, their campers, and wherever else they happen to be by alien beings who subject them to invasive physical procedures that leave scars on their bodies and babies in their wombs. There has never before been a phenomenon like this in recorded history. And it is no respecter of persons. Evangelical Christians are just as routinely abducted as non-Christians, including priests, pastors, prayer "warriors," and "watchmen."

The popular claim that alien abductions can be interrupted by invoking the name of Jesus is patently false. Abduction accounts are filled with instances in which sincere Christians vigorously rebuke their abductors to no avail (the author has personally interviewed believers who have testified to this fact). Being abducted by gray aliens is, to some extent, no

---

[25] In 2020, the Navy released incident reports detailing eight encounters between Navy pilots and UFOs off the US East Coast. See Ralph Blumenthal and Leslie Kean, "Navy Reports Describe Encounters with Unexplained Flying Objects," *New York Times*, May 14, 2020, https://www.nytimes.com/2020/05/14/us/politics/navy-ufo-reports.html.

[26] Especially per the testimony of Colonel Philip J. Corso and physicist Bob Lazar, discussed in detail below.

[27] Manufacturing is a dimension of the UFO phenomenon that is often overlooked. The craft do not merely pop out of thin air, they have to be designed according to precise mathematical specifications and then fabricated through some industrial process. This kind of organization implies a highly sophisticated society with a systemized body of scientific knowledge and a complex language that enables them to conceptualize and engineer technological hardware.

different than being abducted by human traffickers.[28] In both cases, you are taken by force and compelled against your will to lend your body to strangers who sexually abuse you. At least in the case of the aliens, you are returned home after the ordeal little worse for wear.

I have observed that Bible-believing Christians who also happen to be abductees are psychologically oppressed by the demon theory of UFOs. If aliens are demons, they reason, and invoking the name of Jesus is ineffectual, as many have experienced, then they can only conclude that their faith in Christ is inadequate and their soul is in peril. I have also observed that some of the Christian ufologists promoting the demon theory and its invocative solution are abductees themselves wrestling with denial. Their claims are based on their own subjective experiences and the testimony of others who have reported that, while being lifted from their bed during the onset of an abduction, they rebuked the aliens in the name of Jesus and were promptly returned to the pillow. This scenario is not surprising. It is a well-established fact that abductees often only remember the beginning and the end of an abduction episode—the moment they are lifted off their bed and the moment they are gently returned to it. Considering the efficacy of screen memories, it is ill-advised to promote the success of a faith-evoking solution based on the foggy recollection of an incident that is supposed to be forgotten. Alien abductions have no bearing whatsoever on a person's faith in Christ, or lack thereof.

Although aliens are not demons, the interdimensional hypothesis, while largely misconceived, is not without merit. We spent some time in an earlier chapter examining the nature of the universe and our perception of it. We noted that, like the prisoners in Plato's allegory of the cave, we,

---

[28] There may be cases in which an abductee has been liberated from the breeding program through prayer, but if they exist, they are the exception and not the rule. There is no evidence that rebuking a human trafficker in the name of Jesus will stop them from abducting you. Why do we assume that the formula will work on aliens? Many Christians around the world have suffered at the hands of hostile assailants without the benefit of divine intervention. How many Iraqi girls from devout Christian families, sold into slavery after their fathers and husbands were murdered by ISIS insurgents, rebuked their abductors in the name of Jesus before they were put in chains and marched to the slave market? That is not to say that abductees should not pray for deliverance; they should do so, fervently. But the name of Jesus is not a magic wand. We, as Christians, do not brandish invocative words like a wizard but put our faith in the Son of God, who will raise us up at the last day and grant us eternal life in the presence of his Father (see John 6:40).

too, are constrained to see the world in shadows. Due to our perceptual impairment, we cannot directly discern all the facets of the hyperdimensional environment in which we abide, even though we unknowingly interact with them all the time. This is certainly the case at the quantum level, where subatomic particles (or strings) make up the fabric of everyday reality but are completely imperceivable to us—at least without the appliance of technology.

To the degree that our technology becomes more powerful, the hidden world around us becomes more perceivable. Imagine, for example, if we were to install a mirror on the cave wall where the shadows danced in front of Plato's prisoners. As the mouth of the cave was directly behind them, the mirror would enable the prisoners to look outside. They would quickly realize that the animated figures they once believed to be ethereal spirits were merely the dark silhouettes of material beings. The environment outside the cave in which these beings trafficked does not constitute a different world but a previously imperceivable facet of the same world the prisoners had always inhabited.

Some people like to style gray aliens as "interdimensionals" because of their seeming ability to defy the laws of nature. But this is illusory. (As previously noted, the extraordinary abilities of the aliens are contingent on the proximity of their craft.) If we wish to talk of interdimensionals, then we must have a firm grasp on what exactly we mean by *interdimensional*. The word has the quality of a term touted so repeatedly and presumptively that it ceases to mean anything at all. What people probably envision when thinking of interdimensionals are beings who can pass between dimensional worlds just as we pass between the various rooms in our house. Though certainly a favorite plot in science fiction books and fantasy films, the notion has no footing in reality. Extraspatial dimensions do not comprise separate universes but additional facets of the singular universe we all inhabit.

It seems to me that people are conflating several discordant theories: extra dimensions, parallel universes, and alternate realities. Movies and TV shows, such as the Marvel films and the Netflix series *Stranger Things*, have certainly contributed to the confusion. To be sure, these are all different concepts. You do not need extra dimensions to have parallel universes or alternate realities. As the interdimensional hypothesis of UFOs has nothing to do with the hyperspace theory of the universe, it is much more accurately described as a parallel universe or alternate reality hypothesis.

Now, the question is, does a parallel universe or alternate reality actually exist? The answer: *Who knows?*

I do not personally believe in a parallel universe or alternate reality. As much as I wish it were so, you cannot walk through a wardrobe to enter the land of Narnia. There is one universe with one set of physical laws, a singular creation in which all things exist and are bound together by synergistic forces. Though many things are beyond our perception, nothing is beyond nature. The anomalous phenomena occurring in the peripheral of our perception are not an intrusion of supernatural forces from a parallel universe but an imperceivable facet of the same universe in which every creature resides. Hence, there is no such thing as an "interdimensional being," only an extraterrestrial one.

As previously mentioned, the interdimensional hypothesis of UFOs is popular among Christians who are eager to sidestep the existence of extraterrestrials, which they deem to be incompatible with the biblical paradigm—a conclusion the author finds bewildering. How is a being from a different dimension any less extraterrestrial than a being from a different planet? Moreover, it is plainly evident that angels are not human and not terrestrial in origin. Ergo, they must be regarded as both *alien* and *extraterrestrial*. If not, then these words have no meaning. Referring to extraterrestrials as "interdimensionals," like referring to your cat as a "feline," is an exercise in semantics that changes the syllables without changing the facts. It is irrational for a person to axiomatically accept the existence of life in other dimensions, parallel universes, or alternate realities, while simultaneously repudiating the possibility of life on other planets. We have never seen another dimension, another universe, or another reality, but the planets gloss and shimmer every night.

The reason why so many Christians struggle with the notion of intelligent extraterrestrial life is because they are convinced that it contradicts the doctrines of scripture. While the sentiment is understandable, it is also unfounded. The existence of extraterrestrials no more contradicts the gospel of Christ than the existence of angels. The work of Christ pertains exclusively to the sons of Adam. If Jesus did not die to atone for the sins of the angels, then why should we demand that he die for the aliens? Mankind was created for fellowship in the family of God, then corrupted through sin. Alien beings, such as the insectalins, may also have been created for a purpose, peculiar to our own, and then corrupted, even by the same serpent.

Who can know the mind of the Maker or fathom the immensity of his creation? The insectalins might have been conceived to accomplish a specific task in the hierarchy of the kingdom, perhaps related to the maintenance of life's genetic matrix. Does God not employ angels for specific tasks? Are men not also employed in the stewardship of the earth? Should we not expect to find fiercely intelligent entities explicitly designed to perform highly sophisticated functions? Such remarkable beings, if not part of the family, would not be made in the likeness of sons. Their physiology would be suited to their occupation and natural habitat. We need only look to the diverse profusion of life forms on Earth, each species distinct from the other and ingeniously adapted to the environment for which it was designed, if we wish to glimpse the creative impulse of the Architect of the universe. Let us not presume, therefore, to constrain the mind we cannot hope to comprehend.

In the absence of a doctrinal rebuttal to the biblical certainty of extraterrestrial life, Christian researchers usually resort to the outmoded arguments of astronomers from decades past. Much ado has been made over the improbability of an alien race reaching Planet Earth from another star system because of the immense distances that would have to be traversed. The closest star cluster to Earth, Alpha Centauri, is approximately 4.3 light-years, or 25 trillion miles, away. A light-year represents the distance that light travels in one year. Hence, it would take over four years to reach Alpha Centauri traveling at the speed of light. Since it is commonly believed that Einsteinian physics prohibit faster-than-light travel, some scientists argue that contact with an advanced extraterrestrial intelligence from another sector of the universe is virtually impossible. Persistent as it may be, the argument is irrelevant because, as it turns out, the distance is inconsequential.

Although it is highly improbable that you will enter the land of Narnia by pressing through the coats in your wardrobe, it is theoretically possible to transport to the surface of Mars by passing through an Einstein-Rosen bridge, otherwise known as a *wormhole*. Rather than providing access to another dimension, a wormhole provides access to another region within the universe through a dimensional portal. Much like folding a sheet of paper and punching a hole through it with a pencil, by bending the fabric of space-time, two distant points in the universe may be brought together and connected through a wormhole. Traversing the wormhole from point A to point B would result in faster-than-light travel without ever exceeding the speed of light.

Einstein-Rosen bridges are derived in the field equations for general relativity and predicted in string theory, but we do not (officially) possess the technology to test their utility, much less generate them. Some physicists believe that exotic matter is the key to opening a traversable wormhole. In brief, exotic matter is the opposite of regular matter; it has negative energy and a repulsive gravitational field that could, in theory, open and stabilize a wormhole long enough to allow the passage of an aerospace vehicle before it collapses under the force of gravity. Exotic matter has never been found on Earth but is thought to exist elsewhere in the universe.

The bending of space-time is a fundamental principle in Einstein's theory of relativity and a proven reality of physics. An extraterrestrial civilization whose technological knowledge far surpasses our own would likely be able to bypass the vast distances between the stars by warping the space around their craft rather than moving through it.

In the early 1990s, a nuclear physicist named Bob Lazar made headlines with an incredible story. Lazar claimed to have been involved in the reverse engineering of extraterrestrial technology at a secret military installation fifteen miles south of Area 51 in central Nevada. Designated S4, the installation was allegedly equipped with nine hangar bays built into the base of a mountain, each one housing an alien disc of unique design. Some of the discs appeared to be nonfunctioning crash retrievals, with visible damage to their hulls. Lazar was hired to work with one of the functioning models, which he nicknamed the "Sports Model" due to its compact size and sleek exterior.[29] Specifically, he was assigned to the team experimenting with the craft's antimatter reactor.

Without getting into the finer details, Lazar claimed that the reactor was capable of generating a tremendous amount of energy that facilitated the amplification of gravity waves, which warped the space-time around the disc, enabling it to hover in place, move at incredible speeds, and perform otherwise impossible maneuvers. To the degree that the intensity of the gravitational field is increased, the distortion of space-time is also increased. When fully energized, the distortion envelops the entire craft and renders it invisible from every vantage point. By directing the gravity waves, explained Lazar, the alien craft can bend the space-time in front of it and traverse vast distances without exceeding the speed of light. The most critical component of the reactor was a small, triangular piece of exotic matter—Element 115.

For years, skeptics laughed at Lazar's claim that a hitherto unknown heavy metal from an alien planet was being incorporated into the technology of flying saucers, until 2003, when Element 115 (Moscovium) was synthesized by scientists at the Joint Institute for Nuclear Research in Dubna, Russia.[30] The fact that Lazar knew about Element 115 more than a decade before its official discovery is validation of his testimony. Many of the other details surrounding his employment at the S4 installation were also confirmed in subsequent years.[31]

As UFO witnesses sometimes describe the opening of portals out of which flying saucers emerge, it is likely that the extraterrestrials are making use of Einstein-Rosen bridges. The sudden appearance and disappearance of alien craft can now be understood in light of space-time distortion. UFOs are not disappearing into a mysterious interdimensional

---

[29] According to Lazar, the sports model was about sixteen feet tall and forty feet in diameter, with an unpolished stainless steel–like exterior. The door hatch, seats, and general interior of the craft were designed to accommodate persons the size of small children (in other words, the grays).

[30] Just like all elements, Element 115 has various isotopes, most of which are unstable. Although Element 115 is now incorporated in the periodic table, a stable isotope has yet to be successfully synthesized in a commercial lab. See Tim Sharp, "Facts About Moscovium (Element 115)," *LiveScience.com*, December 2, 2016, https://www.livescience.com/41424-facts-about-ununpentium.html.

[31] For the full account of Bob Lazar's testimony, the reader is commended to his autobiographical work, *Dreamland: An Autobiography* (n.p.: Interstellar, 2019).

realm but jumping space by way of dimensional portals in accordance with the principles that govern the known universe. The aliens do not break the laws of physics; they bend them with advanced technology. Interstellar travel is no obstacle to those in possession of this knowledge, be they alien or human.[32]

The focus and scope of the present work does not permit a digression into the classified world of government black projects and special access programs related to the recovery and reverse engineering of alien technology that has given rise to a secret space program and a circumstance that Richard Dolan has coined the "breakaway civilization." It is imperative, however, to highlight one of the more disturbing aspects of this subject matter—the government's bartered acquisition of advanced technology from extraterrestrials.

One of the most intriguing and longstanding legends of ufology relates to a meeting that allegedly took place between President Dwight Eisenhower and a delegation of gray aliens in the mid-1950s. Incredible though it sounds, the incident is regarded as highly plausible by well-researched ufologists and has been affirmed by more than a few notable persons, including the late Bill Cooper (granted, an unsavory character), who served as a briefing team member for the United States Naval Intelligence. Cooper (and others) allege that the rendezvous with the grays took place in 1954 at the Edwards Air Force Base in Southern California. He chronicles the incident in his controversial book *Behold a Pale Horse*:

---

[32] Aside from traversable wormholes and the warping of space-time, there are several other theoretical postulations that could make interstellar travel possible, some of which involve the utility of hyperspace. The concept of hyperspace travel has been widely popularized in the *Star Wars* franchise, where starships equipped with hyperdrives can jump space by traveling through hyperlanes—extraspatial dimensions that provide shortcuts to various sectors of the universe. The science of hyperspace travel as depicted in *Star Wars* movies is not entirely fictitious. Physicists are gradually warming to the idea that extraspatial dimensions could be utilized to traverse the galaxy without exceeding the speed of light—that is, if we can produce enough energy to access them. (See Patrick Johnson, "A Physicist Explains the Science of Hyperspace—And Why Star Wars Isn't Entirely Fiction," *Quartz*, December 2, 2017, https://qz.com/1144624/a-physicist-explains-the-science-of-hyperspace-and-why-star-wars-isnt-entirely-fiction.) In fact, the interdimensional hypothesis of UFOs necessitates some form of hyperspace travel that facilitates traffic between dimensions. Ironically, many IDH proponents vehemently reject the notion of interstellar travel, without realizing that it is automatically built into their worldview. In the interest of avoiding interstellar aliens, they have unwittingly adopted a hypothesis that makes them plausible.

The base was closed for three days and no one was allowed to enter or leave during that time. The historical event had been planned in advance. Details of a treaty had been agreed upon. Eisenhower arranged to be in Palm Springs on vacation. On the appointed day the President was spirited to the base. The excuse was given to the press that he was visiting a dentist. Witnesses to the event have stated that three UFOs flew over the base and then landed. Antiaircraft batteries were undergoing live-fire training and the startled personnel actually fired at the crafts as they passed overhead. Luckily, the shells missed and no one was injured.

President Eisenhower met with the aliens on February 20, 1954, and a formal treaty between the alien nation and the United States of America was signed. . . . The treaty stated that the aliens would not interfere in our affairs and we would not interfere in theirs. We would keep their presence on earth a secret. They would furnish us with advanced technology and would help us in our technological development. They would not make any treaty with any other Earth nation. They could abduct humans on a limited and periodic basis for the purpose of medical examination and monitoring of our development, with the stipulation that the humans would not be harmed, would be returned to their point of abduction, would have no memory of the event, and that the alien nation would furnish Majesty Twelve with a list of all human contacts and abductees on a regularly scheduled basis.[33]

Needless to say, the aliens never provided a list of their abductees to Majesty Twelve.[34] We did, however, receive technological artifacts in

[33] William Cooper, *Behold a Pale Horse* (n.p.: Light Technology Publications, 1991), 202, 204.

[34] Majesty Twelve, also known as Majority Twelve and Majestic Twelve, is a council of individuals strategically selected from government and civilian sectors who are tasked with managing the secret of the alien presence and the research and development of alien technology. Following the Roswell incident in 1947, the group was established that same year by presidential order at the recommendation of Secretary of Defense James Forrestal and Dr. Vannevar Bush, Chairman of the Joint Research and Development Board. The Majestic Documents at majesticdocuments .com provide documented verification of the group's existence.

exchange. Considering its pristine condition, it is plausible that the Sports Model disc and antimatter reactor that Bob Lazar worked on at the S4 facility was an artifact procured through the exchange treaty. Even if the Eisenhower affair is pure myth, there can be no doubt that we have acquired a great deal of technological knowledge from UFO crash retrievals. Credible whistleblowers have emerged over the years claiming that certain aspects of modern technology, such as fiber optics and integrated circuits, were developed from components discovered onboard extraterrestrial craft and then gradually trickled into the commercial sector.[35] Others have revealed that hybrid aerospace vehicles with integrated alien and conventional hardware have been manufactured by defense contractors, such as Lockheed Martin, for covert deployment in the US Air Force. Although there is no way to empirically prove or disprove these claims without hard evidence, the author can personally attest to their veracity.

In the winter of 2013, I was living on the west side of Cleveland, Ohio. One night, around 7:30 p.m., my brother-in-law and I decided to go for a drive and buy some weight-training supplements from a GNC store located at the Brookgate strip mall in the small suburb of Brook Park, where I grew up. As we approached the strip mall, we noticed an aircraft with bright lights hovering above the corner store. At first, we assumed the craft was a large military helicopter, possibly a Black Hawk or Chinook, and wondered if the National Guard was running a drill of some kind. However, when we rolled the windows down to listen for the telltale sound of blades whipping through the air, we heard nothing at all.

When we entered the parking lot, I abruptly hit the brake and cut the engine. Our wonder turned to shock. The craft effortlessly glided from above the store and came to rest about fifty feet above and slightly in front of my car, so as to be entirely visible through the windshield. It was now so close that I could have easily pegged it with a rock. We quickly realized

---

[35] The most famous of these whistleblowers was Lt. Colonel Philip J. Corso. Aside from his distinguished service in World War II, Corso served as an intelligence officer on General Douglas MacArthur's staff during the Korean War and was later assigned to President Eisenhower's National Security Council. In the early 1960s, he was in charge of Foreign Technology in Army Research and Development at the Pentagon. After retiring, Corso went public with his firsthand knowledge of the alien presence. He claimed that many of the most important technological breakthroughs of the late twentieth century were developed from components procured through UFO crash retrievals. He published his testimony in a manuscript entitled *Dawn of a New Age*.

that this was no helicopter. In fact, it was much more reminiscent of an F-117 Nighthawk stealth fighter, but smaller, with rounded edges, stubby protrusions in the place of wings, and no tail. The diamond-shaped fuselage was covered in the same matte-black angular plating as conventional stealth aircraft, but unlike conventional aircraft, it had no propulsion system to speak of—no propellers, no engines, no jets, no exhaust . . . nothing, and despite its close proximity, there was no noise. There were two bright, triangular white lights (my brother-in-law remembers one) positioned at the front of the fuselage, along with a series of smaller green and blue lights. The night was cold and unusually windy. Gusts of wind howled against the doors and rocked the car as we sat gaping through the windshield, but the craft was entirely unmoved, as if encompassed by an invisible force field.

After a minute or two of stunned silence, I suddenly remembered that my brother-in-law was carrying a smartphone with a camera (I only used flip phones back then).

"Tony, your phone!" I exclaimed. "*Your phone!*"

He shook his head, as if waking from a trance, and fumbled for his phone, but as he pulled it from his pocket, it dropped to the floor. By the time he reached down, picked up the phone, and raised it to record a video, the craft had suddenly lifted higher into the air, gently turned on its axis, and begun to move away from us at a smooth and steady pace. We quickly exited the vehicle to keep an eye on it. The freezing wind beat against our faces as we watched it glide over the rooftops of the nearby houses before disappearing behind them.

While driving home that night, I could not shake the feeling that I was *supposed* to see the craft, as if someone knew that I would be in that parking lot at that precise moment. It seemed to have been waiting for me, and when I arrived, it made sure that I had a good look by descending directly over my car. What's more, Tony and I had been discussing UFOs for a couple of weeks prior to the experience. We had often pondered what sort of mechanisms might be powering the alien discs and how far the military had advanced in developing their own hybrid aerospace vehicles with the knowledge acquired from crash retrievals. Indeed, this was a topic of discussion the very day the incident occurred.

In the months and years that followed, I searched through reports of UFO sightings to see if I could find a description that matched the craft we had encountered in Brook Park, Ohio, but to no avail—that is, until the writing of this very chapter, during which time I happened to be reading the book *Hunt for the Skinwalker* by Colm A. Kelleher and George Knapp, in which the following description is recounted by one Tom Gorman (pseudonym), the former owner of Skinwalker Ranch:

> He turned toward the ridge and his jaw slackened. Starkly outlined against the snow-covered ridge was an aircraft that seemed to have just appeared out of nowhere. It was about thirty or forty feet long, and it reminded Gorman of a snub-nosed smaller hybrid version of the F-117 and the B-2. But it was completely silent. There was no wind, and the stillness was uncanny. . . .
>
> The outline of the object, less than a hundred yards away, gave Tom a good view of its short, matte-black wings. It was definitely like a small version of the F-117 "stealth fighter." The odd angled design seemed quite familiar. But Tom knew that the F-117 was extremely noisy. . . .
>
> It hovered silently less than a hundred yards away and only fifteen or twenty feet off the ground. Tom held his breath. The object moved silently away from him without ever increasing its speed and then disappeared into the gloomy night beyond the ridge. Tom heaved a sigh of relief and awkwardly got to his knees in the snow. He looked back several times at the area near the ridge where he had last seen the silent black phantom.
>
> What was this advanced technology? he wondered. Who owned it? And what on earth was it doing there on a ranch in Utah?[36]

Like Tom Gorman, I suspect that what we saw that night was advanced military hardware, the product of black budget projects commissioned

---

[36] Colm A. Kelleher and George Knapp, *Hunt for the Skinwalker: Science Confronts the Unexplained at a Remote Ranch in Utah* (New York: Paraview, Pocket Books, 2005), 51–52.

to reverse engineer extraterrestrial technology. Apparently, the projects have been successful. The craft we witnessed did not employ conventional propulsion systems and was unaffected by the atmosphere around it. We can only surmise that it was enveloped within its own gravitational field, just as Bob Lazar had claimed. The implications are almost unimaginable. The ability to jump space and harness the power of antimatter would give rise to a breakaway civilization and a technocratic ruling class who could not be restrained by any government. Agencies in possession of this technology could be secretly controlling the affairs of Earth and colonizing Mars as I write these words.

The United States is not the only nation to have bartered with extraterrestrials. For reasons we do not have space to enlarge, it would seem that the governing bodies of human civilization worldwide have entered into a treacherous bargain with the grays: we get to develop their technology, and they get to abduct the citizens of our nations.[37] There is a nagging question that ufologists have failed to answer concerning this duplicitous accord: *Why do the aliens need our permission at all?* It's obvious that we are powerless to stop them. The grays can abduct their victims when and where they please without our knowing, never mind our intervention. So why should they inform our political leaders of the abduction program?

The arrangement only makes sense in light of the biblical narrative. The sons of Adam are the gatekeepers of Planet Earth. We may be powerless to stop the grays from trespassing in our domain, but they are not at the top of the food chain. The armies of the kingdom defend our terrestrial dominion. We can, however, choose to open the gates, should we be so foolish, and usher in the Trojan horse. Just like in the days of Jared, when the sons of Cain exchanged their daughters for the knowledge of the watchers, so we have exchanged our reproductive faculties for the technology of the grays. The results will be much the same; the offspring that proceed from the wombs of our women will attempt to usurp the birthright of our species.

---

[37] More than a few leading ufologists are convinced that Eisenhower's rendezvous with the grays is a historical fact, based on an abundance of anecdotal evidence. However, even if the story is fantasy, the fact remains that we have been conveniently provided with alien technology through crash retrievals and permitted to develop and deploy it without interference.

Once the bargain was struck with the grays, so the legend goes, Eisenhower quickly realized that he had made a terrible mistake. The grays had no intention of informing us of their activities and no desire for further communication. The military began to panic. What exactly were the grays up to? And how long could they keep the alien presence a secret from the American people? Rather than disclosing the situation to the public, it was decided that the abductees had to be identified, monitored, and aggressively interrogated.

Dr. Karla Turner, a brilliant abduction researcher who was also an abductee herself, wrote extensively about the government's panicked attempt to figure out what the aliens were doing with the people they were taking. Turner documents a series of compelling military abductions (MILABS), in which various abductees, including her husband, were drugged and dragged from their homes to be interrogated on Army or Air Force bases. It was an ugly affair. Having endured the usual terror of an alien abduction, these unfortunate individuals were then subjected to a military abduction, which was often far worse.

Upon being sequestered to the bases, the abductees were forced to undergo a series of invasive procedures in which their bodies were probed for implants. When discovered, usually in the face and head, the implants were surgically removed. In some cases, the military doctors inserted their own implants into the bodies of abductees, which were likely designed to track them and record biological data. The interrogations were hostile and menacing. The commanders demanded to know what the grays were up to. They verbally and physically abused the abductees in an attempt to extract information they felt was being withheld. Before returning the abductees to their homes, they threatened to kill them, or members of their family, should they ever tell anyone about the abductions, alien or military.[38]

Such was the treatment suffered—and likely still suffered to this day—by many abductees at the hands of their government.

---

[38] Before suddenly dying of an unidentifiable, aggressive cancer in 1996 at the age of 48, Karla Turner authored three books on the abduction phenomenon, all of which are essential reading for abduction researchers: *Into the Fringe: A True Story of Alien Abduction*, *Taken: Inside the Alien-Human Abduction Agenda*, and *Masquerade of Angels*.

The alien abduction program is not new, and it is not old. It has nothing to do with fairies, gnomes, leprechauns, sprites, elves, or any other folkloric creatures from medieval fantasies. The phenomenon is not metaphysical in nature but physical in the most palpable of ways. The program is not irrational or aimless; it is logical, methodical, and diabolical. It was initiated for a purpose and will conclude only when that purpose has been fully accomplished. The purpose is not to deceive us or to save us or to destroy us but to *become* us—to progenerate alien-human hybrids who can blend seamlessly into our society and ultimately supplant us.

The popular television show *Ancient Aliens* has done much to confuse the public regarding the alien question and to conflate the extraterrestrial factions operating on Earth. The show is based on ancient astronaut theory, which propounds that mankind has been in contact with extraterrestrials for millennia. According to the theory, the gods of old were aliens from distant worlds who greatly influenced the course of human civilization and were responsible for the construction of our most impressive ancient monuments. Some ancient astronaut theorists maintain that the human species was not only influenced by the aliens but engineered by them.

Although the television show is pure entertainment, chock full of shoddy research and comical conclusions, there is some biblical truth to its basic premise. Man *has* been in contact with extraterrestrials since the beginning of his existence. For thousands of years, members of the elder race, loyal and insurgent, have been interacting with the offspring of Adam. The pagan gods of old—the dragon and his princes—were indeed ancient aliens influencing the affairs of men.

However, it is a mistake to assume that all aliens are of the same faction. Gray aliens are not members of the elder race. They are not watchers, and they have not been interacting with mankind for millennia. Their presence is a relatively recent development.

It is apparent that the grays are little informed about human civilization and little interested. What they do know has likely been accrued through probing the minds of abductees, who are often instructed to teach the alien hybrids about life on Earth, a task for which the insectalins are evidently ill-equipped. They clearly understand our physiology, but in matters pertaining to our society, they are clueless. These facts do not conform to an ancient race of aliens who have been observing and interacting with humans for thousands of years.

It is logical to infer that the arrival of the grays coincides with the mystery airship phenomenon of the late 1800s. There are few reports of UFO sightings before the turn of the century, and no reports of alien abduction.[39] The arrival of the grays also coincides with another phenomenon that was occurring during this period of time. As previously noted, the turn of the twentieth century was distinguished by an unprecedented acceleration of knowledge that expedited the advancement of many transformative technologies; but scientific progress was only half the story, for this era was also distinguished by an unprecedented surge in the occult, especially in the arcane practice of *spiritualism*.

Traditionally, a spiritualist is one who endeavors to commune with the spirits of the dead (discarnate humans) or to communicate with other denizens of the spirit world. The most common practice employed by the spiritualist is the séance, conducted through the agency of a medium. The reader will have undoubtedly seen an image or film depicting the ritual: the participants of the séance, shrouded in the mystic ambience of candlelight, sit around a table with hands placed palms-down, while the medium—typically a woman—attempts to summon the spirit of a deceased relative, or some other personality from the astral plane, to manifest in their midst (which often occurs through the body and voice of the medium herself). What happens next is entirely dependent on the quality of the medium. More often than not, nothing happens. Sometimes the medium is a fraud, and fakery ensues (such as feigned ectoplasmic discharges). But on occasion, if the medium is true, contact is achieved, though with *whom* is a matter of speculation.

The function of a medium—or psychic, in contemporary parlance—is to be a conduit for contact with spiritual beings. The practice has its roots in the Nephilimic sorcery of the ancient Canaanites, which was both very real and very dangerous.

---

[39] Jacobs and Hopkins have both commented that, based on their research, the abduction program must have commenced in the latter part of the nineteenth century, as there is no evidence of its occurrence before that time. Vallée attempted to draw a correlation between the folkloric traditions of ancient peoples and modern abduction experiences; however, aside from the most superficial of similarities, the correlations are unconvincing.

The famed Witch of Endor, so named in the Book of 1 Samuel,[40] was the last medium to be found in Israel capable of summoning the dead, a practice strictly outlawed by the Hebrew king on pain of death. Saul had driven the sorcerers and mediums from the land, not because they were charlatans but because they were practicing the necromantic mysteries of the Nephilimic tribes whose genetic lineage could be traced back to the offspring of the watchers in the pre-Flood world. The sorcery of the watchers enabled communication with the netherworld, the abode of the dead, and it worked for those who knew how to wield it, as King Saul discovered to his great calamity.[41]

Necromancy had always been viewed as the dark and diabolical art of witches and warlocks, that is, until the nineteenth century, when the historicity of the biblical narrative was undermined and the floodgates of paganism were opened. Beginning in the 1850s and continuing through the 1920s, séances, psychic readings, spirit channeling, spirit healing, automatic writing, trance lectures, and Ouija board parties were all the rage in the West. From the Victorian slum houses in the streets of London to the White House in Washington, DC, paupers and presidents alike were shamelessly engaging in necromancy as if it were as trivial as a tea party.

The widespread publication of occult material (especially the works of Helena Blavatsky) in the United States, the United Kingdom, Spain, France, Italy, Germany, and Russia had amassed an expansive audience. By the latter part of the nineteenth century, there were over one hundred spiritualist periodicals circulating in the United States alone.[42] Newspaper reports confirm that nearly eight hundred American cities and towns were routinely hosting spiritualist gatherings.[43] At the height of the movement, it was estimated that eight million people were practicing some form of the occult in the United States and Europe, a number that would rise

---

[40] See 1 Samuel 28.

[41] Saul instructed the Witch of Endor to call up the spirit of the deceased prophet Samuel. When the medium succeeded to perform the king's command, Samuel informed Saul that he and his sons would be killed the very next day, which happened precisely in the manner it was predicted.

[42] See David Nartonis, "The Rise of 19th-Century American Spiritualism, 1854–1873," *Journal for the Scientific Study of Religion* 49, no. 2 (2010): 361–73.

[43] Ibid. See also Karen Abbott, "The Fox Sisters and the Rap on Spiritualism," *Smithsonian Magazine*, October 30, 2012, https://www.smithsonianmag.com/history/the-fox-sisters-and-the-rap-on-spiritualism-99663697.

considerably by the early twentieth century, when the cities and suburbs of the Western world were as replete with psychic parlors as with barbershops. For many people living at the turn of the century, attending a spiritualist gathering to commune with the dead was as natural as going to church on Sunday morning.

It was precisely during this period of time that the mystery airships began to appear, and the aliens, we may assume, began to identify the best candidates for the breeding program. As previously postulated, it could be that they were looking for individuals whose psychic faculties were more highly developed, allowing for facile telepathic control. It is also possible that they were selecting for a specific genetic marker associated with psychic sensitivity inherent in certain family lines. Such a trait, when enhanced, might enable the hybrids to retain the telepathic capabilities of the grays without necessitating certain aspects of their physiology (e.g., their bulbous craniums).

The synchronicity of the mystery airship phenomenon with the sudden upsurge in occult activity is highly intriguing. Were the grays somehow responsible for the rise of spiritualism in the late 1800s? Or were they drawn to the planet because of it? Is it possible that the collective practice of Canaanitic necromancy by millions of people around the globe authorized, or even invited, their incursion into our realm?

Even if the airships and the séances were entirely unrelated, there is ample reason to conclude that the grays made use of the psychics, and are still making use of them to this day, to dragnet the populace for potential abductees. In her book *Masquerade of Angels*, Turner recounts the true story of Ted Rice, who was a practicing psychic and, as he would come to discover, an abductee. By the end of Ted's spellbinding journey, filled with many vivid abduction encounters, he finally realizes that he was not the spiritual "Light Worker" he had once believed himself to be but a tool in the hands of alien agencies:

> "In my prayers," Ted continued, "I have openly confessed to God that I have been molded, shaped and engineered to be the 'Light Worker' they wanted me to be. I have been in preparation for forty years to do just what I've been doing, which is

fascinating and mystifying people with my remarkable psychic abilities. . . . I overpowered people mentally and left them wide open to invite this invading nightmare into their lives. And I did it all in the illusion and deception that I was really and truly helping my fellow man grow spiritually wiser through my so-called gift."[44]

To some extent, the UFO phenomenon and alien abduction program are one and the same. Most of the disc-, bell-, and walnut-shaped craft darting through our skies are piloted by gray aliens. The smaller discs in particular—presumably deployed for reconnaissance—appear to be designed with only their diminutive anatomy in mind. The larger craft of varying shapes and sizes are specifically fitted for the abduction program, with interiors designed to accommodate humans and hybrids (as well as the taller insectalins).[45] Because the quantity of abductees has been increasing exponentially over time (due to the successive abduction of family lines), we may assume that the production of alien craft is increasing at the same rate to meet the demand—a factor which corresponds to the inevitable upsurge in UFO sightings with each new generation.

Although the grays are likely responsible for the majority of legitimate UFO sightings, they are not the only race in possession of flying saucer technology. Extraterrestrial aerospace vehicles, piloted by both good and bad actors, were undoubtedly cruising the cosmos long before the creation of Adam.

Certain Christian researchers have popularized the view that all UFOs are the product of so-called "fallen angel technology."[46] It is often asserted that fallen angels are forced to utilize a technological means

---

[44] Karla Turner, *Masquerade of Angels*, with Ted Rice (Roland, AR: Kelt Works, 1994), 208–9.

[45] Abductees describe the interior of UFOs with remarkable congruity. The white walls of the alien craft appear to be molded from a plastic-like material, without the need for rivets, bolts, paneling, or any of the other engineering methods that we use in the construction of conventional aircraft. The vessels are not designed for comfort but for efficiency, with only the most essential accoutrements, such as benches extending seamlessly from the walls where abductees are seated before being processed. The interior compartments are curved and smooth. There are no right angles within the craft, not even in the doorways, which are arched and rounded.

[46] The term is often employed to explain other examples of enigmatic knowledge, such as cyclopean megaliths and out-of-place artifacts (OOPArts).

of conveyance because their "wings have been clipped." Aside from the common misconception regarding angels and wings, the presumption that only the bad guys travel in advanced aerospace vehicles is a logical fallacy. Both fallen and non-fallen angels come from the same civilization and are members of the same race. They share the same general appearance, the same heritage, the same language, the same customs, the same knowledge, and the same technology. Hardware has no allegiance. Technology cannot be "fallen." A flying saucer is no more good or evil than your Ford Truck. There is no reason, biblical or otherwise, to doubt that the good guys are not also, on occasion, traversing the skies in UFOs.

Though not encountered nearly as frequently as the grays, tales of a regal, humanlike race of extraterrestrials have surfaced around the globe, including in the Andes mountains among the indigenous Aymara and Quechua peoples, with whom the author has personally spoken. These beings, often referred to as *Nordics* or *Pleiadians*, are typically described as tall, handsome young men with blond (or golden-blond) hair, dazzling blue eyes, and a fair complexion. They are not giants, as some maintain, but have an approximate stature of six and a half to seven feet. In all likelihood, these are members of the elder race, the morning stars.

The biblical narrative seems to insinuate a description of the angels that is consonant with that of the Nordics. On the eve of Sodom's destruction, Lot was sitting in the gateway of the city when he saw two men approaching. He immediately recognized these men as angels.[47] How could this be, unless their appearance was distinct in some way? Sodom was in Judea. The men of Judea were ethnically Semitic, meaning they tended to look like the people of the Middle East today—relatively short (compared to Europeans), with tanned skin, dark eyes, and black or brown hair. Two tall blonds with blue eyes and luminous white skin would stick out like a sore thumb in Sodom. The unique and striking appearance of these men is exhibited in the reaction of the Sodomites, who, being raving homosexuals, gathered together at Lot's door demanding that he bring out his guests so they could have their way with them. No ordinary Semitic men, no matter how handsome, would have attracted this kind of attention in a city bustling with activity.

---

[47] See Genesis 19.

As mentioned earlier, the fallen morning stars are not the grotesque beings we have imagined them to be. Quite to the contrary, they were made in the image of God and are sons of the highest order. Hence, we should expect the dragon princes, and their half-breed progeny, to look like the Nordics. We should also expect to find them, like the Nordics, in command of high technology consistent with the advanced, ancient civilization from which they hail.

According to the Eisenhower legend, after communication was established with the grays, another humanlike extraterrestrial faction, the Nordics, made contact with the US government. "This group," writes Cooper, "warned us against the race orbiting the equator [the grays] and offered to help us with our spiritual development. They demanded that we dismantle and destroy our nuclear weapons as the major condition. They refused to exchange technology, citing that we were spiritually unable to handle the technology we already possessed. These overtures were rejected on the grounds that it would be foolish to disarm in the face of such an uncertain future. There was no track record to read from. It may have been an unfortunate decision."[48]

Whether or not the Nordics made such an overture in the past, a similar scenario is likely to unfold in the future. The gray alien breeding program represents a grave threat to the human species—indeed the gravest we have ever faced. In the late 1990s, Dr. Jacobs began to hear a mantra repeated over and over by many abductees from different walks of life who had never met each other. They spoke of a "Change" that would soon transpire on Earth. "This Change," writes Jacobs, "would consist of human-like hybrids intermingling with humans in everyday life."

> Abductees reported that the aliens had told them that soon "everyone would be together." I had heard this and similar statements often enough to understand that this was part of the aliens' goal. Their activities and communications strongly suggested that they were engaged in a carefully conceived program that was directed toward integrating hybrids into human society. . . .

[48] Cooper, *Behold a Pale Horse*, 202.

Many abductees are now being given new, additional duties. For the last decade, abductees have told me that, although the common abduction procedures still take place, implementing "The Change" has now become almost a full-time occupation for many of them. Even abductees I have known for many years have reported this difference, suggesting that The Change is now either in effect or has expanded greatly over those years.

It is clear now that integration into human society is the aliens' primary goal. All aliens are part of a dedicated program to integrate hubrids into humanity. They perform their duties to fulfill the program's purposes and are all interconnected neurologically. All give allegiance to the insectalins. They do not talk about healing the Earth, or healing or enlightening humans, or joining together with humans in a cosmic community, or anything else that might help humans. They talk about sending aliens to Earth to live here undetected and eventually to supplant humans.[49]

The grays may be thought of as the antithesis of the Borg from *Star Trek*. The Borg are a hostile alien faction that assimilate every race they encounter into their own cyborg collective. It would seem that the operating procedure of gray aliens is precisely the other way around. Instead of assimilating the residents of a planet they wish to acquire into their own collective, they integrate themselves into the populace through hybridization and take over from within. It is a silent coup rather than an open declaration of war. Much more ingenious and insidious than the Borg.

Dr. Jacobs believes that the insectalins are executing a covert operation of planetary acquisition. The hybrids are quietly moving in without our noticing and will use their powerful telepathic capabilities to control us. If they are not stopped, they will eventually supplant the human species on Planet Earth. And this may be their only viable course of action, according to the rules of the game. It is clear that the insectalins are not attempting to wrest the earth away from humanity by force but

---

[49] Jacobs, *Walking Among Us*, 39.

to become human enough to steal the birthright of Adam and inherit the earth by stealth. If their plan were to subdue us by force, they could easily obliterate an entire continent with an antimatter bomb, or some other weapon of mass destruction, and bring humanity to its knees. If they wanted the earth intact, they could release a deadly virus or chemical agent in the atmosphere to exterminate us like cockroaches. Indeed, if the authority of mankind were not enforced by the armies of the kingdom, we would all have been enslaved or perished at the hands of extraterrestrial invaders long ago.

An entire book could be dedicated to the enlargement of the topics discussed thus far, but we must at last bring this long chapter to a conclusion. Our final consideration revolves around this question: How does the program of the insectalins relate to the machinations of the dragon? It is inconceivable that the alien presence has caught the dragon princes (the Nordics) by surprise. They must have anticipated their arrival, or else arranged it. Admittedly, this is a particularly difficult nut to crack, as we are dealing with an intelligence considerably more deft than our own. Rather than commit to a single hypothesis, I humbly offer the following three alternatives:

> » **Alternative A:** The grays are *controlled* by the dragon princes. The breeding program is directly orchestrated by agents of the insurgency. The insectalins are under their command.

> » **Alternative B:** The grays are *allied* with the dragon princes. The breeding program is managed by the insectalins as part of a larger strategy mutually beneficial to both parties. The grays may be one of several alien factions who have joined the insurgency in preparation for the coming war.

> » **Alternative C:** The grays are *autonomous*. The breeding program has been initiated solely by the insectalins for their own objectives. The dragon princes will take advantage of the alien threat to deceive humanity.

Alternatives A and B present a scenario in which the human species is eventually supplanted by alien hybrids, either en masse or selectively. The dragon princes may be orchestrating the usurpation of human authority by installing hybrids into the highest echelons of government in every nation on Earth. The powerful telepathic capabilities of these Manchurian candidates will enable them to rise through the political ranks with ease. Once they are all in position, they will coordinate the formulation of the final world empire in anticipation of the beast. When Apollo is revealed, all authority will be consolidated into his hands.

Alternative C facilitates a scenario in which the heroic progeny of the gods, the Golden Race, will appear to deliver mankind from the alien threat. This contingency coincides with Cooper's account of first contact with the Nordics, who warned us about the grays in advance. The insectalins intend to supplant the human species and subdue the earth by stealth. There is no way that we can stop them; their technology is unassailable, and their hybrids are undetectable. Humanity faces imminent extinction, or at the very least subjugation to insectalin overlords.

Enter Apollo.

The contrast between the hideous gray alien invaders with bulbous heads, spindly limbs, and sinister black eyes and the striking features of the golden-blond saviors who rally to our defense will be stark indeed. Like the Riders of Rohan galloping into battle to break the siege of Minas Tirith just before the city falls to the orcish horde, Apollo and his consorts will make their grand appearance to deliver mankind from certain doom.[50]

Although any of these scenarios are possible, and many others besides, I am more inclined toward Alternatives B and C. The dragon may have had a hand in luring the grays to Planet Earth, but it seems doubtful that he is directly controlling them. The insectalins appear to be laser-focused on achieving their own objectives. It is clear that elements of the United States government are deeply concerned about the advanced capabilities of the grays and the implications of their breeding program. Eventually, the gravity of the situation will become apparent to the defense apparatuses

---

[50] Alternative B might also accommodate this contingency. The dragon may be currently allied with the insectalins but will stab them in the back when the maneuver is most advantageous. This would mean that the grays are being manipulated as controlled opposition and are entirely oblivious to the impending betrayal.

of developed nations worldwide and will require a coordinated response.

When the confrontation begins, we will quickly realize that resistance is futile. The policy of nondisclosure, which until recently was aggressively maintained by the Pentagon, amounts to a silent admission that the grays cannot be deterred. Why make the people aware of a problem for which there is no solution? Even the combined forces of the United States, the European Union, Russia, and China are powerless to avert an adversary who freely traffics in the restricted airspace above our most secret military installations and routinely disarms our nuclear missiles in their silos. Our only hope to defeat such an elusive enemy is to acquire an ally with the same, or greater, capabilities.

Though indomitable by the human race, the grays will quickly succumb to the technological superiority of the elder race. In a display of invincible might, Apollo will vanquish the insectalin invaders and win the affection of the nations. The people will marvel that the gods of old have returned "to reign o'er a world at peace."

The timely arrival of Apollo will be interpreted by the Vatican as the long foretold return of Christ. The Jews will embrace our golden-haired savior as the Messiah, the Muslims as the Mahdi, the Hindus as Bahá'u'lláh, and the Buddhists as Maitreya.

After delivering us from certain destruction at the hands of the grays, Apollo and his consorts, like the watchers before them, will teach us the secrets we were striving to learn and provide us with the final component of our posthuman transformation.

Chapter 12

THE POSTHUMAN PARADIGM

It was the twenty-sixth day of June in the year 2000, the beginning of the second millennium and the dawn of a posthuman paradigm on Planet Earth. The atmosphere in the East Room of the White House was electrified with anticipation. Members of the press, eminent representatives from the scientific community, ambassadors of various nations, and a cadre of politicians were assembled to witness history in the making. At the front of the room stood a single podium emblazoned with the presidential seal, and on each side of the podium were television screens that read: *Decoding the Book of Life—A Milestone for Humanity.*

Prompted by the anthem "Hail to the Chief," the congregation rose from their chairs in homage to the presence of the forty-second president of the United States, Bill Clinton. As the president advanced to the podium, he was followed by two distinguished gentlemen, Craig Venter, founder and president of Celera Corporation, and Francis Collins, director of the National Human Genome Research Institute. A satellite video link was streaming live from the State Dining Room at 10 Downing Street, London, where British Prime Minister Tony Blair had gathered an equally illustrious audience to celebrate the momentous occasion.

President Clinton began his historic speech:

> Nearly two centuries ago, in this room, on this floor, Thomas
> Jefferson and a trusted aide spread out a magnificent map—

a map Jefferson had long prayed he would get to see in his lifetime. The aide was Meriwether Lewis and the map was the product of his courageous expedition across the American frontier all the way to the Pacific. It was a map that defined the contours and forever expanded the frontiers of our continent and our imagination.

Today the world is joining us here in the East Room to behold a map of even greater significance. We are here to celebrate the completion of the first survey of the entire human genome. Without a doubt, this is the most important, most wondrous map ever produced by humankind.[1]

The "most wondrous map" to which the president referred was the sequenced genome of the human species—the blueprint of Adam's genetic architecture. After more than a decade of intensive effort involving an international consortium of twenty institutions employing hundreds of geneticists from around the world, the Human Genome Project was finally consummated. The president's comparison of this remarkable achievement to the bold expedition of Lewis and Clark was perhaps more portentous than he realized. The successful survey of Jefferson's newly acquired territory in the West would eventually open the floodgates of frontier expansion and redefine the borders of a budding nation. In like manner, the successful survey of the human genome was destined to open the floodgates of genetic modification and redefine what it means to be a human being.

The die was cast. Mankind had set in motion the gears of his own inevitable transformation. The "Book of Life" had been decoded and was now open for all to read, for better or for worse.

The consummation of the Human Genome Project marked the beginning of the end of humanity as we know it, but mankind's transformation would not occur overnight. Like all significant technological breakthroughs in

---

[1] The White House, Office of the Press Secretary, "Remarks Made by the President [...] on the Completion of the First Survey of the Entire Human Genome," June 26, 2000, https://www.genome.gov/10001356.

the modern age, human genetic engineering would at first progress at an almost imperceptible pace, until the impetus of necessity and profit compelled momentous evolution. A caterpillar encrusted in his cocoon may appear to be in a state of inactivity, but beneath the chrysalis surface, dramatic change is nevertheless occurring.

Over the last several decades, the development of emerging technologies has been advancing at breakneck speed along the upsurge of an exponential growth curve (as projected by Kurzweil's law of accelerating returns[2]). Among these technologies, there are four whose imminent convergence is predicted to catalyze what analysts are calling the "posthuman revolution." Styled with the acronym "GRIN" (a fitting appellation, as we will see), the intercourse of genetics, robotics, artificial intelligence (AI), and nanotechnology will facilitate enhancements to the full spectrum of human biology, body, mind, and soul and give birth to a *post*human being—*humanity 2.0.*

Although the extraordinary implications of this inevitable eventuality may be lost on the plebeian masses, powerful multinational corporations, prominent futurists, and farsighted investors, perceiving an emerging market of inestimable value, are already preparing to merchandize the upgrades of our species. "For anyone who cares about preserving our humanity," cautions Dr. Leon Kass, the former chairman of President George W. Bush's Council on Bioethics, "the time has come for paying attention."

> Human nature itself lies on the operating table, ready for alteration, for eugenic and psychic "enhancement," for wholesale redesign. In leading laboratories, academic and industrial, new creators are confidently amassing their powers and quietly honing their skills, while on the street their evangelists are zealously prophesying a posthuman future.[3]

---

[2] See Ray Kurzweil, "The Law of Accelerating Returns," *Kurzweil Accelerating Intelligence*, March 7, 2001, http://www.kurzweilai.net/the-law-of-accelerating-returns. Kurzweil's exponential growth models project that technological development in the twenty-first century will continue to progress exponentially; meaning that, instead of experiencing one hundred years of progress over the course of this century, we will experience the equivalent of twenty thousand years.

[3] Leon R. Kass, *Life, Liberty, and the Defense of Dignity: The Challenge for Bioethics* (New York: Encounter, 2002).

Dr. Kass's warning was not heeded. The debate over whether we should act to preserve our humanity before it is too late never ensued. Unbeknownst to the public, in universities and policy think tanks across the globe, professors, scientists, futurists, politicians, and lawyers have been quietly laboring to lay the moral and legislative groundwork for a posthuman paradigm. In an article entitled "The Hybrid Age," Thomas Horn elucidates,

> Most readers may be surprised to learn that in preparation of this posthuman revolution, the United States government, through the National Institute of Health, recently granted Case Law School in Cleveland $773,000 of taxpayers' money to begin developing the actual guidelines that will be used for setting government policy regarding the next step in human evolution—"genetic enhancement." Maxwell Mehlman, Arthur E. Petersilge Professor of Law, director of the Law-Medicine Center at the Case Western Reserve University School of Law and professor of bioethics in the Case School of Medicine, led the team of law professors, physicians, and bioethicists over the two-year project "to develop standards for tests on human subjects in research that involves the use of genetic technologies to enhance 'normal' individuals."
>
> Following the initial study, Mehlman began traveling the United States and offering two university lectures: "Directed Evolution: Public Policy and Human Enhancement" and "Transhumanism and the Future of Democracy," address-ing the need for society to comprehend how emerging fields of science will, in approaching years, alter what it means to be human, and what this means to democracy, individual rights, free will, eugenics, and equality. At the Brookings Institute—the #1 think tank in the world and the #1 policy think tank in the United States—a new series titled "The Future of the Constitution" is likewise examining how the U.S. Constitution and Bill of Rights will need to be amended to ensure rights and privileges for new forms of humans including

genetically engineered homosexual entities. Law schools, including Stanford and Oxford, are hosting annual "Human Enhancement and Technology" conferences to consider the ramifications as well, where transhumanists, futurists, bio-ethicists, and legal scholars are busying themselves with the ethical, legal, and inevitable ramifications of posthumanity.[4]

The guidelines developed by the Case Law School study, initiated in 2006, laid the groundwork for clinical trials in human genetic engineering. Since then, geneticists have been developing gene therapies to target particular genetic disorders, with promising success. In August of 2017, a team of geneticists announced that they had successfully edited out a heritable heart condition in a human embryo.[5] It is important to note that this pivotal breakthrough took place in the United States, where regulations on human embryo experimentation are more prohibitive compared to other nations. (One can only imagine what kind of "breakthroughs" have been achieved in countries with little to no regulation, where aspiring "Dr. Moreau"s can experiment to their heart's content.)

In the wake of this critical achievement, geneticists are now projecting that more than ten thousand known inherited mutations can be eliminated from the human gene pool. Although current federal laws prohibit the gene-editing platform used in the experiment (CRISPR-Cas9) from being tested on living human subjects, the overwhelming benefit of the technology for humanity will eventually tip the scales in Congress and lift the guardrail for clinical trials.

In the foreseeable future, genome modification merchandise will gradually become available to the general public. At first, these controversial

---

[4] Thomas Horn, "The Hybrid Age," *Koinonia House*, February 1, 2012, https://www.khouse.org/articles/2012/1039.

[5] See Pam Belluck, "In Breakthrough, Scientists Edit a Dangerous Mutation from Genes in Human Embryos," *New York Times*, August 2, 2017, https://www.nytimes.com/2017/08/02/science/gene-editing-human-embryos.html. See also Emily Mullin, "2017 Was the Year of Gene-Therapy Breakthroughs," *MIT Technology Review*, January 3, 2018, https://www.technologyreview.com/s/609643/2017-was-the-year-of-gene-therapy-breakthroughs. Several gene therapy techniques were tested and succeeded in curing a range of genetic disorders in 2017, including sickle-cell anemia, cancer (bone marrow and lymphoma), bacterial skin infections (epidermolysis bullosa), and retinal diseases (via the treatment Luxturna).

technologies will be utilized to treat only a handful of peer-reviewed clinical cases; however, as soon as their viability and safety is established beyond doubt, a deluge of commercial interests will force them through the rusted gates of bureaucracy and into the byways of the marketplace. A variety of genetic modifications will become easily accessible to the common man—from simple aesthetic alterations, such as changing the color of one's eyes, to significant upgrades in the physical capabilities of the body and the cerebral capacity of the mind. Even if corporations exercise a measure of caution in the marketing of genome modification merchandise (and caution has never been a virtue of commerce), the Pentagon has already thrown caution to the wind, as the Defense Advanced Research Projects Agency (DARPA) races to deploy genetically enhanced supersoldiers on the battlefield before the Russians and Chinese accomplish the same.[6]

In 2013, DARPA published a solicitation entitled "Advanced Tools for Mammalian Genome Engineering." Despite its ambiguous title, the stated objective of the project leaves no room for doubt as to which species of mammal DARPA intends to genetically engineer:

OBJECTIVE

Improve the utility of Human Artificial Chromosomes (HACs) by developing new selectable metabolic markers for use in human cells, new high-fidelity methods for inserting DNA constructs of at least 50,000 base pairs (bp) in length into defined genomic loci, and new methodologies for facile intercellular genome transplantation.[7]

In brief, the Pentagon wants to improve the powerful gene-editing platform of Human Artificial Chromosomes (aptly abbreviated as HACs)

[6] See Annie Jacobsen, "Engineering Humans for War," *The Atlantic*, September 23, 2015, https://www.theatlantic.com/international/archive/2015/09/military-technology-pentagon-robots/406786; and Eric Tegler, "Russia and China's 'Enhanced Human Operations' Terrify the Pentagon," *Popular Mechanics*, December 16, 2015, http://www.popularmechanics.com/military/research/a18574/enhanced-human-operations.
[7] DARPA / 13.B / ST13B-001, *Advanced Tools for Mammalian Genome Engineering* (SBIRSource online), accessed on July 1, 2019, https://www.sbir.gov/node/413479.

in order to make more significant modifications to the human genome. According to the solicitation, "HACs have the capacity to contain extremely large segments of DNA (potentially up to or surpassing 1,000,000 bp)"[8] and would therefore facilitate an extensive array of enhancements to the biology of human warfighters. Considering that this project was initiated in the year 2013, we may surmise that progress has been made, and not only in the United States.

The wraith of the Cold War is haunting the world once again. In October of 2017, while addressing a gathering of university students, Russian President Vladimir Putin issued the forewarning that genetic engineering will soon lead to the creation of supersoldiers who will "fight without fear, compassion, regret, or pain." He further suggested that this dangerous scenario "might be worse than a nuclear bomb."[9] In light of the Pentagon's admitted interest in "mammalian genome engineering," it is safe to assume that Mr. Putin was not engaging in hyperbole but alerting the world to a new arms race that has been long fomenting in the shadowy recesses of classified military projects.

If the United States and Russia are running neck and neck in the genetic arms race, then China, who routinely disregards the rules, is many paces ahead. In 2015, Chinese scientists took a bold step forward in genetic engineering and became the first to (publicly) edit the genes of a human embryo.[10] Their actions provoked outrage from the global scientific community and urgent pleas not to make a genetically modified baby. The pleas fell on deaf ears.

Just three years later, in 2018, a team of geneticists working at the Southern University of Science and Technology in Shenzhen, China, created the first genetically modified babies.[11] They edited a gene called

---

[8] Ibid.

[9] Mark Hodge, "You're Terminated: Vladimir Putin Warns of Future Sci-Fi Super-Human Soldiers More 'Destructive Than Nuclear Bombs' [. . .]," *The Sun*, October 23, 2017, https://www.thesun.co.uk/news/4746212/vladimir-putin-russia-super-human-soldiers-nuclear-bomb.

[10] See David Cyranoski and Sara Reardon, "Chinese Scientists Genetically Modify Human Embryos," *Nature*, April 22, 2015, https://www.nature.com/news/chinese-scientists-genetically-modify-human-embryos-1.17378.

[11] The scientists involved in the project were subsequently fined and sentenced to three years in prison. See Preetika Rana, "How a Chinese Scientist Broke the Rules to Create the First Gene-Edited Babies," *Wall Street Journal*, May 10, 2019, https://www.wsj.com/articles/how-a-chinese-scientist-broke-the-rules-to-create-the-first-gene-edited-babies-11557506697.

CCR5 in an attempt to make the babies resistant to HIV, smallpox, and cholera. The success of their experiment has yet to be determined, but it is likely that the modifications will now become inheritable by successive generations. These breaches in the ethical boundaries of scientific research were committed by the Chinese in broad daylight. Who knows what scientists working in the secret laboratories of the People's Liberation Army have done in the dark?

Aside from modifying the genes of human embryos, scientists all over the world have been creating genetic chimeras by blending the DNA of various species. In 2011, the *Daily Mail* reported that British scientists had secretly created more than 150 human-animal hybrid embryos. The research was made possible by the Human Fertilization Embryology Act passed in 2008, which legalized the creation of a variety of hybrids, "including an animal egg fertilized by a human sperm; 'cybrids,' in which a human nucleus is implanted into an animal cell; and 'chimeras,' in which human cells are mixed with animal embryos."[12]

In 2019, the Spanish newspaper *El País* published a story about a team of researchers who successfully bred monkeys with human brain cells. According to the article, the controversial project, led by Professor Juan Carlos Izpisúa Belmonte from the Salk Institute in the United States, was conducted in China "to avoid legal issues."[13] In the same year, Chinese scientists announced that they had engineered monkey-pig hybrids and intended to grow human organs inside the creatures for transplantation,[14] which immediately prompted the government of Japan to approve its first human-animal embryo experiments.[15] Not to be outdone by the United Kingdom and China, researchers in the United States have recently created

---

[12] Daniel Martin and Simon Caldwell, "150 Human Animal Hybrids Grown in UK Labs: Embryos Have Been Produced Secretively for the Past Three Years," *Daily Mail*, July 22, 2011, https://www.dailymail.co.uk/sciencetech/article-2017818/Embryos-involving-genes-animals-mixed-humans-produced-secretively-past-years.html.

[13] Manuel Ansede, "Spanish Scientists Create Human-Monkey Chimera in China," *El País*, July 31, 2019, https://english.elpais.com/elpais/2019/07/31/inenglish/1564561365_256842.html.

[14] See Michael Le Page, "Exclusive: Two Pigs Engineered to Have Monkey Cells Born in China," *New Scientist*, December 6, 2019, https://www.newscientist.com/article/2226490-exclusive-two-pigs-engineered-to-have-monkey-cells-born-in-china.

[15] See David Cyranoski, "Japan Approves First Human-Animal Embryo Experiments," *Nature*, July 26, 2019, https://www.nature.com/articles/d41586-019-02275-3.

a mouse that is 4-percent human.[16] Stories like these are now so numerous that they have ceased to elicit alarm in the public. Cross-species genetic engineering is now a mundane fact of life.

Genetic modification represents only one facet of the emerging GRIN technologies. Advancements in the fields of robotics, artificial intelligence, and nanotech are occurring at the same astonishing speed. In August of 2020, *The Independent* stunned the world with the sensational headline "Groundbreaking New Material 'Could Allow Artificial Intelligence to Merge with the Human Brain.'" The article elucidates:

> Scientists have discovered a ground-breaking bio-synthetic material that they claim can be used to merge artificial intelligence with the human brain.
>
> The breakthrough, presented today at the American Chemical Society Fall 2020 virtual expo, is a major step towards integrating electronics with the body to create part human, part robotic "cyborg" beings.[17]

Try to imagine genetically enhanced cyborg beings fighting on the battlefields of the future or competing with your children for the best jobs in the marketplace. As "sci-fi" as these scenarios may seem, the development of the technologies that will make them a routine fact of life is inevitable.

In other words, dear reader, Jack is out of the box, and he's not going back in.

In the philosophy of technology, there is a theory called the "technological imperative" (otherwise known as the "inevitability thesis"), which posits that once a technology is introduced into society, what follows is the inevitable development of that technology. To put it another way, when

---

[16] See Anthony Cuthbertson, "Scientists Make 'Human-Mouse Chimera' that's 4% Human," *Independent*, May 22, 2020, https://www.independent.co.uk/life-style/gadgets-and-tech/news/human-mouse-cells-embryo-disease-a9528181.html.

[17] Anthony Cuthbertson, "Groundbreaking New Material 'Could Allow Artificial Intelligence to Merge with the Human Brain,'" *Independent*, August 17, 2020, https://www.independent.co.uk/life-style/gadgets-and-tech/news/artificial-intelligence-brain-computer-cyborg-elon-musk-neuralink-a9673261.html.

set in motion, the developmental progression of any useful technology is unavoidable, unstoppable, and irreversible, even if it poses a catastrophic risk to society itself.

The most salient example of the technological imperative at work is the development and deployment of the atomic bomb. In 1917, the pioneering research of British physicist Ernest Rutherford laid the groundwork for artificially induced nuclear reaction and eventuated the splitting of the atom.[18] Few among Rutherford's colleagues in the scientific community of that day could have imagined the ruinous mushroom cloud that was fated to rise on the shores of Japan nearly three decades later. On the sixth of August 1945, the whole world witnessed the megadeath capabilities of nuclear fission, as *Little Boy*[19] detonated in the atmosphere over Hiroshima, instantly vaporizing much of the city, along with tens of thousands of its inhabitants. The total annihilation of Nagasaki would follow three days later by way of another fission bomb, dubbed *Fat Man*.

Rather than provoking an immediate moratorium on nuclear technology, the grisly aftermath of Hiroshima and Nagasaki ignited an international arms race. What began as a modest pursuit to understand the building blocks of matter ended in the frenzied proliferation of a weapon so powerful that at the height of the Cold War, both the United States and the Soviet Union could lay waste the whole earth many times over. Even in the wake of the catastrophic nuclear meltdowns at Chernobyl in 1986[20] and Fukushima in 2011[21]—evincing the volatility of nuclear power plants—mankind continues to tiptoe the atomic tightrope.

Despite the alarming probabilities for nuclear holocaust, at least nine countries around the world are forging nuclear weapons as you read these words, and over thirty-one countries are utilizing nuclear power plants

[18] In 1932, Rutherford's colleagues, Ernest Walton and John Cockcroft, would eventually succeed in splitting lithium atoms using accelerated protons.
[19] *Little Boy* was the nickname of the uranium fission bomb detonated over Hiroshima, Japan, on August 6, 1945.
[20] On April 26, 1986, a nuclear reactor exploded at the Chernobyl Nuclear Power Plant in the Ukrainian SSR, Soviet Union. The incident caused widespread fallout of radioactive material over the USSR and Europe.
[21] On March 11, 2011, an earthquake-induced tsunami flooded Japan's Fukushima Daiichi Nuclear Power Plant, leading to power outages, explosions, and multiple reactor meltdowns. The impact of radioactive contaminants released into the surrounding environment, including the Pacific Ocean, has never been fully evaluated.

for energy. No matter what the cost, no matter how high the stakes, the development of nuclear technology will progress ever onward, until its maximum utility has been exhausted. The indomitable impulse of the technological imperative demands no less.

The sequencing of the human genome was tantamount to the splitting of the atom, inasmuch as it inaugurated the first steps on a long road leading to an inevitable destination of unimagined consequence. Just like Ernest Rutherford and the scientific community of his day, modern geneticists are pursuing the development of genomic technologies with noble intentions. Few of these brilliant men and women have envisaged the impending fallout of the posthuman paradigm, billowing on the horizon like a mushroom cloud.

In the 1980s, the first home computers began appearing in the average American household. It was the dawn of the Information Age. In the 1990s, those same households were interfacing with the global computer network, otherwise known as the World Wide Web. By the year 2010, even the isolated Maasai tribesman herding his cattle through the plains of Tanzania was cruising the information highway on his smartphone.

Who could have imagined in the 1980s that miniature computers, millions of times more powerful than the combined computing resources available to NASA during the Apollo missions, would eventually be stowed in the pockets of ordinary people the world over? And that these people would be able to instantaneously access the full compendium of human knowledge with a flick of their finger?

The Information Age has transformed human society in profound ways and facilitated the rise of another Tower of Babel paradigm on Earth. Men of every tribe, tongue, and nation are becoming increasingly unified in language (binary code) and purpose, so that "nothing they plan to do will be impossible for them."[22] The networking of individuals and organizations through the matrix of the World Wide Web has accelerated the proliferation of knowledge and expedited the development of technology to such a degree that scientific breakthroughs, once requiring centuries of successive collaboration, are now realized within the span of mere decades.

---

[22] Genesis 11:6 (NIV).

Today we are on the cusp of the next transformative age, the *Hybrid Age*, in which the conflux (or *hybridization*) of emerging technologies will give us the tools to radically alter the sociobiological construct of the human species.

In the Hybrid Age, men will merge with their machines to transcend the limitations of their bodies. The computing technology we hold in our hands will be integrated into our brains, and we will surf the web with our minds rather than our fingers. Synthetic organs will be ready for installation in medical facilities when our natural organs fail, and cybernetic prosthetics will replace lost or damaged limbs. Nanobots will patrol our vascular highways to destroy pathogens and provide maintenance to our cells. Diseases will be cured by editing defective genes, and superhuman abilities will become possible through engineering new ones. Our babies will be designed rather than conceived, and artificial wombs will emancipate women from the bearing of children and the curse of Eve. Hereditary genetic disorders will become obsolete. The average life expectancy in the developed world will soar to over one hundred years old. This is only a sampling of the utopian vision cast by futurists for the Hybrid Age. Some of it will surely come to pass, but not without a price.

Just ten years after the completion of the Human Genome Project, anyone with the know-how could modify the human genome for less than one thousand dollars. Today, a growing movement of "biohackers" are setting up high-tech do-it-yourself bio labs in the basements, kitchens, and garages of their homes to rewrite the DNA of living organisms—including themselves—with the power of CRISPR[23] gene-editing technology.

Many of these citizen scientists hold no formal degree. The knowledge of their craft is acquired online by accessing the same resources available to doctoral students studying at the highest levels of the most prestigious universities. In fact, the biohackers have a distinct advantage over their degree-bound counterparts: they are members of a rapidly expanding international community conducting a broad range of genetic experiments in the privacy of their homes and then uploading their "DNA mods" to

---

[23] Short for Clustered Regularly Interspaced Short Palindromic Repeats, CRISPR technology is a simple yet powerful tool that facilitates precise and permanent genetic modifications to the genomes of any living organism by utilizing the natural defense mechanisms of bacteria and archaea.

the web for the communal benefit of their biohacking comrades. In this way, the community can crowdsource genetic engineering while avoiding the red tape that impedes university and corporate research.[24]

The motivations driving the biohacking community are as varied as the hackers themselves. Many are content with engineering new kinds of bacteria for the brewing of better beer (including glow-in-the-dark beer). Others enjoy genetically modifying their pets (yes, they make their pets glow in the dark too). The more serious biohacker may be seeking a cure for a debilitating disease afflicting his body or that of a loved one, while the most ambitious of all dream of enhancing themselves with the superhuman abilities of their comic book heroes.

Although the motivations of the biohackers are varied, they share a common goal: to arm the masses with CRISPR gene-editing technology and incite a global "Biohacking Revolution." The implications of such a revolution are both exhilarating and alarming—exhilarating because personalized medicine may finally break the choke hold of Big Pharma over the necks of the infirm and their physicians; alarming because DNA mods would then become as easily accessible as aspirin and ibuprofen.

Among the many tools in the GRIN-tech toolbox, genetic engineering poses the greatest threat to the preservation of humanity. Whereas robotic, AI, and nano technologies will eventually enable significant upgrades to an individual's physical and cerebral capacity, germline genetic engineering will enable permanent alterations to the hereditary profile of the human species at large. Within one generation, engineered heritable genes could propagate through the human populace on Planet Earth and irreparably corrupt the genome of mankind forever.

Now that man is in possession of the tools to exercise his will to power and direct the course of his own evolution, the birth of overman is imminent. Within a few generations, posthumans will walk the earth. The transition from human to posthuman will advance incrementally, one technological step after another. Humanity has already entered into the initial stages of this transitional phase, which we may think of in terms of a pregnancy. At this moment, humanity 2.0 is an embryo gestating in

---

[24] See Delthia Ricks, "Dawn of the BioHackers," *Discover Magazine*, October 5, 2011, http://discovermagazine.com/2011/oct/21-dawn-of-the-biohackers.

the womb. The rudimentary constituents of his anatomy are present. All that is required to complete his development and effectuate his delivery are nourishment and time.[25] When the hour of labor draws near, our Promethean "midwives" (Apollo and his consorts) will make their grand appearance (corresponding with the previously defined alien threat) to guide the posthuman through the birth canal and into the world.

The transitional phase between human and posthuman is called *transhuman*. Today, a growing international consortium of leading academics, law professors, bioethicists, and military advisors are members of a *transhumanism* movement (also known as *Humanity Plus*, or *Humanity+*), which advocates expedited development and implementation of human enhancement technologies. According to Horn, one of the leading researchers on the subject, transhumanists intend to use "genetics, robotics, artificial intelligence and nanotechnology (GRIN technologies) as tools that will radically redesign our minds, our memories, our physiology, our offspring, and even perhaps—as Joel Garreau, in his bestselling book *Radical Evolution*, claims—our very souls."[26] *ExtremeTech Magazine* underscores the primary motivation of the movement—eternal life:

> Transhumanism is a cultural and intellectual movement that believes we can, and should, improve the human condition through the use of advanced technologies. One of the core concepts in transhumanist thinking is life extension: Through genetic engineering, nanotech, cloning, and other emerging technologies, eternal life may soon be possible. Likewise, transhumanists are interested in the ever-increasing number of technologies that can boost our physical, intellectual, and psychological capabilities beyond what humans are naturally capable of.[27]

---

[25] The gestational metaphor is popular among transhumanists. For example, Humanity+, a leading transhumanist organization, describes itself on its website as a "think tank of educators, entrepreneurs, and innovators incubating Humanity's future" ("Humanity+ Home," *HumanityPlus.org*, accessed on January 5, 2020).

[26] Horn, *Zenith 2016*, 212.

[27] Sebastian Anthony, "What Is Transhumanism, or, What Does It Mean to Be Human?" *ExtremeTech*, April 1, 2013, https://www.extremetech.com/extreme/152240-what-is-transhumanism-or-what-does-it-mean-to-be-human.

The injunction that we *can* and *should* "improve the human condition through the use of advanced technologies" is piously touted by transhumanists everywhere, many of whom argue that we have a moral obligation not only to mitigate suffering but to eliminate death. The master morality of Nietzschean philosophy is clearly the bedrock of this ideal. Indeed, the very concept of directed evolution is an expression of the will to power. If it were simply Darwinian, as they claim (most transhumanists do not like to be associated with Nietzsche), it would lack the moral imperative that is a defining feature of the movement. Evolution through natural selection doesn't give a flying flip if humans evolve or go extinct. It has no purpose, no direction, and no destination. From where, then, do transhumanists derive their moral injunctions? Who is to say that the pursuit of techno-immortality is even moral at all?

Ironically, some transhumanists believe that the Bible supplies the inspiration for their ambitions. Members of the Christian Transhumanist Association claim to be compelled by the doctrines of scripture. "We believe," they affirm on their website, "that the intentional use of technology, coupled with following Christ, will empower us to become more human across the scope of what it means to be creatures in the image of God."[28] This bizarre transhumanist theology is plainly antithetical to the gospel of Christ. Transhumanists are not interested in remaining human or retaining the image of God. To the contrary, the very goal of transhumanism is posthumanism. Hence, Christian transhumanism is a contradiction in terms. The work of Christ is meaningless to those who intend to evade death through the salvific power of technology.

One of the most vocal evangelists of the transhumanist movement, a futurist by the name of Zoltan Istvan, has been traversing the United States in his "Immortality Bus," modified to resemble a coffin (presumably to remind people of their impending demise). The slogan painted on the side of the bus reads, "Live Forever with Transhumanism." He deployed the Immortality Bus in 2016 during his bid for the presidency as the sole candidate for the newly minted Transhumanist Party.[29]

---

[28] Christian Transhumanist Association, "The Christian Transhumanist Affirmation," accessed on January 5, 2020, https://www.christiantranshumanism.org.

[29] Personally, I think his bus would have been better suited to the campaign of Hillary Clinton, but with the subtraction of the letter *t* from the word *Immortality*.

Istvan ran for office on what was undoubtedly the most ambitious promise ever dared by a politician: eternal life for all. After failing to garner the votes in 2016, he relaunched his campaign in 2020, pledging, if elected, to immediately devote the resources of government to the development of life-extension technologies. Despite his promises of immortality, Zoltan Istvan has yet to capture the hearts of the American people; but the future looks bright for the Transhumanist Party. As life-extension technologies become progressively more feasible, the message of transhumanism will become increasingly more compelling.

In 2017, *NBC News* published an article entitled, "Godlike 'Homo Deus' Could Replace Humans as Tech Evolves." Authored by science journalist Dan Falk, the article featured the work of transhumanist professor Yuval Noah Harari. Writes Falk,

> Evolution is a slow affair, taking some 5 million years to turn a chimpanzee-like creature into us. But what happens when we push down the accelerator and take command of our bodies and brains instead of leaving it to nature? What happens when biotechnology and artificial intelligence merge, allowing us to re-design our species to meet our whims and desires?
>
> Historian Yuval Noah Harari explores these questions in his runaway bestseller, "Homo Deus: A Brief History of Tomorrow," a kind of sequel to his 2014 book, "Sapiens." The title of his new book suggests a startling stage in our evolution: Homo sapiens ("wise man"), far from being the pinnacle of creation, is a temporary creature, one soon to be replaced by Homo deus ("god man").
>
> "It is very likely, within a century or two, Homo sapiens, as we have known it for thousands of years, will disappear," Harari told an audience at the Carnegie Council for Ethics in International Affairs recently. "Not because, like in some Hollywood science fiction movie, the robots will come and kill us, but rather because we will use technology to upgrade ourselves—or at least some of us—into something different;

something which is far more different from us than we are different from Neanderthals."[30]

Professor Harari's vision of the god man, *homo deus*, is a portrait of apotheotheism—the synthesis of Darwinian evolution, Nietzschean philosophy, and Luciferian theology—but it is also a portent of things to come. The professor hints at a scenario that is quietly contemplated but rarely articulated by futurists. If a portion of humanity evolves into *homo deus*, what happens to those who elect to remain *homo sapiens*? Clearly, a new dystopic class system will be instituted at the emergence of the god man, otherwise known as the overman, a circumstance that Nietzsche gleefully anticipated.

The social castes of the future will be composed of two groups, which we shall designate as *Neo* (new) humans, and *Nea* (neanderthalic) humans. As the Neo humans will be physically and intellectually superior to the Nea humans, they will occupy the most important positions in society and govern the affairs of state. Because they are unwilling, or unable, to evolve, Nea humans will be viewed with contempt, the vestigial refuse of human evolution, and ultimately eliminated from the social body. In her book *The Revelation Alternative to Armageddon*, Barbara Marx Hubbard, channeling her spirit guide, forecasts the hostility in store for the Nea humans:

> Out of the full spectrum of human personality, one-fourth is electing to transcend with all their heart, mind, and spirit, One-fourth is ready to so choose, given the example of one other who has made the commitment, One-fourth is resistant to election. They are unattracted by life ever-evolving. Their higher self is unable to penetrate the density of their mammalian senses. They cannot be reached. . . . They go about their business, eating, sleeping, reproducing, and dying. They are full-fledged animal/humans. One-fourth is destructive.

---

[30] Dan Falk, "Godlike 'Homo Deus' Could Replace Humans as Tech Evolves," *NBC News*, May 31, 2017, https://www.nbcnews.com/mach/technology/godlike-homo-deus-could-replace-humans-tech-evolves-n757971.

They are born angry with God. They hate themselves. They project this hatred upon the world. They are defective seeds. . . . Now as we approach the quantum shift from creature-human to co-creative human—the human who is an inheritor of god-like powers—the destructive one-fourth must be eliminated from the social body.[31]

Hubbard's spirit guide is careful to reassure her coevolving comrades that they will not have to do the dirty work themselves:

Fortunately you, dearly beloveds, are not responsible for this act. We are. We are in charge of God's selection process for Planet Earth. He selects, we destroy. We are the riders of the pale horse, Death.[32]

All of this is reminiscent of Revelation 17, where men are compelled to worship the image of the beast and receive his mark, or face the dire consequences. It is the author's opinion that the mark of the beast is much more than a chip implanted in the hand or a barcode imprinted on the forehead. To worship the image of the beast and receive his mark is to become like Apollo, a posthuman hybrid modified with the genetic markers of the Golden Race.

The advantages of being reborn in the image of Apollo—extended life and godlike powers—will be extraordinarily enticing. The vast majority of people will eagerly line up to receive their evolutionary upgrade, but not everyone will comply. The fact that some will resist, and pay for their resistance with exclusion from commerce,[33] is proof of the principles hitherto established, namely, that the birthright of Adam cannot be wrested from us by force; it must be willfully abdicated. The mark of the beast, therefore, will be a choice advertised with the same allurement as the fruit from the tree of knowledge: *eat and become like the gods!*

---

[31] Barbara Marx Hubbard, *Book of Co-Creation: Part III, The Revelation Alternative to Armageddon* (n.p.: New Visions, 1980), 59–60.
[32] Ibid., 60.
[33] See Revelation 13:17.

An old and reliable adage assures us that *nothing in life is free*. Everything has a cost. The humanitarian benefits of biotechnology are very great. We all applaud when doctors discover new and innovative ways to cure children afflicted with degenerative diseases or when our veterans are fitted with state-of-the-art prosthetics to mend their broken bodies. The desire to alleviate human suffering is noble, and the full inventory of our technological toolkit should be mustered to the task. The question is, how far are we willing to go in our crusade to improve the human condition? Are we willing to surrender the very hallmarks that make us human in order to extend our lives?

The astonishing scientific breakthroughs of the last century have been attributed to the singular genius of mankind. We believe that our technological advancement has been achieved entirely on our own, but we are gravely mistaken. In truth, we have been deliberately provided with the blueprint to build the mechanism of our own demise. Behold the cunning of the serpent: we were first convinced to deny the biblical origin of our species so that we might be persuaded to discard the image we bear by means of the technology we were guided to develop, thereby divesting ourselves of the dominion it guarantees. GRIN, indeed!

Just like Esau, the offspring of Adam are about to sell their birthright for a bowl of stew.

Chapter 13

JACOB AND ESAU

In this final chapter, I am faced with the daunting task of a painter who, having added so many colors to the palette, must now apply them to the canvas and bring to life the portrait he has carried around in his head. Fortunately, the biblical narrative provides me with a template in the form of a familiar story—Jacob and Esau.

The story begins with Rebekah, the wife of Isaac and daughter-in-law of Abraham, who is barren. Isaac prays for his wife, and she becomes pregnant with twins, but when the time comes to deliver the babies, something rather bizarre occurs:

> The first came forth red, all his body like a hairy mantle; so they called his name Esau. Afterward his brother came forth, and his hand had taken hold of Esau's heel; so his name was called Jacob.[1]

I remember how perplexed I was as a young lad in Sunday school when my teacher glibly recited these verses, as if what they were describing was perfectly normal. I suppose that, being a twin myself, I was especially alarmed to discover that the first boy to emerge from Rebekah's womb looked like the red spawn of Bigfoot. Twins are supposed to resemble one another, are they not? Something was wrong with this picture.

---

[1] Genesis 25:25–26 (RSV).

Even if Jacob and Esau were fraternal twins as opposed to identical twins, the fact that one of them was red and hairy like a mantle should give us pause.

As previously established, *Esau* means "red." He would later be called *Edom*. *Jacob* means "heel holder" or "supplanter," because he had taken hold of Esau's heel. He would later be called *Israel*. The story of Jacob and Esau revolves around the concept of a birthright. In ancient times, a father, before passing away, would bequeath his patriarchal authority and material possessions to his firstborn son as an inheritance—a birthright. Once given, the blessing of the birthright could not be rescinded; it could, however, be abdicated. As Esau was born first, the birthright belonged to him.

When Isaac was on his deathbed and blind, the time came to bestow the birthright to Esau. However, Rebekah favored Jacob and persuaded him to fool his father by impersonating his brother so that the birthright would pass to him instead. Jacob, realizing that his father would likely touch him to confer the blessing, made the obvious observation, "Behold, my brother Esau is a hairy man, and I am a smooth man."[2]

The word *hairy* in this instance comes from the Hebrew *sa'iyr*, which is most commonly associated with a male goat. Esau wasn't hairy like a man; Esau was hairy like a goat.[3] Rebekah's solution to the problem removes all doubt that Esau was *inhumanly* hairy—she covered Jacob's arms and neck in goat skins.

There are a few people alive today (about fifty) suffering from a rare genetic disorder called hypertrichosis, otherwise known as "werewolf syndrome," which causes their bodies to be covered in an inordinate amount of thick hair. It is possible that Esau was born with hypertrichosis, but the double phenomenon of being a twin and having the genetic disorder is very rare indeed. There is, however, another possibility: Esau was not entirely human.

It cannot be coincidental that both Abraham's wife, Sarah, and Isaac's wife, Rebekah, were barren. Neither is it coincidental that in both cases

---

[2] Genesis 27:11 (RSV).

[3] Incidentally, *sa'iyr* can also mean "satyr" or "faun," imbuing it with a more diabolical connotation, e.g., "They shall no longer sacrifice their sacrifices to the goat demons [*sa'iyr*] with which they play the harlot" (Leviticus 17:7, NASB).

an ill-begotten elder sibling threatened the continuity of the family line. In the first case, it was Ishmael, and in the second, Esau. Furthermore, we must not fail to recognize the parallels between Cain (and Abel), Ishmael (and Isaac), and Esau (and Jacob). Every one of these sibling contenders was directly influenced by Satan, who intended to corrupt the bloodline of the Christ and usurp the birthright of Adam. Just as John had beheld, the dragon was ever poised to devour the male progeny of the woman. Had Cain, Ishmael, or Esau received the birthright instead of their younger brothers,[4] then the birth of Christ would have been prevented and the Dragon Slayer Prophecy forestalled.

Sarah, because of her barrenness in old age, was tempted to doubt the promise of God and persuaded Abraham to produce an heir through Hagar, her Egyptian handmaiden. Ishmael was born as a result. But the scheme failed as soon as Sarah's womb miraculously came to life and Isaac was conceived. Having learned from his previous mistake, the dragon, it seems, took a more direct approach with Rebekah.

What was the cause of Sarah's and Rebekah's barrenness? Of course, the condition could have been perfectly natural, and this would seem the most logical conclusion, if it were not for the red monstrosity that emerged from Rebekah's womb. Is it possible that the dragon was tampering with the reproductive faculties of these women? Was Esau the product of in vitro fertilization? Could the same procedure of artificial insemination employed by gray aliens today account for the hybrid creature that pre-empted Jacob through the birth canal three thousand years ago? These questions, though highly speculative, are worth pondering in light of the abduction phenomenon and the breeding program it entails.

As with Cain, it is ironic that Esau's carnal passions became the undoing of the dragon's carefully laid plan. The birthright would have safely passed to Esau had his ferocious appetite not interfered:

> Once when Jacob was cooking stew, Esau came in from the field, and he was exhausted. And Esau said to Jacob, "Let me

---

[4] Cain, who according to John was "of the evil one" (1 John 3:12, ESV), would have received the birthright from his father had he not been banished from the family for killing Abel. Consequently, the birthright fell to Seth.

eat some of that red stew, for I am exhausted!" ... Jacob said, "Sell me your birthright now." Esau said, "I am about to die; of what use is a birthright to me?" Jacob said, "Swear to me now." So he swore to him and sold his birthright to Jacob. Then Jacob gave Esau bread and lentil stew, and he ate and drank and rose and went his way. Thus Esau despised his birthright.[5]

We can imagine the dragon standing there, facepalming with dismay as he witnessed Esau surrender the prize for a bowl of stew. It is important to recognize that Esau had to abdicate his birthright before Jacob could appropriate it. Had Esau not sold his birthright to Jacob with an oath, then the blessing of Isaac would have been nullified.

In yet another twist of irony, Esau's hallmark hairiness would deal the dragon his final blow. While Esau was away hunting, Rebekah covered Jacob's hands and forearms in goatskins and clothed him in his brother's garments, reeking with his peculiar odor, before sending him into his father's tent to secure the blessing. The ruse succeeded. Isaac, believing him to be Esau, conferred the birthright to Jacob and appointed him to rule over his siblings and all the family of Abraham.

Isaac was the promised son of Abraham and a prototype of the coming Messiah. The sacrifice of the Father's Only Begotten Son was foreshadowed in his command to Abraham, "Take your son, your only son Isaac, whom you love, and go to the land of Moriah, and offer him there as a burnt offering on one of the mountains of which I shall tell you."[6] Abraham was not engaging in infanticide, as atheists are fond of asserting, but play-acting the plan of God for the salvation of mankind. It was never God's intention that Abraham sacrifice his son. The performance was meant to be interpreted as a message: the Father was going to send his own beloved Son to die for the sins of the world. Moriah means "chosen by Yahweh." Abraham and his descendants were the chosen bloodline through whom the Son of Man, the seed of the woman, would come.

The writer of Genesis portrays Jacob as a usurper, and indeed he was, but had he not supplanted his brother Esau in the hierarchy of the

---

[5] Genesis 25:29–34 (ESV).
[6] Genesis 22:2 (ESV).

family, then Israel would never have produced the Messiah, and mankind would not have a kinsman redeemer. In consideration of this fact, we are compelled to view the story from a higher vantage. In truth, Esau is the usurper, whose ill-begotten birth preempted the promised seed and imperiled the fulfillment of the Dragon Slayer Prophecy. Jacob grabbed Esau's heel and took back what rightfully belonged to him, and to all of us—the birthright of Adam. As we will see, Jacob, like his father Isaac, was an archetype of Christ. The symbolic sacrifice of Isaac was a fore-token of Christ's first coming and sacrificial death, and Jacob reclaiming the birthright from Esau, a harbinger of his return at Armageddon and triumph over Apollo, the hybrid son of the dragon.

The story of Jacob and Esau is the roadmap for understanding the unfolding of events at the end of the age. As the dragon cannot seize the birthright of mankind by force, he must persuade us to sell it for a bowl of stew. He must also present a claimant to the throne of Adam who is human enough to inherit the seal of his authority. This is why the dragon intends to produce a male child with a human woman, just as the watchers did in the pre-Flood world.

As previously established, dominion of the earth does not belong to one man, or even to one family line, but to the whole of mankind. The birthright is inherent in our genome. We are all the offspring of Adam, replicated with the seal of his likeness and endowed with the authority it guarantees. The wholesale purchase of the human birthright would require universal (or majority) consent from the human populace at large.

Abdicating our authority to the dragon is one thing; selling him our birthright is quite another. The first can be achieved through a voluntary transaction, but the second necessitates a genetic transformation.

Recall that the prime objective of the Great Plan is to usher in a New Golden Age and enthrone the ten kings of the Golden Race—the human-hybrid progeny of the seven dragon princes, with Apollo as lord over all. These kings, subordinate to their fathers, will lead the nations into kinetic war with the kingdom of heaven, culminating at Armageddon.

As outlined in a previous chapter, the New Golden Age will come to pass with the confluence of three essential components: (1) the estab-lishment of a new religion that impels men to become like the gods,

(2) the disclosure of a hostile alien presence and the arrival of the Golden Race, and (3) the development of GRIN technologies and the emergence of posthumanity. The third component, the posthuman paradigm, is the key to usurping human dominion on Planet Earth.

The only way that we can effectively sell our birthright is to willfully relinquish the genetic markers that make us human. This is precisely the goal of posthumanism—to discard the body of Adam in order to attain the attributes of the gods; to dispense with the mortal and moral inhibitions of the human condition and evolve into overman. In times past, such a lofty ambition was little more than a pipe dream. Today, it is a vision of the future.

Men of old pined to become like the gods but were far removed from the technology that could make their lofty aspirations possible. We stand, now equipped with the GRIN toolkit, but a few paces from the same forbidden fruit that seduced our primordial parents. Soon we will pluck it from the branch and press it to our lips. But just as Eve had to be coaxed by the serpent to commit the act, so Apollo and his consorts will guide us into becoming the gods of our own design. However, apotheosis has a price. Our divinity will cost us our humanity. This is the Faustian bargain we will strike with the devil.

Indeed, Faust is a fitting analogy. According to the classic German legend, Faust was an accomplished scholar and famed magician who grew increasingly dissatisfied with his life and decided to make a deal with the devil. Not content with the meager indulgences of his mortal condition, Faust craved the food of the gods—perpetual youth, unlimited knowledge, and uninhibited pleasure. His appetite for apotheosis impelled him to summon Mephistopheles, an emissary of the devil. When Mephistopheles appeared, Faust proposed a bargain: he would sell his soul in exchange for what he desired. Playwright Johann Wolfgang von Goethe, in his theatrical rendition of the tale, specifies Faust's request—he wanted to become *der übermensch*, the overman.

At first it went well for Faust. His mind was infused with transcendental knowledge, and he attained everything his heart desired. But when the hour of his death was nigh and payment of the bargain due, the devil came to claim his soul and dragged him down to hell.

Like Faust, modern man is growing increasingly dissatisfied with the limitations of human biology. We hunger for perpetual youth, unlimited knowledge, and uninhibited pleasure. Driven by the will to power, we will endeavor to direct the course of our evolution and discard the body of Adam in order to become the overman. Before the end of the age, we will surrender our humanity in pursuit of immortality, and thus, sell our birthright for a bowl of stew.

What happens when we are no longer human enough to possess the birthright of our species? If we forfeit the image of the Elohim, the seal of authority inherent in our genome, who will defend our dominion on Earth? Who will restrain the alien agencies intent on taking over?

For thousands of years, the adversaries of mankind have been kept in check by the armies of the kingdom, who defend and enforce our dominion on Earth. But our authority is contingent on the image we bear. As soon as we discard the genetic markers that make us human, those forces will withdraw and leave us to our fate.

In light of this principle, we may now understand the mystery of the "restrainer" mentioned in Paul's letter to the church at Thessalonica. The reader will recall that the Thessalonians were greatly distressed because they believed that the Lord had come to rapture the righteous and they were left behind. Paul, irritated by their ignorance, admonished them to remember that Christ will not return until the rebellion occurs and the man of lawlessness, the son of destruction (Apollo) is revealed.

> Do you not remember that when I was still with you I told you these things? And you know what is *restraining* him now so that he may be revealed in his time. For the mystery of lawlessness is already at work. Only he who now *restrains* it will do so until he is out of the way. And then the lawless one will be revealed, whom the Lord Jesus will kill with the breath of his mouth and bring to nothing by the appearance of his coming. The coming of the lawless one is by the activity of Satan with all power and false signs and wonders, and with all wicked deception for those who are perishing, because they refused to love the truth and so be saved. Therefore God sends

them a strong delusion, so that they may believe what is false, in order that all may be condemned who did not believe the truth but had pleasure in unrighteousness.[7]

In the author's opinion, the *restrainer* is Michael, a mighty prince of the elder race who commands the armies of the kingdom and enforces the dominion of mankind on Planet Earth. The *strong delusion* concerns the gospel of Apollo, who will impersonate Christ and declare himself to be the son of god and savior of the world. As long as Michael restrains him, Satan cannot operate openly on Earth. However, when the offspring of Adam abdicate their birthright by becoming posthuman, then Michael will withdraw his hand, and all hell will break loose.

The transition from human to transhuman to posthuman will not transpire as a single event but as a sequence of events over time. It is imperative, according to the rules of the game, that we take these steps ourselves. In the same way that Esau had to willfully abdicate his birthright before Jacob could usurp it, so we will have to make a conscious choice to become posthuman through the implementation of our technology.

In the beginning, we will use our technologies to mitigate the deficiencies of our genome. Gene therapies will successfully cure many genetic disorders, and minor cybernetic enhancements will improve certain physical and cognitive abilities. However, due to the quickening pace of degeneration, more extreme modifications will be necessary to counter the decline. As we inch ever closer to error catastrophe, it will become increasingly apparent that the human genome is no longer viable. Once we reach the end of our genetic rope, we will require an infusion of supplemental DNA from an outside source.[8]

Enter a new breed of men sent down from heaven to supply our need.[9]

Our desire to become like the gods will be greatly intensified when the progeny of the gods appear. Apollo and his golden-haired siblings will arrive precisely in the hour of insuperable crisis. They will first deliver us

---

[7] 2 Thessalonians 2:5–12 (ESV), emphasis added.

[8] It is possible that the insectalins have already reached this point, and they are using human DNA to slow the genetic decline of their species. As the whole universe of matter is subject to entropy, all living things are expiring together, including the grays.

[9] In accordance with the Sibylline oracle from Virgil's *The Eclogues*, as cited in chapter 9.

from the insectalin invasion and then help to redress the genetic apoc-alypse we face as a species.[10] To the amazement of all, they will disclose that their fathers, the dragon princes, were the original progenitors of mankind, who engineered the first human beings by splicing segments of their own DNA into the genome of a primitive hominoid species indig-enous to Planet Earth. They, as the offspring of god and man, will offer to upgrade our genome in the same way—by mingling their DNA with ours so that we may become like them.

At this point, having already modified our biology in significant ways, we will be far along the path of posthumanism. Indeed, the coming of Apollo will be triggered by our genetic transformation. The recipience of Apollo's genetic markers will consummate the final step in our evolution out of Adam and make the change immutable.[11]

The blood of the dragon's only begotten son, so to speak, will be offered for the salvation of mankind. Apollo will be presented as the prototype of the new man—humanity 2.0. In order to enter the kingdom of Apollo, you must be born again. The old man, Adam, must die if the new man is to be resurrected to eternal life in the image of the beast. Only members of the New Golden Race may be citizens of the New Golden Age. Those who reject rebirth will be marked as obsolete and unable to participate in Apollo's Atlantean world order. They are, in the words of Hubbard's spirit guide, "unattracted by life ever-evolving" and "defective seeds" who must be "eliminated from the social body."[12]

Those who receive the mark of the beast will become ineligible for salvation through the work of the cross. The gospel of Jesus Christ has but one proviso—you must be human. The Son of God became a man to save mankind. Posthumans, by definition, are irredeemable. Jesus is a kinsman redeemer only for the offspring of Adam, his *human* brethren. This is why those who receive the mark are inexorably damned.

---

[10] Alternatively, Apollo will disclose that the grays, under his direction, have been laboring to create hybrids for the preservation of the human species, or something to this effect. In addition, there may also be catastrophic natural disasters occurring on the planet that Apollo helps to amend.

[11] There is also the very real possibility that the grays are conspiring with Apollo to supplant the human species once the change happens. They become more human as we become less; they seize the birthright when we relinquish it.

[12] Barbara Marx Hubbard, *Book of Co-Creation,* see chapter 12 for full quotation.

In the last days, there will be scarcely a human being left on Earth. The mark of the beast will be irreversible and hereditary, leading to the near extinction of the human species. However, a remnant of mankind will persevere until the return of Christ. While discussing the end of the age with his disciples, Jesus tells them,

> For then there will be great tribulation, such as has not been since the beginning of the world until this time, no, nor ever shall be. And unless those days were shortened, no flesh would be saved; but for the elect's sake those days will be shortened.[13]

The phrase "no flesh would be saved" may also be rendered, "no flesh would be *able to be* saved." This situation is reminiscent of the pre-Flood world, in which all flesh was corrupted. It is not incidental that Jesus invokes Noah a few verses later:

> But as the days of Noah were, so also will the coming of the Son of Man be.[14]

The days are shortened for the sake of the elect, not to save their *lives* but to preserve their *humanity*. If the days were not shortened, then there would be no candidates for salvation left on Earth. No flesh would be *able to be* saved. All flesh would be corrupted.

A curious verse in Revelation 9 seems to anticipate a grim predicament for the posthuman:

> In those days men will seek death and will not find it; they will desire to die, and death will flee from them.[15]

This bizarre scenario is perfectly conceivable within the context of the GRIN technologies currently under development. Extreme genetic and cybernetic enhancements to human biology could make dying a difficult

<hr>

[13] Matthew 24:21–22 (NKJV).
[14] Matthew 24:37 (NKJV).
[15] Revelation 9:6 (NKJV).

affair for posthuman beings. Considering that the transhumanist prime objective is to live forever through the power of technology, it is not hard to imagine the lengths to which they will go to cheat death. How ironic that men who seek to live forever will one day give anything to die.

Transhumanists today are already excited about the prospect of uploading their consciousness into synthetic bodies, including nanotech bodies that might be capable of surviving even the most catastrophic of injuries. As it happens, surviving a catastrophic injury is a prophetic signature of the beast:

> And I saw one of his heads as if it had been mortally wounded, and his deadly wound was healed. And all the world marveled and followed the beast.[16]

Just as Jesus authenticated the message of the gospel by rising from the dead, so Apollo will "authenticate" his counterfeit gospel by miraculously recovering from a deadly wound. The incident will further provoke the nations to worship the beast and will serve as a proof of concept demonstrating the benefits of being reborn in his likeness. When given the opportunity, the masses, enraptured with the prospect of immortality, will eagerly line up to receive the genetic markers of the Golden Race.

The mark of the beast is a clever ploy to irrevocably divest the human species of their birthright and seize the title deed of Planet Earth. The hybrid son of the dragon will hijack the authority of Adam and usurp the throne that belongs to the Son of Man. Apollo will rule over a planet virtually bereft of human beings. Indeed, he will be more human than the posthumans subjugated to his dominion. When once he has consolidated power, he will prepare for war with the Prince of princes, as predicted in the oracle of Daniel:

> When rebels have become completely wicked, a fierce-looking king, a master of intrigue, will arise. He will become very strong, but not by his own power. He will cause astounding devastation and will succeed in whatever he does. He will

---

[16] Revelation 13:3 (NKJV).

destroy those who are mighty [and] the holy people. He will cause deceit to prosper, and he will consider himself superior [exalt himself]. When they feel secure, he will destroy many and take his stand against the Prince of princes. Yet he will be destroyed, but not by human power.[17]

The surface layer of this prophecy pertains to the aforementioned Greek tyrant, Antiochus Epiphanes (c. 215–164 BC), who persecuted the Jews, slaughtering eighty thousand of them within a three-day period. However, the deeper meaning points to Apollo, of whom Antiochus Epiphanes was but a presage. As noted earlier, *Epiphanes* means "god manifest." Like Antiochus, the beast will exalt himself as god, being the son of god, and will receive his authority from his father:

So they worshiped the dragon who gave authority to the beast; and they worshiped the beast, saying, "Who is like the beast? Who is able to make war with him?"

And he was given a mouth speaking great things and blas-phemies, and he was given authority to continue for forty-two months. Then he opened his mouth in blasphemy against God, to blaspheme His name, His tabernacle, and those who dwell in heaven. It was granted to him to make war with the saints and to overcome them. And authority was given him over every tribe, tongue, and nation. All who dwell on the earth will worship him, whose names have not been written in the Book of Life of the Lamb slain from the foundation of the world.[18]

It is important to recognize that the beast is endowed with the author-ity of the dragon, his inhuman father, *and* with the authority of Adam, through his human mother. Because he attains his authority legally, and is human enough to appropriate it, he is permitted to rule for a short time[19] and to persecute the saints in the same way that the emperors of Rome

---

[17] Daniel 8:23–25 (NIV).
[18] Revelation 13:4–8 (NKJV).
[19] Specifically, forty-two months. See Revelation 13:5.

did in the first and second centuries. However, the purpose of the beast is not merely to persecute the saints but to prosecute a war.

Recall the conspiracy of Psalm 2:

> Why do the nations rage, and the people plot a vain thing? The kings of the earth set themselves, and the rulers take counsel together, against the Lord and against his anointed, saying, "Let us break their bonds in pieces and cast away their cords from us."[20]

The "kings of the earth" are the hybrid beast kings, and the "rulers" are their fathers, the dragon princes. They, and the posthuman denizens of Apollo's empire, are conspiring to make war with the powers of heaven. As in the first rebellion, the dragon will muster a formidable army. Many morning stars will defect and join his ranks.[21] The old alliances will be renewed, the ancient ruins will be rebuilt, and the dragon's Edomite confederacy will be revived in all its strength.

Though I cannot supply a scriptural text to buttress the postulation, I suspect that the kings of the earth and their fathers, the rulers, will plan a two-pronged attack designed to defend the empire of Apollo and resist the return of Christ. The dragon princes will deploy their extraterrestrial forces from fortifications on Mars and elsewhere in the solar system. On Earth, the beast kings and their posthuman legions will field the armaments of the elder race. Flying discs will patrol the outer atmosphere of the planet, while mile-wide mother ships prepare to repel the armies of the kingdom should they break through the dragon's first line of defense.

Emboldened by their overwhelming force of arms, the nations will rage with inhuman madness and comfort themselves in the delusion that the dragon princes and their half-breed sons are mightier than the powers of heaven.

But the Lord will look on with a smile.

---

[20] Psalm 2:1–3 (NKJV).

[21] The defection of morning stars well acquainted with the majesty and might of the King is a testament to the dragon's own magnetism and influence. One does not brave the dreadful consequence of sedition without an assurance that the defecting side can win. The dragon's power at the end of the age will be great enough to instill such confidence.

He who sits in the heavens shall laugh; the Lord shall hold them in derision. Then he shall speak to them in his wrath, and distress them in his deep displeasure: "Yet I have set my King on my holy hill of Zion."

"I will declare the decree: The Lord has said to me, 'You are my Son, today I have begotten you. Ask of me, and I will give you the nations for your inheritance, and the ends of the earth for your possession. You shall break them with a rod of iron; you shall dash them to pieces like a potter's vessel.'"[22]

Per John's vision of the woman and the dragon, Michael will preemptively assault the dragon's fortifications and throw down his forces from their interplanetary strongholds, confining them to the earth.

Rejoice, O heavens and you who dwell in them! But woe to you, O earth and sea, for the devil has come down to you in great wrath, because he knows that his time is short![23]

Before Christ returns to dash the nations to pieces like a potter's vessel, the earth will resemble a dystopian nightmare. There will be no atheists in the New Golden Age. As predicted by Blavatsky, all will worship the dragon and the sun (Apollo). The God of Abraham, Isaac, and Jacob will be blasphemed as a tyrant and imposter. Jesus will be hated, his name outlawed, and those who follow him hunted like wild animals. Apollo will rule the planet with no one to oppose him.

In Revelation 5, John is caught up to the throne room of heaven to witness a scene of tremendous implication:

Then I saw in the right hand of him who sat on the throne a scroll with writing on both sides and sealed with seven seals. And I saw a mighty angel proclaiming in a loud voice, "Who is worthy to break the seals and open the scroll?" But no one in heaven or on earth or under the earth could open the scroll or

[22] Psalm 2:4–9 (NKJV).
[23] Revelation 12:12 (ESV).

even look inside it. I wept and wept because no one was found who was worthy to open the scroll or look inside.[24]

Have you ever wondered why John weeps over this scroll? Why does it elicit such profound sorrow? John's reaction always seemed so irrational to me, until I realized that this scroll is the title deed of Planet Earth. John is weeping because mankind has lost dominion of the realm he was created to rule, and no one is able to reclaim it for him.

But that is not how the scene ends.

You see, dear reader, even if there are no more human beings left on Earth, there is still a Son of Man seated at the right hand of the Father in heaven. Just when it appears that all is lost for the offspring of Adam, Jacob grabs hold of Esau's heel:

> Then one of the elders said to me, "Do not weep! See, the Lion of the tribe of Judah, the Root of David, has triumphed. He is able to open the scroll and its seven seals."
>
> Then I saw a Lamb, looking as if it had been slain, standing at the center of the throne, encircled by the four living creatures and the elders. The Lamb had seven horns and seven eyes, which are the seven spirits of God sent out into all the earth. He went and took the scroll from the right hand of him who sat on the throne. And when he had taken it, the four living creatures and the twenty-four elders fell down before the Lamb. Each one had a harp and they were holding golden bowls full of incense, which are the prayers of God's people. And they sang a new song, saying: "You are worthy to take the scroll and to open its seals, because you were slain, and with your blood you purchased for God persons from every tribe and language and people and nation. You have made them to be a kingdom and priests to serve our God, and they will reign on the earth."[25]

---

[24] Revelation 5:1–4 (NIV).
[25] Revelation 5:5–10 (NIV).

Jesus is able to take the scroll and open its seals because *he* is a son of Adam, the root *and* the offspring of David,[26] a legal inheritor of the human birthright and a rightful claimant to the throne of his ancestors. He has all authority in heaven as the Son of God and all authority on Earth as the Son of Man.[27]

Upon taking the deed from the hand of his Father, the Lamb begins to break its seven seals, one by one. With the breaking of each seal, a new catastrophe is unleashed on the nations. Wars, famines, plagues, and cataclysms rock the earth.

The wardens of the kingdom watch the obliteration of the bestial empire with bated breath, as the Son waits for his Father's command:

> The Lord says to my lord: "Sit at my right hand until I make your enemies a footstool for your feet."
>
> The Lord will extend your mighty scepter from Zion, saying, "Rule in the midst of your enemies!" Your troops will be willing on your day of battle. Arrayed in holy splendor, your young men will come to you like dew from the morning's womb. . . .
>
> The Lord is at your right hand; he will crush kings on the day of his wrath. He will judge the nations, heaping up the dead and crushing the rulers of the whole earth.[28]

Finally, when the nations lie in smoldering ruin, a trumpet blast will peal through the air, and the seed of the woman, the Dragon Slayer, will rise from his throne and march forth with the armies of heaven to reclaim the earth for the sons of Adam. Apollo will gather what forces remain in the valley of Armageddon to make his stand against the Prince of princes, the King of kings and Lord of lords:

> Then I saw heaven opened, and behold, a white horse! The one sitting on it is called Faithful and True, and in righteousness

---

[26] See Revelation 22:16.
[27] See Matthew 28:18.
[28] Psalm 110:1–3, 5–6 (NIV).

he judges and makes war. His eyes are like a flame of fire, and on his head are many diadems, and he has a name written that no one knows but himself. He is clothed in a robe dipped in blood, and the name by which he is called is The Word of God. And the armies of heaven, arrayed in fine linen, white and pure, were following him on white horses. From his mouth comes a sharp sword with which to strike down the nations, and he will rule them with a rod of iron. He will tread the winepress of the fury of the wrath of God the Almighty. On his robe and on his thigh he has a name written, King of kings and Lord of lords.

Then I saw an angel standing in the sun, and with a loud voice he called to all the birds that fly directly overhead, "Come, gather for the great supper of God, to eat the flesh of kings, the flesh of captains, the flesh of mighty men, the flesh of horses and their riders, and the flesh of all men, both free and slave, both small and great." And I saw the beast and the kings of the earth with their armies gathered to make war against him who was sitting on the horse and against his army. And the beast was captured, and with it the false prophet who in its presence had done the signs by which he deceived those who had received the mark of the beast and those who worshiped its image. These two were thrown alive into the lake of fire that burns with sulfur. And the rest were slain by the sword that came from the mouth of him who was sitting on the horse, and all the birds were gorged with their flesh.[29]

This sanguinary scene was also beheld by Daniel, who foresaw the coming of the Lord, the vanquishment of the beast kings, and the bequeathal of Adam's dominion to the Son of Man, just as Enoch had predicted thousands of years before:

And as I looked, the beast was killed, and its body destroyed and given over to be burned with fire. As for the rest of the

---

[29] Revelation 19:11–21 (ESV).

beasts, their dominion was taken away, but their lives were prolonged for a season and a time.

I saw in the night visions, and behold, with the clouds of heaven there came one like a son of man, and he came to the Ancient of Days and was presented before him. And to him was given dominion and glory and a kingdom, that all peoples, nations, and languages should serve him; his dominion is an everlasting dominion, which shall not pass away, and his kingdom one that shall not be destroyed.[30]

Writes Enoch,

And thus the Lord commanded the kings and the mighty and the exalted, and those who dwell on the earth, and said: 'Open your eyes and lift up your horns if ye are able to recognize the Elect One.'

And the Lord of Spirits seated him on the throne of his glory, and the spirit of righteousness was poured out upon him, and the word of his mouth slays all the sinners, and all the unrighteous are destroyed from before his face. And there shall stand up in that day all the kings and the mighty, and the exalted and those who hold the earth . . . And one portion of them shall look on the other, and they shall be terrified, and they shall be downcast of countenance, and pain shall seize them, when they see that Son of Man sitting on the throne of his glory.

And the kings and the mighty and all who possess the earth shall bless and glorify and extol him who rules over all.[31]

When the final trumpet sounds in Revelation 11, John hears loud voices in heaven, declaring,

---

[30] Daniel 7:11–14 (ESV).
[31] 1 Enoch 62:1–3, 5–6 (RHC).

"The kingdom of the world has become the kingdom of our Lord and of his Christ, and he shall reign forever and ever." And the twenty-four elders who sit on their thrones before God fell on their faces and worshiped God, saying, "We give thanks to you, Lord God Almighty, who is and who was, for you have taken your great power and begun to reign. The nations raged, but your wrath came, and the time for the dead to be judged, and for rewarding your servants, the prophets and saints, and those who fear your name, both small and great, and for destroying the destroyers of the earth."[32]

The phrase "destroyers of the earth" can also be translated "corruptors of the earth,"[33] which is evocative of the genetic corruption wrought by the watchers in the pre-Flood world. Christ returns in the aftermath of judgment by fire, which, like the Flood, rids the earth of hybrid usurpers. In both cases, human dominion is restored to the remnant of mankind; in the first, to Noah and his offspring, and in the second, to Christ and his saints who endure to the end.[34]

The return of Christ at the end of the age is the final fulfillment of the Dragon Slayer Prophecy. After eons of leading men and morning stars into rebellion, war, and ruin, the mighty dragon prince will be utterly crushed by a son of Adam born from the womb of a daughter of Eve.

He laid hold of the dragon, that serpent of old, who is the Devil and Satan, and bound him for a thousand years; and he cast him into the bottomless pit, and shut him up, and set a seal on him, so that he should deceive the nations no more . . .[35]

Jesus is the hero of humanity who restores our realm, rectifies our condition, and reconciles us to God. Because of Adam's sin, man was sundered from the divine family, condemned with the dragon, and subjected to

---

[32] Revelation 11:15–18 (ESV).
[33] See "Strong's G1311 – *diaphtheirō*," Blue Letter Bible, accessed on May 12, 2020, https://www.blueletterbible.org/lang/Lexicon/Lexicon.cfm?strongs=G1311&t=KJV.
[34] See Revelation 20.
[35] Revelation 20:2–3 (NKJV).

decay, degeneration, and death. The Son of God became a man to redeem
the sons and daughters of Adam, deliver them from condemnation, and
lead them back to the Father's house.

The gospel of Jesus Christ is elegantly depicted in the Parable of the
Prodigal Son, who is emblematic of Adam and, by extension, all of mankind. Once a beloved sibling in the Father's house, enjoying the fare and
fellowship of his table, man squandered his inheritance and became
indentured to the swineherd, eating the slop of pigs. But God, because of
his great love, made a way of reconciliation for those who, like the prodigal
son, recognize their depravity and repent:

> "The son said to him, 'Father, I have sinned against heaven
> and against you. I am no longer worthy to be called your son.'
>
> "But the father said to his servants, 'Quick! Bring the best
> robe and put it on him. Put a ring on his finger and sandals
> on his feet. Bring the fattened calf and kill it. Let's have a feast
> and celebrate. For this son of mine was dead and is alive again;
> he was lost and is found.'"[36]

The robe and sandals with which the prodigal son is clothed represent
the righteousness of Christ and the resurrection; the ring that is placed
on his finger is the seal of the royal house; the feast is the wedding supper
of the Lamb.[37]

The return of mankind to the family of God is the crux of the gospel
and the purpose of the Christ. In order to reconcile us to the Father, the
Son of Man wore our flesh, the body of Adam, and, taking our sin upon
himself, nailed it to the cross:

> He himself bore our sins in his body on the tree, that we might
> die to sin and live to righteousness. By his wounds you have
> been healed.[38]

---

[36] Luke 15:21–24 (NIV).
[37] See Matthew 22; Revelation 19.
[38] 1 Peter 2:24 (ESV). See also Philippians 2:5–11; Colossians 1:21–23; Hebrews 2:14–18.

The grisly visage of a disfigured man crucified on a tree with a crown of thorns pressed into his brow is a vivid portrait of the origin and penalty of Adam's sin. By eating the fruit from the tree of knowledge, Adam brought the blight of death upon his race and the curse of futility upon his realm:

> "Cursed is the ground because of you; through painful toil you will eat food from it all the days of your life. It will produce thorns and thistles for you, and you will eat the plants of the field. By the sweat of your brow you will eat your food until you return to the ground, since from it you were taken; for dust you are and to dust you will return."[39]

"Fit objects, then," notes Pember, "are the thorn and the thistle to remind man of the curse. And keeping their origin in view we can see a deep significance in that awful scene when our Lord suffered himself to be crowned with thorns, so that even his enemies set him forth as the great Curse-bearer; when he wore on his bleeding brow that which owed its very existence to, and was the sign of, the sin which he had come to expiate."[40]

"Surely he has borne our griefs and carried our sorrows," wrote Isaiah seven hundred years before Jesus of Nazareth was beaten and flogged as he carried his cross to the hill of Golgotha, "yet we esteemed him stricken, smitten by God, and afflicted. But he was pierced for our transgressions; he was crushed for our iniquities; upon him was the chastisement that brought us peace, and with his wounds we are healed."[41]

Never, not in all the ages of the earth, not in the good deeds of any man, not in story, not in poem, not in song, has there ever been an expression of love to rival the cross of Christ. That the Son of God, the very Singularity of all creation, humbled himself to be born into our condition so that he might bear our curse, suffer our affliction, and pay the penalty for our sin, is a love that simply cannot be fathomed by the human heart.

"In this the love of God was made manifest among us," wrote John, who stood at the foot of the cross as Jesus convulsed with pain and

---

[39] Genesis 3:17–19 (NIV).
[40] Pember, *Earth's Earliest Ages*, 132.
[41] Isaiah 53:4–5 (ESV).

struggled to breathe, "that God sent his only Son into the world, so that we might live through him. In this is love, not that we have loved God but that he loved us and sent his Son to be the propitiation for our sins."[42]

Life in Christ is the antidote to death in Adam. Jesus, the Son of God, is the second Adam,[43] who was born into the world to succeed where the first Adam had failed and in so doing restore all that was lost. Tempted in every way by the same seducing serpent, Jesus did not succumb to sin but obeyed his Father with perfect devotion, even consenting to be crucified like a common criminal. "As one trespass led to condemnation for all men," wrote Paul to the Romans, "so one act of righteousness [the cross] leads to justification and life for all men. For as by the one man's disobedience the many were made sinners, so by the one man's obedience the many will be made righteous."[44]

Just as those who are born from the first Adam inherit the condemnation of his trespass—alienation and death—so those born of the second Adam through the resurrection will inherit the justification of his righteousness—reconciliation and everlasting life:

> For as by a man came death, by a man has come also the resurrection of the dead. For as in Adam all die, so also in Christ shall all be made alive.[45]

The rebirth of the resurrection is a reset of the human race to the blueprint of Adam as he was before the fall. The fallen Adam, the body of sin, was crucified with Christ so that those who die believing in him might also be raised in him, and born again as sons of God:

> For if we have been united together in the likeness of his death, certainly we also shall be in the likeness of his resurrection,

---

[42] 1 John 4:9–10 (ESV).

[43] Adam was a son of God. The only other son of God in the line of Adam was Jesus of Nazareth; all others were sons of Adam. Thus, Jesus is the second Adam (see Romans 5; 1 Corinthians 15).

[44] Romans 5:18–19 (ESV).

[45] 1 Corinthians 15:21–22 (ESV).

knowing this, that our old man [fallen Adam] was crucified with him, that the body of sin might be done away with.[46]

Jesus did not cease to be human when he rose from the dead, and neither will we. Indeed, we will be more human than we are now. Every defect in our genome, accrued over thousands of years of degeneration, will be remedied at the resurrection. Through Christ, mankind will be completely restored to his Edenic glory in the family of God. Every human faculty that was lost or diminished as a result of the fall will be fully reactivated. We who are presently shackled to the grave and languishing in the decay of our mortal bodies will one day be liberated from the blight of death to live forever in the amaranthine bliss of paradise.

The posthuman gospel of humanity 2.0, the self-made second Adam, is a circumvention of the cross of Christ. Rather than enter through the door,[47] posthumans will attempt to scale the wall of paradise and steal the fruit from the tree of life. In their fervor to attain immortality, they will foolishly defy the only one who has the power to grant it.

> "I am the resurrection and the life; he who believes in me, though he die, yet shall he live, and whoever lives and believes in me shall never die."[48]

The resurrection is the rectification of the human condition. Jesus Christ *is* humanity 2.0.

---

[46] Romans 6:5–6 (NKJV).

[47] Jesus said, "I am the door. If anyone enters by me, he will be saved, and will go in and out and find pasture. The thief does not come except to steal, and to kill, and to destroy. I have come that they may have life, and that they may have it more abundantly" (John 10:9–10, NKJV).

[48] John 11:25–26 (RSV).

For more information about Timothy Alberino, including updates on upcoming projects, media appearances, and publications, visit:

TIMOTHYALBERINO.COM

Index

purpose of evolution 198, 200–201, 207, 209, 211, 273
transhumanism
  Christian movement 273
  Homo deus 274–76
  objective 272, 288
  political party 273–74
  will to power 199–201, 207, 271, 273, 285
Corso, Philip J., *see* US government involvement *under* aliens
cosmology
  ancient traditions
    Hebrew 43, 49, 126
    Near Eastern 90–92, 93, 94–95
    North American 93
    Scandinavian 91, 93
    South American 93
  axis mundi 92, 93–94, 97
  biblical symbolism 94–95
  hermetic gates 91–92, 97, 143, 148, 203
  hermeticism 165, 181, 205
  world tree 58, 92
CRISPR, *see under* genetics: genetic engineering
Crowley, Aleister 198, 213
  beliefs 202, 204, 209–10
  Book of the Law 204–5
  Horus 203–4, 205
  marriages 202–3, 205, 206
  modern culture, influence on 207–8
  Thelema 204–5, 207–8
    Abbey of 206
  upbringing 202

D

DARPA, *see* genetic engineering: military use *under* genetics
Darwinism
  Darwin, Charles 173, 208, 212
  evolution, theory of 105–6, 107–8, 114, 172–73
    microevolution 166
    natural selection 116, 198–99, 273
  see also conscious evolution
David (biblical figure) 117, 188
  progenitor of Christ 3, 50, 52–53, 85, 179, 293–94
  psalmist 41, 74, 178
Dead Sea Scrolls 127–28
Deborah, Song of 54–55, 57
deluge, the, *see* Flood, the

demigods, *see under* paganism
demons 26, 79
  ancient beliefs 28, 86, 203, 280
  comparison to aliens 5, 218, 228, 232–35
  definition 100, 123, 161–62
  demonic possession 25, 28, 34–35, 142, 229
    examples of 35, 63, 162, 203
dimensional theory, *see under* physics
Dionysus 192, 199
divorce 99, 205–6
DNA, *see under* genetics
dominion (defined) 78–80
dominion (over Earth) *see under* birthright (of Adam)
Dominionism 87
dragon, the
  aspects of 37–38,
    devil, the 65, 82–83, 100–1, 154, 284, 292, 297
    Leviathan 48–49, 182
    Lucifer 40–41, 44, 155, 181–82, 191, 205
    morning star 40, 100
    Optimus Maximus 180
    prince (fallen) 37–40, 43, 54, 61, 85, 100–101
      power of the air 86–87, 218
    Satan 15, 41–42, 48, 50, 52, 80, 82–87, 100–101, 103, 153–54, 176, 179–81, 285–86, 297
    serpent 44, 51, 65, 99–102, 111, 153–54, 181, 238, 277, 284, 297, 300
    Tyre, king of 38–39
  condemnation of
    exile 49–50, 63–64, 74, 80, 110–11
    fall from grace 41, 49–50
    incarceration 8–9, 62, 80
    man's share in 12, 68, 158
dragon princes
  confederation of 41, 48–49, 179, 182, 205
    Edom, shattered vessels of 58, 61–64, 205
    influence on mankind 81, 192, 248, 256–57
    hexagram symbol 81–82, 182, 205
    spawn of 154, 176, 182, 283, 287, 291
  see also condemnation of *under* dragon, the
Dragon Slayer Prophecy 50–53, 82–84, 166, 281–83, 297
  in Eden 50, 99–102, 111

Z

Scripture Index

Made in the USA
Monee, IL
05 April 2022

94178976R00194